PRACTICAL HANDBOOKS FOR COLLECTORS

OLD CLOCKS

OLD CLOCKS

By

H. ALAN LLOYD

FOURTH EDITION

LONDON · ERNEST BENN LIMITED
NEW YORK · DOVER PUBLICATIONS INC

First edition *1951*
Second edition (*revised and reset*) *1958*
Third edition (*revised*) *1964*
Second impression *1965*
Fourth edition (*revised and enlarged*) *1970*

Published by Ernest Benn Limited
Bouverie House · Fleet Street · London · EC4
& Dover Publications Inc
180 Varick Street · New York *100 14* · N Y

Distributed in Canada by
The General Publishing Company Limited · Toronto

© Dondi Horological Limited *1970*
Printed in Great Britain

ISBN *0-510-05301-7*
ISBN *0-486-22662-X* (U.S.A.)

Note to Fourth Edition

Although the preparation of the new material now incorporated was undertaken by the author, the actual production, and therefore proof reading and final oversight of details, has been carried out since his death in the summer of 1969.

He had not at that time provided an intended short preface to this fourth revised edition, but it is certain he would have wished to emphasise that he regarded the research for the two appendixes as of sufficient importance to be added to a practical handbook. Their importance and bearing on the early history of clock-making are obvious and will produce a fitting memorial for the author of this book and the pioneers of horology.

Acknowledgements for kind permission for reproduction should be made to the British Museum for *Plate 79c* and to the Royal Society for *Plates 80a, b* and *c*. The reproductions of the Dondi MS are from the Bodleian Library, and all photographs of the reconstruction are the copyright of Dondi Horological Limited.

The publisher is also indebted to Dr. F. A. B. Ward for his final reading of the proofs of the new material.

January 1970

Preface to Third Edition

The resetting for this edition has provided the opportunity to make a number of corrections and additions. Thanks are due to the many readers who have written and for their continued expression of interest.

1964

Preface to First Edition

THE past few years have been very active in horological research and many interesting items have been brought to light, thus rendering the Author's book in the 'Chats' Series out of date in many respects.

The present book has a much wider range, including as it does Continental examples, especially in that early period of clock-making, the fourteenth, fifteenth and early sixteenth centuries, where there are abundant examples of very interesting work, whilst we, here in England have little or nothing to show. We have the oldest surviving mechanical clocks at Salisbury and Wells, but these, while made in this country, cannot be proved to have been the work of an Englishman. The bishop who ordered them had been recently translated from the Continent and may well have imported a Continental clockmaker; we have many records of Continental public clocks from the beginning of the fourteenth century. What we do know, thanks to the researches of Mr. Howgrave-Graham, is that judging from decorative resemblances, in all probability these two clocks were the work of one man and this probability is supported by the fact that the bishop in question was translated from Salisbury to Wells just at this same period. Richard of Wallingford is the only Englishman of whom we have record in these early days.

A chapter on American Clocks is included and in the preparation of this the Author acknowledges, with many thanks, the considerable assistance he has received from Mr. Walter M. Roberts, President of the National Association of Watch and Clock Collectors.

As before, no attempt will be made to describe in detail any complicated clocks, these, when occasionally introduced, are so done to illustrate a particular feature incorporated. Those interested in complicated clocks are referred to the author's *Some Outstanding Clocks Over 700 Years, 1250–1950*, recently published.

1

This book will remain discursive rather than scientific. In a way the author has followed the lead of the first author of a book on clocks in English, John Smith, most gloriously English of English names. This little book published in 1674, entitled *Horological Dialogues*, takes the form of an imaginary conversation between a clock-owner and a clockmaker and deals with the current problems of setting up and maintaining clocks.

In the present book the author asks his reader to imagine that all the clocks illustrated form his collection, which he has divided into types and periods for the convenience of display and dissertation. ('Heaven forbid,' ejaculates my wife, 'that we should own all those clocks. We have quite enough; we live in a house, not in a museum.' And she is quite right.) The author is taking the reader round and explaining how evolution and design progressed through the ages.

When we come to a particularly interesting piece which has historical connexions, or is by a particularly famous maker, we shall pause on our tour and deal with that point; there will be no stern chairman to rap the table with his gavel and say: 'Gentlemen, the point before the meeting is . . .' But these temporary digressions will not displace any of the clocks on the shelves, and we shall pick up our narrative of evolution and design just where we left off to traverse the bypaths.

Of course, in spite of a generous allowance of plates and many pages of text, there are many omissions both of examples of clocks and in biographical and historical matter. One may criticise and say that there is a big gap in the series here, or that this or that type has been omitted entirely; or another that there should be more biographical notes or a fuller glossary of horological terms, etc. All too true, but, in the words of the second-hand-clothes dealer who, when his customer brought back a coat and complained that it was full of moth, replied, 'Vot do you expect for thirty shillings?—'umming birds?' The author always feels that illustrations are the heart and soul of books of this nature and he has sacrificed some things to achieve greater completeness in this direction. He hopes that the reader will agree.

The reader also will find a certain amount of repetition in the text; this has been done rather than have too many references back.

Where known, measurements are given; these are only given as a rough guide, since all photographs have been scaled down to uniformly sized blocks. In many instances they have been scaled off from the photographs; where only one dimension, such as that of the dial, has been known they are therefore only approximate.

The most usual questions put by the beginner about an old clock he has inherited or acquired are, 'How old is it?' and 'How much is it worth?' Old clocks do not differ from other *objets d'art*, nor do their owners differ from other human beings; or do they? (The sister of a famous collector, on being introduced to my wife and myself, turned to my wife and said, '*You* are normal, aren't you?') Most owners think that their geese are swans, so the answer is generally, 'Not half as old as you think' and 'Nothing like as much as you hope.' In this matter we generally have to join up with the Irishman, who when asked, after he had killed his pig, what it weighed replied, 'Not as much as I expected; I never thought it would.' Most really fine pieces have been rediscovered during the last fifty years and now the urge to hold something more than paper-money has brought so many into the market who have no real interest in or knowledge of it, that prices are out of all proportion and the real connoisseur is left sadly to look on.

There are, however, still occasional finds to be made. One of the fine early pieces illustrated in this book was bought, just before the war, for £3. Further, there are many fine pieces by the lesser well-known makers, which horologically are just as interesting as some of the less elaborate pieces by the great makers.

The question of dating examples has always been difficult. We get a certain trend in design but, unless we have some documentary evidence, dates must always be approximate. The author states in advance that he will not be drawn into any controversy on this point. Further, it is often difficult to convince those ignorant of the subject that their ideas are quite wrong. The author had the greatest difficulty once in persuading a friend, who claimed descent from an Elizabethan clockmaker, of the same name, that a clock he owned did not date from that period, because someone who had little or no knowledge had told him so, and he liked to believe it. The type of clock could not have been earlier than Charles II, and it was in fact a George III piece.

Obviously, the earlier the clock the greater its interest and value as a general rule; but there are many exceptions, mainly those pieces which incorporate the first use of later developments in the craft and which are the work of those later masters, who, not content with the results already achieved by others, have gone on to devise those later improvements.

But the interest in any subject, and clocks in particular, does not lie in acquiring the rare and expensive, which are usually, but not always, also beautiful both in design and manner of execution. Such possessions are of necessity limited to the very few by reason of the fact that very few genuine examples exist; prices have reached such levels that a book dealing only with the 'aristocrats' of the clock world would have a practical interest for very few.

No, the vast majority of owners of old clocks have inherited them from their ancestors and this gives them a personal value that cannot be appraised in the sale room. It is to these owners of clocks, in the main, that this book is addressed in the hope that, by studying the different points brought out, such as the progress in design of cases, hands, spandrels, dials, etc., they may be able with reasonably certainty to date their own possessions, and, with these as a nucleus, start a collection based on some specific idea.

Clocks by makers residing in a particular locality, clocks of a shape particularly admired, such as basket or balloon, etc., clocks showing the evolution of design over a chosen period; all these could form the basis of a collection. Just to acquire anything because it happens to be old is not, in the author's opinion, collecting; it is merely performing the functions of a dealer who has to keep a large stock to satisfy a catholicity of tastes; a collector should be strong-minded enough to discriminate between what fits into his plan and what does not.

In writing a book of this sort the author is dependent on many people for help, especially in the matter of illustrations, and thanks are due to the following for the items enumerated:

Thureau-Dangin: The Sumerian numeration. Biographical details of John Shelton: Mr. T. W. Robinson, late Librarian Royal Society. Details of the travels of Shelton's clock: Professor Cope of Philadelphia University. The Librarian of the Royal Society for access to their shelves.

Fig. 8 is from Ungerer's *Horloges Astronomiques*. Hessisches Landesmuseum, Frontispiece, *Plate 45c, d, 46a*; Mrs. Oakden Fig. 10, *Plate 24d*; Bodleian Library *Plate 1b*; Musee des Arts decoratifs, Paris *Plate 2a, b*; Dr. E. Gschwind *Plate 2c, d*; British Museum *Plate 3*; Herzog Anton-Ulrich Museum, Brunswick *Plate 4a, 5, 6, 12*; Dr. H. von Bertele *Plate 4b, c* and *d, 19a*; The Ilbert Collection *Plate 7, 9a, 14b, 26c, 39c, 40a, b, 46b, 47*; Banff Museum *Plate 8*; Rosenborg Museum, Copenhagen *Plate 9b*; the late Captain H. Vivian *Plate 9d*; Science Museum, London *Plate 10a, 21*; Dr. E. Morpurgo *Plate 10b, c, d*; Bavarian National Museum *Plate 13*; Germanisches Museum, Nuremberg *Plate 14a, 45a, b*; Mr. E. Brooks *Plate 14c, d, 19d*; Dr. Newland *Plate 15b*; Mr. John Huddleston *Plate 15c*; Zwinger Museum, Dresden *Plate 15d*; Mr. P. Dawson *Plate 12c, d*; Fitzwilliam Museum, Cambridge *Plate 17b*; Mr. W. Stopher *Plate 18a, 43c*; the late W. Iden *Plate 17d, 22b, c, 23c, 35c, d, 37a, 38a*; Lord Harris *Plate 17a, 18b, c, d, 20b, 22a, 37b, 43a, d, 44a*; Mr. G. F. Hutchinson *Plate 17c, 24a*; the late Earl of Leicester *Plate 19c*; The President, Queens' College, Cambridge *Plate 20a, 37d*; the Rev. Dinsdale *Plate 20c, 41c, d*; the late J. C. Hirst *Plate 22d, 26b, 39d*; by gracious permission of Her Majesty, the Queen *Plate 25a, c, d, 38c*; the Master of Trinity College, Cambridge *Plate 25b, 39b*; Mr. James Oakes *Plate 26a*; Vienna Clock Museum *Plate 27d*; Mr. L. H. Cooper *Plate 28c, 44c*; The Mond Nickel Co. Ltd. *Plate 29c, 44d*; the Hon. Mrs. B. Ionides *Plate 30, 33b*; Mr. B. Partridge *Plate 31a, 40d*; Mr. C. E. Thornton *Plate 32b, c, 41b*; Mr. A. Greenwood *Plate 33a*; Mr. W. Gibson *Plate 34d*; Mrs. van Zwanenberg *Plate 33c, 41a*; The Royal Society *Plate 35a, b*; Dr. Solbeck-Stojaneck *Plate 36b*; Mr. C. W. Glossop *Plate 42a*; the late A. K. Marples *Plate 42b*; Mr. Ernest Watkins *Plate 43b*; Mr. M. Dineley *Plate 44b*.

From the author's collection *Plate 1d, 9c, 11, 15a, 16a, b, 19b, 23a, b, 24b, 28d, 31c, 37c, 38b, d, 39a, 40c, 42c, d, 46c, d*.

American Philosophical Society and Geo. H. Eckhardt *Plate 48*; George H. Eckhardt *Plate 49b*; Old Stourbridge Village *Plate 49a, d*; C. A. Currier, M.D. *Plate 49c*; J. Cheney Wells Collection, Courtesy Mr. Barney *Plate 50a, b*; D. K. Packhard *Plate 51a, b, c, d*; W. M. Roberts *Plate 52c, d*; *Plate 52b, 53c, d*,

F. Mudge Selchow; *Plate 53a, 54a, b,* R. C. Morrell, Bristol Clock Museum; *Plate 54c, d,* Dr. A. G. Cossidente.

All the other Plates not enumerated are acknowledged, with much gratitude to the late Malcolm Webster, who gave me free run of his extensive stock and let me choose the examples needed; he also gave me valuable advice. Fig. 9 is from a drawing by Mr. F. Janca.

Limpsfield 1958

Contents

7

Illustrations

9

12 Hans Buschmann, Year Spring Clock, 1651–2; Back view, Mainspring and Movement

13 Dials of J. G. Mayer's Clock, c. 1660; Back Plate and Movement

14 German Lantern Clock, c. 1560
    J. B. Alberti, Italian Lantern Clock, 1685
    van Stryp, Early Dutch Pendulum Clock; Movement

15 Edward East, Pediment Clocks, c. 1660; c. 1670; Early cased Clock, c. 1665
    Jobst Burgi, 'Architectural' case, c. 1610

16 John Hilderson, Pediment Clock, c. 1665; Movement
    Wm. Knottesford, Clock, c. 1685; Back view

17 Joseph Knibb, Wooden Basket Clock, c. 1685
    Thomas Tompion, Wooden Basket Clock, c. 1685
    Joseph Windmills, Basket Clock, 1698
    John Shaw, Double Basket Clock, c. 1695

18 Samuel Watson, Wooden Basket Clock, c. 1690
    Joseph Knibb, Wooden Basket Clocks, c. 1685; c. 1695
    Daniel Quare, Wooden Basket Clock, c. 1695

19 Peter Garron, Three train Clock, c. 1705
    Thomas Tompion, Wooden Basket Clock, c. 1705
    George Graham, Inverted Bell Clock, c. 1715
    Joseph Antram, Three train clock, c. 1715

20 Edward East, Cased Lantern Clock, c. 1664; Hanging Clock, c. 1670: Clock spoilt by 'modernisation'

21 William Clement, Turret Clock, 1671; Back view

22 Ahasuerus Fromanteel, long-case, c. 1680: Johannes Fromanteel, long-case, c. 1675: Edward East, long-case, c. 1685: Joseph Windmills, long-case, c. 1690

23 Wm. Clement, long-case, c. 1685; Movement
    John Clowes, long-case, c. 1685

24 Christopher Gould, long-case, c. 1690: Wm. Osborne, long-case, c. 1705: Jas. Drury, grandmother, c. 1710: George Graham, long-case, 1728

25 Thomas Tompion, year long-case, c. 1695; Movement
    Richard Street, long-case, 1708
    Equation Kidney and Rocker Arm, c. 1695

B

39 William Osborne, Dial, *c.* 1705 : Richard Street, Dial, *c.* 1708 :
    Daniel Quare, Dial, *c.* 1710 : George Graham, Dial, *c.* 1720

40 Quare Equation Movement, *c.* 1710 ; Back view : William
    Tomlinson, Dial, *c.* 1735 : Thomas Budgen, Dial, *c.* 1740

41 Finney, Dial : John Benson, Dial, *c.* 1775 : Helm, Dial,
    c. 1785 ; Perpetual Calendar

42 Thomas Lister, Dial, *c.* 1805 : William Bothamley, Dial,
    c. 1785 : Edward East, Back Plate, *c.* 1660 : John Hilder-
    son, Back Plate, *c.* 1665

43 Joseph Knibb, Back Plate, *c.* 1685 : Henry Jones, Back
    Plate *c.* 1680 : Samuel Watson, Back Plate, *c.* 1690 :
    Daniel Quare, Back Plate, *c.* 1695

44 Claude du Chesne, Back Plate, *c.* 1715 : George Graham,
    Back Plate, *c.* 1725 : Justin Valliamy, Back Plate, *c.* 1775 :
    Back Plate, *c.* 1820

45 Monastic Night Alarm Clock, *c.* 1400 ; Behind the Dial :
    J. P. Treffle Night Clock, *c.* 1675 ; Back view

46 Dial and below movement Pendulum in 45 *c.* : Italian
    Night Clock, *c.* 1680 : Joseph Knibb, Night Clock, *c.* 1685

47 P. T. Campani, Night Clock, 1683 ; Movement : Three
    Early Nineteenth-century Night Clocks

48 Rittenhouse Clock, 1769 and Dial

49 Simon Willard, Tall Clock, *c.* 1785 : R. Shearman, Tall
    Clock, *c.* 1800 : John Osgood, Corner Tall Clock,
    c. 1797 : Joshua Wilder, Grandmother Clock, *c.* 1800

50 Simon Willard, Wall Clock, *c.* 1770 : Movement of Wall
    Clock : Simon Willard, Banjo Clock, *c.* 1810 : Move-
    ment of Banjo Clock

51 Anon. Banjo Lyre Clock, *c.* 1825 : Anon. Lyre Clock, *c.* 1830 :
    Benjamin Morrill, Mirror Wall Clock, *c.* 1820 ; Movement

52 David Wood, Shelf Clock, *c.* 1800 : Simon Willard, Light-
    house Clock, *c.* 1822 : Eli Terry, Shelf Clock, *c.* 1816 ;
    Wooden Strap Movement

53 Atkins & Downs, Mirror Shelf Clock, *c.* 1831 ; Wooden
    Movement : Joseph Ives, Wagon Spring Clock,
    c. 1825 ; Movement

CHAPTER ONE

Early Methods and Mechanical Development

How and when primitive man came to take cognisance of the passing of time can only be surmised. Not being nocturnal in habit, he would rise with the sun and retire at dusk. How did the recording of Time begin? Who made, and how were they made, those first efforts in numeration in order that some record might be kept of the motion of the heavenly bodies; for undoubtedly these inspired the earliest efforts at mathematics and astronomy.

We are now nearing the completion of the second millenium of the Christian era; the birth of Jesus seems incredibly remote and the civilisation and knowledge of those days we look upon as very primitive, except so far as moral precepts are concerned. Yet we have to double this period and then add it to our present reckonings, bringing us to 4000 B.C. in order to arrive at the time that it is estimated that the Sumerian civilisation began; when the Sumerians first started counting on their 10 fingers and thumbs.

Finding 10 not easily divisible, they introduced a unit of 6, which is divisible by 2 and by 3, and formed a system based on a combination of 10 and 6. They then took 60 as another unit and, based on this, they arrived at $2 \times 60 = 120$, $3 \times 60 = 180$, up to $10 \times 60 = 600$. This, again, was taken as a further unit and we get $2 \times 600 = 1200$, $3 \times 600 = 1800$, up to $6 \times 600 = 3600$ or 60^2. This was taken as finality and the word for it was Sar, or a circle, whole, totality. Later they increased their reckoning up to 60^3, 216,000.

This has frequently been accepted as the origin of the circle of 60 degrees of 60 minutes each, but this is not so. The division of the circle originated in space measurements in the celestial sphere, which were eventually converted into time measurements. The division of the day into two periods of 12 hours each is generally credited to the Babylonians.

In the twentieth chapter of the Second Book of Kings, verse eleven, we read, 'And Isaiah the prophet cried unto the Lord: and he brought the shadow ten degrees backward, by which it had gone down in the dial of Ahaz.' This is again recorded in the thirty-eighth chapter of Isaiah, verse eight, reading, 'Behold, I will bring again the shadow of the degrees, which is gone down in the sun dial of Ahaz, ten degrees backward. So the sun returned ten degrees, by which degrees it was gone down.' These passages have sometimes been taken to indicate that sundials, as we know them, were in use in early biblical times; but the marginal notes in the Authorised Version give the alternate translation of the Hebrew rendered 'dial' as degrees, and the Revised Version gives the rendering steps. The Rev. J. R. Dommelow in his *One Volume Bible Commentary* writes, 'Probably a platform surrounded by steps and surmounted by a pillar, the shadow of which fell upon a smaller or larger number of steps according as the sun mounted or declined in the sky.'

It is not within the scope of this book to trace these early efforts to record time. Let it suffice to say that one of the earliest known surviving time-measuring instruments is an Egyptian shadow clock of the tenth or eighth centuries B.C., of which a copy is in the Science Museum, in London; the original is (or was) in Berlin. This was not, as might be supposed, a vertical erection, but a horizontal T-shaped piece, the cross-bar being slightly higher than the tail. As the sun made its daily apparent motion from east to west, rising and declining in the heavens, the shadow of the cross-bar would be thrown on the tailpiece, gradually shortening towards midday and lengthening again as the shadow travelled down the scale in the afternoon.

There are three kinds of day, two natural and one artificial, viz. the sidereal day, the solar day and the mean day. Astronomers have at all times used the sidereal day, that is the time taken by the earth to revolve once, so that any given fixed star again passes the observer's meridian. This period is fixed at 23 hours 56 minutes 4 seconds mean solar time. The mean solar day is longer, because it is measured by the passing of the sun across the observer's meridian, and while the earth has been completing its daily revolution it has been also completing a day's travel in its annual orbit around the sun, which adds, on an average, 3 minutes 56 seconds to the sidereal day. The stars are so far distant compared with the distance between the sun and the earth that this error is negligible in estimating sidereal time. The sun, which is approximately 93,000,000 miles away from the earth, is really only a very near star.

It will be noted that the expression *mean solar day* has been used; the length of the apparent solar day as shown on a sundial varies each day. Because the earth's orbit around the sun is elliptical, owing to the effect of gravity, the daily travel of the earth in its orbit varies. In January, when the earth is nearest the sun, it travels its fastest, whereas in July the earth is at the farthest point in its elliptical course and, therefore, travels at its slowest speed. When farthest from the sun the earth is said to be in its apogee, and when nearest in its perigee.

Another factor is that the sun's apparent motion is not along the celestial equator, but in a plane inclined to it at an angle of approximately $23\frac{1}{2}°$; this causes a daily varying effect. Some-times these two causes operate together, that is, both tend to increase or diminish the length of the day, and sometimes they operate against each other, the one tending to increase the length of the day and the other to shorten it, or vice versa. The combination of these two causes is a daily variation between mean time as shown by the clock and apparent time as shown on a sundial. This is known as the equation of time, and will be dealt with when we consider equation clocks.

But while astronomers have always known the variation be-tween sidereal and solar time, and divided the day into twenty-four equal parts between the passing of the meridian of any given star, they were, until the general standard was raised by the resurgence of education at the period of the Restoration, a category apart. For the masses there was no standard; in some places, such as Nuremberg and district, the so-called Nurem-berg hours of light and darkness were kept. These were equal in duration but varied in number with the season. The twenty-four hours were divided between eight hours of darkness and sixteen of daylight at mid-summer and eight hours of daylight and sixteen of darkness in the middle of the winter. In between, public notices decreed on what dates an hour should be added to or subtracted from the daylight period. Clock dials were often painted, partly light blue and partly dark blue, representing day and night; movable shutters then indicated the proportion of daylight to darkness for the month in question. This system was abandoned early in the seventeenth century. According to Albrecht, in *Die Raeder Uhr*, there is in the Germanisches Museum in Nuremberg a wooden clock with its original dial of date 1630 having a simple twelve-hours dial. Presumably this clock is by a Nuremberg maker, but this is not stated. In the near-by town of Rothenberg the old method of reckoning carried on until early in the nineteenth century.

In Egypt and in the Middle East the time was divided into an equal number of periods, usually six, of light and dark, the length of each period would, therefore, vary daily with the seasons. This method of reckoning time was practised in Japan until 1873; they used clocks with foliot balance, a type which will be described later, having two escapements and two foliots, the one for daylight hours and the other for the night hours; the former would cut out at dusk and set in motion the latter. Every month the clockmaker would call and adjust the weights of each foliot, lengthening the period of the daylight hour and shortening that of the night, or vice versa.

We have, however, wandered somewhat from the theme of very early time-recording methods. As the reader has been warned in the Preface, this is a discursive book, and it will at times wander off into branch discussions. Besides shadow clocks, which were useful only in sunshine – here we must remember that early civilisation started in the Middle East, Egypt and the Mediterranean countries, where there is usually plenty of sunshine – the Greeks and Egyptians developed water clocks, or *Clypsedræ*, as they were called by the Greeks. These usually worked on the principle of the filling or the emptying of a vessel at a controlled speed, and they had the advantage of being useful at night or in cloudy weather.

The burning of graduated candles or of oil contained in a marked glass vessel was another rough-and-ready method of telling the passing of the hours. These methods were later supplanted by the sand-glass, which gave more accurate results (see *Plate 1a*). This shows a series of four glasses of the Renaissance period, so filled to empty in $\frac{1}{4}$, $\frac{1}{2}$, $\frac{3}{4}$ and 1 hour respectively. As will be seen from the illustration, these early glasses were cast in two pieces and joined together in the middle by bands. Up to the eighteenth century, and even in some country parishes into the nineteenth century, these sand-glasses were used in church pulpits to remind the preacher of the passing of time and, if need be, to restrain his eloquence. In the parish church of Titsey, Surrey, near where the author lives, there is still a stand of four sand-glasses on the wall by the pulpit; but as the church has a quarter chiming clock, the sand-glasses have largely lost their usefulness.

With present-day sermons of ten, fifteen, or twenty minutes as the rule, it is difficult to realise the patience with which our forebears sat listening to sermons of two hours' duration or more, and twice a day at that very often, if we are to accept the evidence of the habits of the times as given to us by Samuel Pepys.

We can imagine the Presbyterian, Dr. Bates, using such a glass when preaching his farewell sermon at St. Dunstan's on August 17th, 1662; this being the last Sunday before the application of the Act of Uniformity. Samuel Pepys writing in his *Diary* says:

'17th (Lord's Day). Up very early, this being the last day that the Presbyterians are to preach, unless they read the new Common Prayer and renounce the Covenant, and so had a mind to hear Dr. Bates' farewell sermon, and walked thither . . . to St. Dunstan's, where it not being seven o'clock yet, the doors were not yet open. . . . At eight o'clock I went and crowded in at a back door among others, the church being half full almost before any doors were open publicly . . . and so got into the gallery beside the pulpit and heard very well. His text was "Now to the God of Peace" the last Hebrews and the 20th verse: he making a very good sermon. . . . Besides the sermon, I was very pleased with the sight of a fine lady that I have often seen walk in Graye's Inn Walk, and it was my chance to meet her again at the door going out, and very pretty and sprightly she is. . . . After dinner to St. Dunstan's again; and the church quite crowded before I came, which was just at one o'clock; but I got into the gallery again, but stood in a crowd and did exceedingly sweat all the time. . . .'

Sermons were so long that it was possible to visit several churches on a Sunday sampling the sermons at each. Another entry, for November 9th, 1662, reads:

'9th (Lord's Day). . . . Then up, and after being ready

walked to my brother's where my wife is, calling at many churches, and then to the Temple, hearing a bit there too. . . .'

We can imagine the parson, at the end of the first hour, taking the sand-glass and turning it over on its central pivot, taking a deep breath and preparing for the second hour.

Just when clocks, as we know them with trains of wheels, came into use it is impossible to say. They were first used for monastic purposes at a time when the life of the whole community was regulated by the canonical hours. Unfortunately the monks did not consider posterity. They used the same word, horologium, to denote anything that recorded the passing of time whether it be a sundial, water-clock, or any other type, or a mechanical, weight-driven clock as we know it today. Thus there is no guide to the exact date of the change over to weight-driven clocks. It would, of course, be gradual, spreading outwards from the place of its origin.

It would seem correct to suppose that turret clocks were the first to be made. They would be installed in the monastery tower, at first without any dial visible from the outside, and the sexton would strike the necessary number of strokes on the bell. Even if they had had dials very few of the general populace could have read them.

A great deal of controversy has raged over the exact location of the first turret clocks. Some say they started in Italy, some that South Germany was their place of origin. Mr. R. P. Howgrave-Graham, who has perhaps done more to elucidate this problem than anyone – at any rate as regards England – considers the earliest English clock, of which anything has survived to come down to us, to be the old Salisbury Cathedral clock recently discovered by Mr. T. R. Robinson, of date about 1386, being just older than the more widely known clock at Wells Cathedral dating about 1392. He has recently discovered evidence that these two clocks were by the same maker.

The clock from Dover Castle, now in the Science Museum in London, was long thought to be one of the oldest surviving in England, but recent research has shown that this clock is probably of mid-seventeenth-century origin. Turning to the Continent, in 1277 has produced the *Liber del Saber Astronomico Alfonso X de Castille*. This was a book containing the collected writings of Hispano-Moorish authors of the day; it also repeated, probably, the writings of earlier centuries from Arabia and the Near East. In this is depicted a Mercury clock not unlike the seventeenth-century water clocks we sometimes see in which the drum is divided into compartments by radial pierced plates, the water or mercury percolating through the small holes and acting against a weight, giving to the drum a slow but continuous motion, unbroken by any escapement. Since the Court of Alfonso X was the centre of learning at that time, it may be fairly well assumed that the mechanical clock, as we now know it, had not yet been invented.

Opposed to this, Giovanni de Dondi of Padua, about 1350 constructed a weight-driven-balance clock as the motive force for his famous astronomical clock. (*Plate 1b.*) In his detailed description of this clock he says that the ordinary clockwork part is only shown diagrammatically since it is a common clock, of which several types are known. It would seem, therefore, that in the 75 years between 1277 and 1350 the mechanical clock had been invented and become quite common.

Dante makes reference to a clock in his *Paradiso*, which would appear to be a mechanical clock; the *Paradiso* was written around 1320. A clock is also reputed to have been made in Padua by Dondi's father in 1344. Those interested in this aspect of horology are referred to Drummond Robertson's *The Evolution of Clockwork*, perhaps the most exhaustive work on the subject, at any rate in English.

Strasburg Cathedral has been the location of three famous clocks, the first, by an unknown maker, being finished about 1354. This was succeeded by the second, constructed between the years 1571 and 1574 by the famous brothers Isaac and Joseph Habrecht, members of a famous family of clockmakers, from the designs of Conrad Dasypodius, Professor of Mathematics at Strasburg University.

This clock, after many years of inactivity, was replaced by the present clock by Schwilgué, which was finished in 1842. This is one of the marvels of the present time. In its astronomical recordings it even takes in the precession of the equinox, the gearing of which, according to Ungerer, has a ratio of 1 : 9,451,512.

When constructing the second clock in 1574 Habrecht used an automaton in the form of a cock, which crowed and flapped its wings when the clock struck. This cock was part of the original clock of 1354, and was in sufficiently good order to be used again two hundred years later; it is today preserved in the museum at Strasburg. The device of a crowing cock is often incorporated in early clocks to record the hours and probably derives from Our Lord's warning to Peter, that he should deny Him before the cock crew.

Thus we see that, if by 1350 clocks had attained such a degree of perfection that automata capable of functioning over several hundred years were incorporated in them, they must have attained a considerable degree of refinement by that date. The location of this clock at Strasburg favours the South German school of thought as the origin of turret clocks. As we have seen independent thought was active contemporaneously in Italy.

In his *Origin de l'Horologe à Poids* the late M. Charles Frémont illustrated automata which are dated around 1250, but these were not applied to clocks.

The easiest form of motive power which would appeal to the early investigator would be the falling weight. Indeed, today, this is still an ideal method as it gives an even and steady pull. How to control this force was the problem; who solved it no one knows, and no one, probably, ever will. Whatever his name, he was, in the author's opinion, a perfect genius; he had no antecedent work to guide him.

Recently Drs. Joseph Needham and Derek Price have discovered a chinese manuscript of 1088 which describes a water clock where a stream of water flows into a cup at the end of an adjustable steelyard which tips when the requisite weight of water has been introduced. This unlocks a train allowing it to go forward one step and then locks it again as the empty cup returns to its original position, each interval being $\frac{1}{4}$ hour. Regulation was by adjusting the weight of water necessary to tip the steelyard, by altering the position of the counterpoise. A tube sighted on to a selected star gave the sidereal day as the time standard for regulation. Here we have a definite escapement, functioning at a constant interval to unlock and relock a train of wheels.

The inventor of the verge escapement in all probability had no knowledge of this Chinese clock so that we can credit him, as well as his Chinese predecessor, as being a man of genius.

The invention is known as an escapement because it allows one tooth of the crown wheel to escape at a time, thus enabling it to make a fractional turn before locking the wheel again. The word verge is probably derived from the Latin *verga* a wand or staff. This root appears in the word verger, he who precedes the church procession with his wand or staff of office.

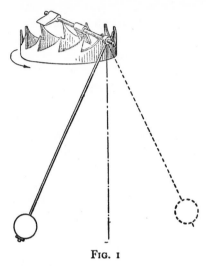

Fig. 1

Fig. 1 shows the form of the verge escapement as later adapted to the pendulum; it consists of a wheel with an uneven number of saw-like teeth, known as the crown wheel – a very apt description. Across this is positioned a staff or arbor, as it is termed in horology, with two pallets set in it at right angles to each other. As the foliot, seen in *Plate 1c*, swings in one direction, one pallet on the arbor releases a tooth of the crown wheel, but the second pallet has now become locked on the crown wheel, causing a check to the swing of the foliot and setting it swinging in the opposite direction.

The term foliot is possibly derived from the old French *esprit follet*, a goblin associated with Puck and represented by the ceaseless to-and-fro motion. This raises the query, was the inventor a Frenchman? In the absence of any more substantial proof of early activity in France, this does not seem likely. The clock in the Palais de Justice in Paris, originally constructed by Henri de Vic, and of which all parts have at different times been renewed once or more times, was for a long time accepted as one of the earliest clocks, if not the earliest. According to Drummond Robertson the real name of the maker was Heinrich von Wiek, and he came from the upper reaches of the Rhine or Lorraine in 1362 to start the work. These details do not lend much support to the theory of a French invention of the verge escapement, which Dondi says was widely known in 1350.

An illustration of a very early foliot-balance clock is given in *Plate 1c*. This is an example of a very early chamber clock without alarm or strike, and dates from the middle of the fifteenth century. Final regulation was effected by the alteration of the position of the weights on the crossbar; in the picture the upper pallet is free and the lower one is engaging one of the teeth of the crown wheel. The driving weight and rope are not shown; the rope would pass over the grooved wheel to the left of the bottom, or great wheel, in the illustration. It will be noted that the foliot balance and pallet arbor are suspended by a thread which allowed a free swing. This gave a further means of regulation; by altering the position of the thread on the notched arm the angle of incidence of the pallet to the crown wheel is changed, longer contact giving a slower release of each tooth and vice versa.

The use of silk for suspending pendulums actuated by a crutch was maintained on the Continent two hundred years later for the suspension of the pendulum after its invention in 1657, but it was not employed in England.

The clock will hang on a hook driven into the wall and passing through the upper ring at the back, a vertical position being maintained by the two lower distance pieces. It will be seen that the arbor of the great wheel passes through the front plate and engages with the toothed periphery of the dial, thus revolving the dial so that each hour in turn passes before a stationary pointer or hand, not visible in the photograph, instead of the hand revolving in front of a stationary dial, as is the custom today.

We have already remarked that, probably, the earliest clocks were used for monastic purposes; they were simple alarm clocks which let off every hour. This served to call the attention of the sexton and, if necessary, to awaken him. He then proceeded to strike the necessary number of hours on the monastery bell, which would be quite independent of the clock. 'Old Time, the clock setter, that bald Sexton Time,' says Shakespeare in *King John*.

These early clocks had to serve the sexton day and night. We therefore often find knobs set into the dial enabling the time to be ascertained by touch, with a double knob set at the 12 or 24, according as the dial was made to record 12 or 24 hours. The use of raised indicators on clock and watch dials is still in use today in what are known as blind men's watches. The Italians reckoned the time in twenty-four equal hours starting at sunset; the South Germans, twice times twelve, starting at midnight. As we have already seen, in Nuremberg and district they had their own method of calculating time.

The question of precedence between the balance and foliot is quite uncertain, nor can we attribute either one or the other to any definite locality. An example of a balance is seen in *Plates 1b and 9a*. The balance wheel has the same reciprocating action as the foliot balance, but regulation was by means of the driving weight. A cylindrical copper sheath would be nearly filled with lead, leaving a space at the top into which more or fewer lead shot could be placed, until the necessary degree of accuracy of going was achieved. One such early weight is seen in *Plate 9c*. The crown wheel in these clocks still remained vertical.

Up to this time clocks and their housings were constructed entirely of metal, the movements of iron and the housings either of iron or, in the case of the finer products, of gilded brass. Fig. 2 shows an illustration from Jost Aman's *Book of Trades* showing 'The Clockmakers'. It was published in Nuremberg in 1658 and brings this point out. The narrow strip plates were riveted or wedged. It was the second half of the sixteenth century before wood was used for the making of cases on the Continent; in England a century later.

Turret clocks were, from the earliest days, made entirely of wrought iron and of the cage type (*Plate 21*). The modern 'bench' type, i.e. a cast-iron horizontal bed with the various trains positioned side by side, was not adopted until later. The earliest found by the author is in the church of Notre-Dame at Versailles dated 1763, but this type was not generally adopted until Big Ben was designed by Lord Grimthorpe, then Edmund Beckett Denison, in the eighteen-fifties.

c

Confector horologij.   Vrmacher·

FIG. 2

The earliest domestic clocks were also all of wrought iron, both movements and housings, as we see in *Plate 1d*. In the sixteenth century, on the Continent, housings began to be made of brass, as mentioned above, and often elaborately engraved and gilded. In England, with a few exceptions at the end of the sixteenth century, this change did not take place until after the turn of the seventeenth century. A transitional clock with iron frame and brass dial and side plates is seen in *Plate 9a*.

Great strides were made on the Continent during the sixteenth century, in Italy, South Germany at Augsburg and Nuremberg, and also in Strasburg, where the noted family of Habrecht were living. The famous Strasburg clock, already referred to, showed the hour, the day, the month, all the festivals of the Church, the motion of the sun, the moon and the celestial globe, as well as the daily passage of the stars across the heavens. It also embodied various automata which performed at the hours as well as the cock already referred to. This clock was about fifty-five feet in height.

The museums and private collections of Europe contain many examples of elaborate astronomical chamber clocks of this period, varying in height from six to about twenty inches. Many of these show minutes as well as hours and often have each minute engraved on the dial.

As we shall see in the chapter on early Continental clocks, Jobst Burgi's cross-beat escapement allowed a very high degree of accuracy for a time standard uncontrolled by a pendulum, and it is thought that Tycho Brahe's and Kepler's accuracy of observation was, at any rate in part, due to the improved accuracy of Burgi's clocks.

England was right behind during the sixteenth century, only turret clocks being made; with few exceptions domestic clocks were not made in this country until the seventeenth century, and the minute hand not really adopted until after the introduction of the pendulum in 1658. From a practical point of view this was of little importance, since the degree of timekeeping was so poor that a single-handed clock showing the quarters was as effective as anything else.

The use of brass for housings was followed by the adoption of this alloy for the trains in the first quarter of the seventeenth century. This statement must be qualified to the extent that brass is never used on to brass. The wheels of the movements would be of brass engaging into steel pinions mounted on steel arbors. Strange as it may seem, it is the steel pinion that wears quicker than the brass wheel. It is thought that grains of dust or dirt embed themselves in the softer brass and have an abrasive action on the harder steel. In dealing with wheels and pinions, we should remember that while wheels have 'teeth', pinions have 'leaves'.

Since wrought iron or steel was the principal medium for the construction of these early clocks, it is quite natural that clockmakers belonged to either the Blacksmiths' or Locksmiths' Guild, according to the size of clock that they were making.

In 1657, Salomon Coster of The Hague made a clock for the celebrated mathematician Christiaan Huygens, which incorporated a pendulum. This was an invention of as great importance to the craft as any, and should be ranked with the verge escapement, the anchor escapement and the fusee – to which reference will be made later. The name pendulum is derived from the Latin *pendulus*, hanging down. Huygens' clock was spring-driven.

To whom belongs the honour of the invention of the pendulum has been the subject of dispute, at times very acrimonious,

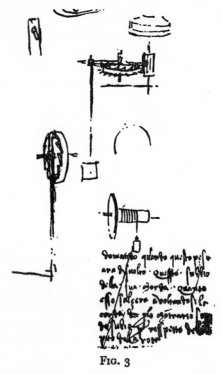

FIG. 3

especially between the contemporary claimants. There is no doubt that a pendulum driven by a weight was invented by Galileo; Tycho Brahe, the famous Danish astronomer, is also reputed to have used a form of pendulum, but in both these cases it is considered that an observer had to count the beats and that they were not geared into a clock as we know it today. As we have just read, it is probable that Tycho Brahe used Burgi's cross-beat escapement. There can be no doubt that several different brains were at work independently at different times. Leonardo da Vinci, that incomparable genius, centuries before his time, had sketches of the pendulum in his note-book[1] at the end of the fifteenth century (Fig. 3), and certainly Galileo's model was working before 1657; but, as stated before, these pendulums were in all probability only accurate oscillants, the number of vibrations to be counted by an observer, a very tedious and uncertain business. The writer is satisfied that Huygens did first apply the pendulum to clockwork and that his work was independent of Galileo's. Further reference will be made to the invention of the pendulum later.

The spring as a motive force came into use about the middle of the fifteenth century. There is in the Musee des Beaux Arts in Antwerp a portrait of a man in the costume of about 1450 in the background of which is shown a clock suspended from the wall by a chain and having no weights. It would appear to be definitely spring driven. The invention of the fusee as an equaliser to the declining force of a spring has long been credited to Leonardo da Vinci on the strength of drawings in his notebooks, but Professor Zinner, of Bamberg, has recently found in the Stuttgart Museum a manuscript by Paulus Alemanus (Paul the German), written in Rome about 1477 in which at least seven clocks with fusees are deleniated, showing clearly that at that date the fusee was in common use. Leonardo's sketch books date about 1485–90. A spring, when fully wound up, exerts a greater pull than when it is nearly run down, so that an uncontrolled spring-driven clock would go too fast when fully wound and too slowly when nearing the end of its time. To counteract this a fusee is used.

The term *fusee* is derived, according to the *Century Dictionary*, from the old French *fusee*, a thread. In medieval Latin, *fusata* was a spindle full of thread or yarn, an expression derived from the word *fusus*, a spindle. Since the first fusees were wound with catgut, the likeness to a spindle full of thread is very obvious.

The principle of the fusee (Fig 4) is that of the lever: when the spring is fully wound the pull is on the smallest diameter; as the spring uncoils, the extra leverage due to the increased diameter equalises the force transmitted to the train. The invention of the fusee will be referred to in the next chapter. The fusee is an invention of the first importance, it is still in

---

[1] Leonardo always wrote backwards. These copies of his sketches have been laterally inverted to allow the writing to be read without a mirror.

use in high grade clocks after five hundred years. We can appreciate its age better if we relate it to contemporary events, the Wars of the Roses and Jack Cade's rebellion.

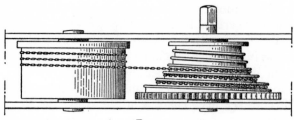

FIG. 4

It has in the past been generally accepted that spring clocks carried on the person were first made by Peter Henlein of Nuremberg about 1510; but we may have to accord that honour now to Italy. Professor Morpurgo, of Amsterdam and Rome, has found old manuscripts dated 1488, originating from Milan, that refer to an 'orologio' to be carried on the person in conjunction with a costly habit.

The fusee, equalising the pull of a spring encased in a barrel does not appear to have been adopted by the early German makers; these adopted a device known as the 'stackfreed' (Fig. 5). This consists of a stiff spring carrying at the end a

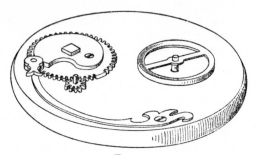

FIG. 5

small roller which bears against a shaped cam mounted on a toothed wheel, not fully cut. A pinion on the mainspring arbor strikes the stop on the wheel after a few turns, thus utilising only those turns of the spring that are most nearly equal in force and then obliging the owner to rewind. At the same time the lessening distance of the edge of the cam from the centre of revolution, decreases the resistance from the roller on the end of the spring, and so counteracting the decreasing force of the spring during these first few turns.

Just what the derivation of the word *stackfreed* is the author has failed to ascertain; even that monument of erudition the *Oxford Dictionary* fails to help us in this case, merely giving a mid-eighteenth-century French writer as the first to employ the word and stating that it is probably a corruption from the low German or Dutch.

A mid-sixteenth-century clock from the author's collection is illustrated in *Plate 1d*. The wheelwork is wholly of iron and, in this case, the housing framework as well. It is weight-driven, and one of the grooved wheels to take the cord can be seen at the back in the lower part of the going train The foliot balance with the notches for the regulating weights can clearly be seen, but the vertical pallet arbor, whose pallets engage the teeth of the vertical crown wheel, is hidden by the foremost corner pillar. Outside the framework at the back is the 'locking plate' or 'count wheel' of the striking train, and above it the 'fly' or air brake that revolves at high speed and acts as a governor to the speed of the falling weight during the actual period of striking. This type of striking arrangement is the earliest known. Like the verge escapement, it was a flash of genius on the part of its inventor, the air brake being a particularly bright idea. This method is still used today, mainly in turret clocks, but also, in France, for domestic clocks.

A pin lifts the locking arm, which can be seen locked in a notch, and allows it to fall again after each stroke of the hammer; while the clock is striking, the count wheel is turning, and the intervals between the notches is so graduated that the locking arm can fall on the rim of the locking plate one less than the necessary number of blows to record the hour. At the last blow it falls into the next notch and stops the locking plate from turning further, thus stopping the striking train until the next hour is reached, when a pin will again lift the locking arm allowing the striking train again to function. In the illustration ten has struck. Revolving anti-clockwise there are spaces for eleven and twelve, when come the small notches for the early hours.

It will be noticed that the whole construction is held together with wedges or rivets; metal screws had not yet appeared in horology.

We left the development of the pendulum to follow the history of the fusee; we must now return to the pendulum, its effect on contemporary horology and the improvements brought to it. Once invented, its considerably enhanced time-keeping caused the owners of foliot or balance-wheel clocks to have them converted. This was quite an easy thing to do. It involved changing the position of the crown wheel from the vertical to the horizontal, so that it would have a horizontal pallet arbor to the end of which would be fixed the pendulum rod, at first a direct and rigid connexion, not suspended on a silk thread and moved by a crutch as was the early Continental practice already referred to.

As a result of this easy possibility of conversion, it is today very difficult to find any clocks that have their original foliots or balance wheels. Many old clocks which had been converted from balance wheel to pendulum have of recent years been restored to their original form, but this must always leave its traces in the matter of empty or filled-in holes in the top and back plates, since, as already explained, the lay-out of the crown wheel had to be changed from vertical to horizontal and then back again to vertical. Care should be taken to make inquiries on this point of restoration when acquiring any clock with a foliot or balance.

Having made the great forward step of the introduction of the pendulum, the next move was to improve the type of escapement. The ideal pendulum swings entirely freely of any outside interference; but, of course, such a pendulum would soon come to rest through air resistance if it had no impelling force. This is provided by the motive force of a weight or spring through the wheels, or train as it is called in horology, of the clock.

The nearest to the ideal is that escapement which leaves the pendulum free for the greatest length of time. Although we acknowledge the inventor of the verge escapement as one of the greatest geniuses of his day, we are forced to admit that his invention is the worst possible escapement in that it never leaves the pendulum free. The teeth travel up the whole length of the pallet and as soon as one pallet is free of one of the teeth of the crown wheel the other pallet engages.

The modifications of escapements are legion, some very good, some not so good. For our purpose we shall deal only with two more, the anchor and the dead beat. They, or slight variations of them, are used in the vast bulk of clocks of interest to the average collector.

First in order of time was the anchor escapement, so called because the curved arm and the two pallets resemble the base and flukes of an anchor (Fig. 6). This type of escapement allowed the teeth of the escape wheel to escape with a much smaller arc of swing of the pendulum, 4° or 5° as compared with 35° to 40° required for the verge escapement.

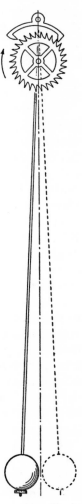

With the wide arc of swing of the verge escapement, pendulum lengths had to be kept very short, and they rarely exceeded the approximate ten inches necessary to give a half-second beat. This new type of pendulum, which was not directly connected to the pallet arbor, but suspended from a cock at the back of the clock by a thin flexible spring strip, allowed a much longer pendulum to be used without its swing becoming unwieldy. This fact, combined with the better time-keeping inherent in the anchor escapement, led rapidly to the adoption of the approximately thirty-nine-inch pendulum, beating one second as the standard. This enabled the second hand to be introduced. The term *second* was originally called the *second minute*, showing that it was the second division of the hour by sixty. John Wilkins, Bishop of Chester, writes in 1650: 'Four flames of an equal magnitude will be kept alive the space of sixteen second minutes.'

Just as many clocks were 'modernised' by the conversion from the balance wheel to verge when the pendulum was first introduced, so those who had not already converted their balances, and many who had either converted balance clocks or had verge lantern clocks, had them converted to anchor escapement with 'Royal'

Fig. 6

pendulums, as they came to be called, since it was considered that this was an appropriate name for these 'more richer kinds of pendulum'. Whether these converted clocks beat exactly one second or some odd fraction of a second would, of course, depend on the train of the clock converted; but since the clocks were not provided with second hands, this would not matter.

The invention of the anchor escapement has been frequently attributed to Robert Hooke, a most versatile genius of the seventeenth century, who from 1662 till his death in 1705 was Curator of Experiments with the then newly formed Royal Society. His industry was prodigious and he was always producing before the Society his ideas on many subjects, many of which were only the first conception of an idea and never developed or perfected.

For years writers have made this attribution, one copying from another until it has become almost legendary, but the writer, who admittedly at first 'followed the crowd', has failed to find any evidence to substantiate the claim. Indeed such scanty contemporary evidence as is available is to the contrary and distinctly favours the rival claimant, William Clement.

The earliest writer in England on horological subjects was John Smith. We could scarcely find a more ordinary and utterly English name. In 1675 he published his *Horological Disquisitions*, a little volume of 120 pages 16mo, detailing an imaginary conversation between a craftsman and a layman concerning the care and use of clocks. In this there are only very brief allusions to the thirty-nine-inch one-second pendulum. On page 34, in answer to a query as to the right method of setting up a long-case clock, he writes: 'In setting up long swing Pendulums, after you have taken them from the coffin, open it, and make free all things that are fastened, etc.' The author, by the way, deprecates this connexion of clocks with coffins; he prefers to think of them as living things. On pages 47 and 48 there are further references to the long pendulum:

'Q. Have you nothing more to deliver concerning Pendulums?

'A. Nothing more concerning these ordinary ones, I confess; something more might be delivered concerning the richer kinds. . . .

'Q. Is the long pendulum subject to variation as the short one is?

'A. No; being once brought to a true time it alwaies keeps it, for it moveth in so small an arch, that it is unpossible for it to move less without standing. . . .'

No mention is made of any inventor of the long pendulum or any controversy on this point, but that the anchor escapement is clearly meant is shown by the reference to the small 'arch' of swing; also it is quite evident that by 1675 the long seconds pendulum had become well established in use.

In 1694 Smith published his second book, *Horological Dialogues*. When writing this he was apparently aware of the rival claims made for the invention, for he writes on pages 2, 3 and 4:

'At length, in *Holland*, an Ingenious and Learned Gentleman, Mr. *Christiaan Huygens*, by Name, found out the Way to regulate the uncertainty of its Motion by the Vibration of a Pendulum.

'From *Holland*, the fame of this invention soon past over into *England*, where several eminent and ingenious Workmen applyed themselves to rectify some Defects which as yet was found therein; among which that eminent and well-known Artist Mr. *William Clement*, had at last the good Fortune to give it the finishing Stroke, he being indeed the real Contriver of that curious kind of long Pendulum, which is at this Day so universally in use among us.

'An invention that exceeds all others yet known, as to the Exactness and Steadiness of its Motion, which proceeds from Two Properties, peculiar to this Pendulum: The one is the weightiness of its Bob, and the other the little compass in which it plays: The first of these makes it less apt to be commanded by those accidental differences of Strength that may sometimes happen in the Draught of Wheels, and the other renders the Vibrations more equal and exact, as not being capable of altering so much in the distance of its Swinge, as those other kind of Pendulums are, who fetch a larger, and, by consequence, a less constant Compas.

'For Pendulums that swing or vibrate very far out, as all Crown-Wheel Pendulums do, are apt, by reason of many Accidents that happen to vary much in the Distance they swing, and that's the reason they do not always go or move the same Pace, a larger Vibration taking up more Time to be performed in, than lesser ones do: But the Vibrations of this Pendulum of Mr. *Clement's* contrivance is so very exact and steady, that, when 'tis well in Order, and the Air of the same Consistence, it shall in Five hundred or a Thousand Revolutions of its Index, keep so equal a Time, that no Human Art can discover the least considerable Difference in any of its Revolutions, an excellence to which no other known Motion can as yet pretend, and for which, I think, it will not be improper now, at last, to call it the *Royal Pendulum.*'

Here we have a very emphatic contemporary opinion that William Clement was the *real* contriver of the anchor escapement, written by a man who fully realised the importance of the discovery and the desirability of giving honour where honour was due.

Two years later William Derham, a parson, at one time a Canon of Windsor, wrote his *Artificial Clockmaker.* On page 96 of this book he also attributes the invention to Clement, writing: 'For several years this way of Mr. Zulichem's was the only method, *viz.* Crown-Wheel Pendulums, to play between two cycloidal cheeks, etc. But afterwards Mr. *W. Clement*, a *London* Clockmaker, contrived them (as Mr. *Smith* saith) to go with less weight, an heavier Ball (if you please) and to vibrate but a small compass. Which is now the universal method of the Royal Pendulum. But Dr. *Hook* denies Mr. *Clement* to have invented this; and says that it was his Invention, and that he caused a piece of this nature to be made, which he shewed before the *R. Society*, soon after the Fire of *London.*'

It will be noted that here is another contemporary writer agreeing that Clement was the inventor; Derham in a marginal note refers to Smith's attribution on page 3 of his *Horological Disquisitions* given above.

The recording by Derham of Hooke's claim is the only piece of written contemporary evidence that has so far been discovered to support the attribution to Hooke, and this is very definitely negative in character. A careful search through the records of the Royal Society papers, both those published and the unpublished Hooke manuscripts, has not revealed any evidence that Hooke ever produced anything approaching the principle of the anchor escapement before the Royal Society.

In view of Derham's statement, particular attention was paid to the period at the end of 1666, shortly after the Great Fire. Already before the Fire, on June 13th, 1666, there is the entry: 'Mr. Hooke exhibited a new contrivance of a circular pendulum, applicable to a watch, and moving without any noise and in continued and even motion without any jerks.'

It should be noted that at this period the going train of a clock was designated the watch part and the striking train the clock part, from the Latin *clocca*, a bell; it was some forty or fifty years later that the pocket watch, at first so designated, became generally known as a watch, and that the term was dropped in connexion with clocks.

On August 8th and again on August 22nd, 1666, Hooke was urged to produce his circular pendulum; the Great Fire intervened in September and we have no further entry until October 31st, 1666, when 'Mr. Hooke produced an inclining pendulum, which, though short, should perform the office of a long perpendicular one, the several degrees answering to the several dimensions of length.'

Here it should be noted that the wide arc of swing of the verge escapement made long pendulums impracticable unless there was ample space; Huygens did at one time make a clock with a verge escapement having a seconds pendulum, reducing the amplitude by an intermediate gearing.

On November 21st, 1666, Hooke presented a paper dealing with the ratio of the times of swing of a pendulum through the various portions of its arc and related these to the motions of a circular pendulum, but there is no mention of any form of escapement to lessen the arc of swing of the pendulum. On the same day 'Mr. Hooke shewed the society another kind of pendulum, which being perpendicular and short, by counterpoising performed the part of a long one.' Here again we have an effort to get a longer period of swing combined with a small arc.

'December 12th, 1666. Mr. Hooke produced a new sort of pendulum made after the manner of a beam, and so contrived, that by placing the beam nearer or farther below the centre of motion, the pendulum may perform its vibrations in any time assigned. . . .' Here we have the basis of the metronome of today, the bugbear of the author's childish and ineffectual efforts on the piano.

On January 1st, 1666–7, February 14th, 1666–7, January

2nd, 1667–8, May 6th, 1669, and October 28th, 1669, there are references to the circular pendulum, pendulums without any check at all, and 14-feet pendulums beating two seconds with an arc of swing of half an inch, which was less than 1°. None of these can be connected with the anchor escapement.

Nevertheless, as we can conclude from the above quotations, Hooke seems to have been fully alive to the desirability of combining a small arc of swing with a long period to improve timekeeping; what today is known as 'circular error'. He has been given the reputation of trying to appropriate, on occasion, the inventions of others; but here we may well have a case of 'I realised years ago that it was necessary to reduce the arc of swing of the pendulum and was working on this problem before the Fire of London', leading, after Clement had solved the problem, in 1671, as we shall see later, to the claim 'That's nothing new; *I* had that idea years ago'.

Gunter, in his *Early Science at Oxford*, volume one, page 232, makes the bare statement that Hooke invented the anchor escapement about 1675, but he makes no attempt to support this statement from any source whatever. This assertion is clearly wrong, as we have seen from Smith's book of 1675 that the long pendulum with its small arc of swing was already well established by that date.

As opposed to the negative evidence in favour of Hooke, we have, besides the positive statements of Smith and Derham, further positive evidence in favour of Clement in the shape of a turret clock, now in the Science Museum in London, signed and dated 'Guiliemus Clement Londini, Fecit 1671' (see *Plate 21*).

This has always had a recoil escapement and the date has been fully authenticated. A full description of the clock appears later.

If Clement had merely applied Hooke's invention of the anchor we should have expected frequent communications between the two men during the early years of application, but Hooke, in his diary which starts on March 10th, 1671–2, only once mentions Clement, on August 30th, 1672, and then only in connexion with the supply of a bell clapper for a turret clock. Clement was at this time still a member of the Blacksmiths' Guild.

The author is somewhat shy at introducing this rather technical passage into a book of a popular nature; but the invention
of the anchor escapement was as great a step forward in horological science as that of the verge escapement; and, like it, it
embraced entirely new principles which were the inventor's
idea. It led the way to the dead beat escapement and many
other variants and improvements both in escapements and
pendulums, which would have been quite impossible of application to the verge escapement.

Let us give honour where honour is due.

The next stage in escapement development,
made possible by Clement's invention, was an
important one which held the field for about
two and a quarter centuries. If you watch the
second hand of the average old long-case clock
you will notice after each 'tick' or 'tock' a slight
shudder, or recoil as it is termed, due to the
jarring when each pallet of the anchor engages
a tooth of the escape wheel. Although considerably less than the interference with the pendulum
in the verge escapement, it is very definite
interference and effects the time-keeping quite
considerably, in spite of Mr. Smith's eulogies
'that when 'tis well in order and the air of the
same consistence, it shall in Five hundred or a
Thousand revolutions of its Index, keep so equal
a Time, that no Human Art can discover the
least considerable Difference in any of its
revolutions. . . .'

About 1715 George Graham invented the
dead beat escapement. In this escapement the
pallet beds 'dead' on to the escape wheel
tooth; there is no jar or recoil (Fig. 7). This
escapement is more expensive to make. It is still
used in better quality domestic clocks, but its
principal use was in connexion with regulators,
i.e. clocks sufficiently accurate to be used for
astronomical observations and as master-clocks,
and remained the most usually adopted
escapement for time-keeping of the highest

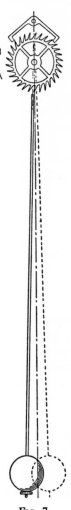

FIG. 7

accuracy until the end of the nineteenth century, when a German, named Riefler, introduced a different type. With this we shall not deal here, since it was only used in observatory clocks and did not have any general application. Let it suffice to say that Riefler did not entirely supplant Graham; many observatories retained their dead beat clocks.

Besides improvements in the design of escapements, clock-makers also sought to improve the pendulum. We have already seen the great stride forward made by the adoption of the Royal pendulum beating one second. In its first stages this consisted of an ordinary iron wire, suspended by a piece of flat spring, which is slipped through a narrow slit in the cock fixed to the back plate of the clock. The bob is a leaden lenticular mass, faced with brass. Regulation is made by screwing up or letting down a 'rating' nut, which travels on the threaded finial of the pendulum rod.

In the early bob pendulums used with verge escapements, which were usually pear-shaped, although some early makers, such as East, often used more ball-shaped bobs, it was not possible to tap the thread in the interior of the hole drilled through the bob to receive the pendulum rod. The hole was plugged with wood, which in turn was drilled the exact size of the pendulum rod and which then took up the fine threads cut in the pendulum rod itself; allowing an adjustment to be made by turning the whole bob.

These simple pendulum rods made no allowance, or compensation as it is called, for expansion or contraction owing to heat or cold. Graham made some experiments in 1715 with the expansion of metals, but did not pursue them. In 1721, in the course of some other experiments, he noticed the extraordinary high rate of expansion of mercury (quicksilver). He therefore made a bob for his pendulum of a glass jar containing mercury suspended in a brass frame attached to a brass pendulum rod (*Plate 26c*). By trial and error he ascertained the exact amount of mercury necessary in the jar, so that its upward expansion in heat would raise the centre of oscillation of the pendulum to the same extent as the expansion of the brass rod lowered it, with, of course, the converse in cold weather. (Note. The centre of oscillation of a pendulum is not quite the same as its centre of gravity, but we need not deal with that difference here.) Graham mercury pendulums are still in use today in high-grade clocks.

About the same time as Graham was experimenting with the differential expansion of metals in London, the brothers John and James Harrison, sons of a Yorkshire carpenter were making similar experiments which resulted in the invention of the grid-iron pendulum (*Plate 35*). This invention has always been credited to John Harrison, but it would now seem more likely that it was the work of the younger brother, James. John Harrison came to London in 1728 bringing the grid-iron pendulum with him. The brothers had found out that the expansion of brass to steel was approximately in the ratio of 3 : 2. He saw, therefore, if he had a brass rod 6 feet long and a steel one 9 feet long and joined them together at their lower ends, the upper ends would remain 3 feet apart whatever the variation of temperature. However, 9 feet was too long for convenience in a pendulum, so they devised the method of cutting his rods into lengths, three of steel and two of brass. In the illustration it will be noted that there are nine rods; in order to avoid distortion the four outer on one side are duplicated on the other side; we have therefore steel, brass, brass, steel fixed to the outer grid, and steel, brass, steel, brass, steel in the central grid, which is free to move within the guide plates.

This type of pendulum, again, is still in use in high-grade clocks today. John Harrison's life-work was to devise a time-piece which would go sufficiently accurately to enable the determination of the longitude of a ship at sea. After many years of effort, and possibly as many spent in wrangling with his adjudicators, and after the personal intervention of King George III, who was very interested in clocks and watches, he was finally awarded the whole of the £20,000 prize offered in Queen Anne's time for the solution of this problem, which had been the bane of navigation from time immemorial. Latitudinal position was easy to determine from the stars or sun, but to determine one's longitude necessitated very accurate time-keeping, from which could be calculated the number of degrees traversed to the east or west from a known starting-point. Harrison first used his grid-iron in compensating the balance of his first timepiece in 1735.

D

There was another application of this differential of expansion adopted by John Ellicott in 1752. In this the expansion of the rod downwards raises the bob by means of levers within the bob, and vice versa. It was never widely adopted; we shall therefore not go further into a detailed description of its working.

Thus we have outlined the early efforts at time-recording, at the control of clocks and the main improvements that the ordinary collector or others interested are likely to encounter. In the following chapters we shall deal with the different specimens of clocks illustrated and follow their progression through the years, seeing the effect of inventions on their design, the modifications due to social and economic causes, the influence of design and fashion on them until, finally, we come to the period where machinery and mass production, if only on a limited scale, rob the craft of individuality and interest from a student's point of view. The interest shifts to that of the engineer and workshop specialist.

CHAPTER TWO

Some Early Continental Clocks 1350-1650

IN this period the Continent was far ahead of England. Our early examples of clocks made in England, Salisbury and Wells cathedral clocks, were in all probability made by a foreigner invited to England for this purpose. It is due to the researches of Mr. R. P. Howgrave Graham that we know that the Bishop of Salisbury in 1386 was one Erghum, who came from Bruges to England on appointment to the See. We also know that this same bishop was translated to Wells and was there in 1392 when that clock was made. Mr. Howgrave Graham has also ascertained that the two clocks are, in all probability, by the same craftsman, since they both carry similar decorative or maker's marks. Now we know that there are many records of public turret clocks on the continent from the early days of the fourteenth century; also as we shall see later, in 1350 clocks were considered so common that no particular description of them was deemed necessary. What more likely than a desire by Bishop Erghum, who had been used to having clocks in his churches and cathedrals, that he should send for his clockmaker and commission clocks first in Salisbury and then in Wells.

The only Englishman of whom we have any record is Richard of Wallingford, who about 1340 is said to have constructed an elaborate astronomical clock. All trace of this has disappeared, all we know is that about two hundred years later, Leyland saw it, and from his description, it was apparently still in going order. Some have contended that this machine was the same as Wallingford's 'Albion' (all by one), which appears to have been a type of Equatorium, but the fact that Leyland refers to the clock showing the ebbing and flowing of the sea, infers to the author's mind, a mechanical astronomical clock.

During the years 1348–62, Giovanni de Dondi was working on his famous astronomical clock, which showed with a great degree of accuracy, the motions of the sun, moon and the five planets, as well as the nodes. It also had a perpetual calendar for the fixed feasts of the church and a perpetual calendar for the movable feasts, a feat not since achieved until Schwilgué, in 1842, made the third Strasbourg clock. By this time the Gregorian calendar was in use and the feat was much more complicated. This book is not dealing with complicated astronomical clocks, but the ordinary weight-driven verge escapement mechanical clock, which formed the motive force for all the astronomical dials, as is seen in *Plate 1b*. It will be noticed that Dondi uses a balance. Now this is the earliest depiction of a mechanical timepiece known to us, so it will be seen that the question of priority as between balance and foliot is an open question. It will also be noticed that Dondi only indicates the general lay-out; no details of pivots, bearings or plates are given. Dondi left the fullest possible description of just how he made the astronomical parts of his clock and for this the horological world owes him a great debt. In this he says that (and remember that we are dealing with a man writing in the middle of the fourteenth century), as clocks are quite common, and as there are several types quite well known, it would be a waste of time for him to give further details of this clock, for if he who is studying the manuscript, with a view to making a reproduction, cannot complete this clock by himself, he is wasting his time in contemplating any further work. Now as we have seen in 1277 the mechanical clock was not known. Its spread after its invention must have been very rapid. A notable feature of Dondi's clock is that it is made entirely of brass; in the two hundred pages of manuscript iron is not mentioned.[1]

In *Plate 2* are seen two early spring driven clocks with fusees. The small one has a date 1504 engraved on the little door. If this date be genuine it would make it the earliest surviving example of the fusee. At all events it is very early and is included here to show the very pointed type of fusee employed at the outset. The little door opens to show to what extent the fusee has run down. The clock is in the Musee des Arts Decoratifs, in Paris. The other illustration shows a mid-sixteenth-century clock with its travelling case of tooled morocco leather. It shows the hours of the day and night and has an astrolabe dial that would allow for the rising and setting of certain named stars

[1] See Appendix I.

to be ascertained as well as the temporal hours of the night. From the revolution of the ecliptic circle the times of the rising and setting of the sun could be ascertained. In both cases the movements are all of iron; especial notice should be taken of the very fine balance of large diameter in the larger clock. The smaller has a foliot. The travelling clock is engraved for the latitude of Toledo, and is presumably of German make for export.

Another interesting piece made for the latitude of London and dated 1560 is seen in *Plate 3*. The maker's mark, a form of 'M' is not identifiable, but since the inscriptions are in French, presumably it was made in France. It is not intended in this book to enter into detailed descriptions of complicated astronomical dials, this aspect of horology is fully dealt with in the author's *Some Outstanding Clocks over 700 Years 1250–1950*, recently published. The object of the inclusion of this example is to give an illustration of how astrology, which entered so intimately into all details of daily life, was often introduced into horology. The signs of the Zodiac are engraved around the base of the drum containing the movement, and each sign has its legendary figure engraved upon it:

Aquarius (The Water-carrier)		Virgo (The Virgin)	August
	January	Libra (The Balance)	September
Pisces (The Fishes)	February	Scorpio (The Scorpion)	
Aries (The Ram)	March		October
Taurus (The Bull)	April	Sagittarius (The Archer)	
Gemini (The Twins)	May		November
Cancer (The Crab)	June	Capricornus (The Goat)	
Leo (The Lion)	July		December

The concentric circles on the top of the drum represent the different celestial spheres. First come air and fire that were supposed to surround the earth, then the seven spheres of the sun, moon and five planets, followed by that of the Firmament, or the fixed stars. Beyond that a sphere representing the *Chrystalineum* or the year of $365\frac{1}{4}$ days and finally the sphere of the *Primum mobile*, to account for a slow motion independent and in the opposite direction to the others which was later identified with the precession of the equinoxes.

The front dial will indicate sidereal time and will show the hour, position of the sun in the ecliptic, rising and setting of the sun and the principle stars, phases of the moon, &c. The back dial is for direct observation of the sun; the rectangular engraving is for the measuring of vertical and horizontal heights.

Reverting to the twelve signs: often under each sign is engraved the word *Bonum*, *Medium*, or *Malum*, preceded by the initial letter of the sign in question. In the Middle Ages, and even up to the end of the seventeenth century or after, astrology

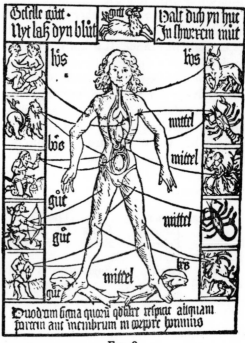

Fɪɢ. 8

played a great part in the life of the people; the influence of the stars and planets was good, fair, or bad, according to the month of happening. Surgical operations were supposed to be influenced by the month of their operation. Fig 8 shows a diagram which was originally on the first Strasburg clock, indicating in which months certain organs should be operated on.

Incidentally the ancient Greek and Roman philosophers considered that every hour of the day was under the influence of one of the seven planets then known to them. It must be remembered that the earth was considered fixed and the sun was thought to be a planet like the others, viz., the Moon, Mercury, Venus, the Sun, Mars, Jupiter and Saturn, giving them in order of their distance from the earth. As previously mentioned, the sun is really only a very near fixed star.

Each day of the week was allotted to the god represented by that planet which was supposed to influence the earth at the hour of midday to one p.m. on that day, each succeeding hour being influenced by the planet next distant from the earth. Starting with the moon as influencing the period midday to one P.M. on 'Monday' we get:

Saturn	Jupiter	Mars	Sun	Venus	Mercury	Moon
						1
2	3	4	5	6	7	8
9	10	11	12	13	14	15
16	17	18	19	20	21	22
23	24	1	2	etc.		

giving Mars (French: *mardi*) as the deity for the second day. Following this round, we get Mercury for the third day (Fr. *mercredi*); Jupiter – Jove – for the fourth (Fr. *jeudi*); Venus for the fifth (Fr. *vendredi*); Saturn for the sixth (Fr. *samedi*); and the Sun for the seventh (Fr. *dimanche*), being derived from Dies Dominico, or The Lord's Day. English and German names of the days of the week are derived from their own gods, but, according to the Oxford Dictionary, these gods are identified with the Greco-Roman gods. Tuesday comes from the fem. gen. of O.E. Tiw, the name of an ancient Teutonic god identified with Mars. Wednesday is Woden's day; Woden was the god of eloquence and also had the facility for rapid movement from place to place, the same attributes as Mercury. Thursday, Thor's day, the god of thunder, as was Jove. Friday, according to these experts, does not come from Freyja, but from the goddess Frig, wife of Odin. The name is the feminine of the old Teutonic adjective *frijo*, beloved, loving; here we have our link with Venus.

On the pillar of this clock are marked nine columns, of which seven are for each day of the week, the remaining two being marked '*Heures du jour*' and '*Heures de la nuit*'. The former has roman numerals I to XII and continuing with I and II, the latter runs from III to XII, with the last four spaces blank. In the planetary columns, the last four signs are repeated at the top of the next column, to preserve continuity.

Clocks rolling slowly down an inclined plane, with gravity as the motive force have generally been attributed to the latter half of the eighteenth century, but in the Museum at Brunswick is to be found the clock illustrated in *Plate 4a*, made by Isaac Habrecht of Strasburg, who died in 1620. It will be recalled that Habrecht, with his brother, Josias, was the maker of the second Strasburg clock, to the designs of Conrad Dasypodius.

During 24 hours the clock travels slowly down its inclined plane, which is about three feet long. It has then to be lifted up and placed again at the top of the incline, a very simple method of winding. The hand is fixed and is read against the revolving chapter ring.

Another discovery of the last few years, made by Dr. H. Von Bertele, partly from researches in his native Vienna and partly from visits to other Continental museums, is that of Jobst Burgi's Cross-Beat escapement. This discovery has thrown light on certain, hitherto inexplicable, reference to manuscripts of the mid-seventeenth century which referred to a *libramentum duplice*, or double escapement. Within about 60 years of its invention it was superseded by that of the pendulum. The cross-beat was for some years a closely guarded secret and was only practised by Burgi and a few of his pupils, mainly in northern European plain. With this invention Burgi achieved a very greatly improved time standard over the standard verge escapement, the only other then known alternative. In the early models the very fine teeth on large escape wheels and their precise adjustment to the two pallets of the cross arms, allowed for accurate adjustment, but in his latest designs, each pallet could be adjusted separately.

Plate 4c and *d* shows a delightful little clock, about 6¼ in. high. At the top, in front can be seen the two arms of the cross-beat escapement, which, geared together, oscillate in opposite directions. In this case they are not separately adjustable and regulation is by means of setting up or letting down the mainspring. In the view of the back-plate it will be noted that the key has to be inserted into a square hole in the winding arbor, instead of the arbor protruding and fitting into the winding key. *W* is the winding arbour and *S* is for adjusting the setting of the mainspring, the degree to which this is altered is shown by a scale engraved on the spring barrel, and seen through the heart-shaped opening *T*. *R* is a lever to slacken the mainspring tension. The clock is by Fransisco Swartz of Brussels and dates about 1630. It is an early example of the introduction of the minute hand.

The remaining illustration in *Plate 4* is one of the religious type of clock that became popular in Roman Catholic countries in the 'Counter Reformation' period. It shows Christ roped to a pillar for the flagellation. The date is about 1610. The hours are shown on a revolving band around the sphere on the top of the column, the quarters being indicated on the small horizontal dial on the base of the clock. A fusee chain is used instead of gut.

As previously mentioned, Burgi's cross-beat escapement was not generally known and others assayed to find a better time standard than the verge escapement. In several cases this took the form of a rolling ball, really a development of the idea of the inclined plane clock that we have just been considering. These ball clocks were often of complicated design, the path of the ball was often tortuous and the method of restoration of the ball various, in fact many of the designs seen on paper would have very little hope of mechanical performance. A Monsieur Grollier de Sevière, who died aged 90 in 1680, designed or collected many examples of rolling-ball clocks and these were set out in book form by his grandson, of the same name in 1719.

The clock of this type illustrated in *Plates 5* and *6* was made in 1601 by Christoph Rohr of Leipzig. The date has been fixed by documentary evidence. A steel ball is released at the top of the run, when it reaches the bottom it falls into a trap and is directed inwards. In its inward passage it strikes the curved trigger seen in *Plate 5b* and more clearly in the enlarged section *Plate 6a*. The ball rolls into a cup attached to the linked chain running in a groove in the side of the vertical tube. The trigger releases the spring drive to the wheel driving the chain, which goes at once into motion and carries the ball to the top in such a time as will make the descent and ascent combined, one minute. There is only one ball; a second cup, which will descend to be ready in position when the ball again reaches the end of its travel can just be seen, upside down catching the highlight in the centre of the dark shadow under the top plate in *Plate 5b*. The other long chain serves to drive the carousel on the top. Every three hours the knights and foot soldiers parade before the turbaned Turk, who vigorously beats the drum in front of him with a hammer in each hand. The clock shows the hour, quarter, date and day of the week.

Before leaving this chapter on early Continental clocks it will be interesting to include an example which shows that, in the opinion of some at any rate, old ideas are best. It will be recalled that one of the earliest subsidiary methods of regulation of a weight-driven verge escapement clock was to alter the position of the thread suspending the pallet arbor and so to alter the angle of incidence between the pallet and the crown wheel. A most interesting development of this idea applied to a spring-driven clock is seen in *Plate 7*, a clock by Hans Kiening of Fuessen in Bavaria, of date about 1590.

The clock takes the form of a book, the inner hand indicates the hour, one revolution in 24 hours, and the longer hand indicated the quarters, with subsidiary marks for every five minutes and seven and a half minutes, or half quarters. Above is a dial indicating the extent to which the spring has run down, a very early example of the 'up and down'. The shutters indicate the number of hours of day and night, the Nuremberg hours, incidentally they also indicate the times of sunrise and sunset. From the illustrations it will be seen that this clock combines the stackfreed principle of a shaped cam fixed to a toothed wheel driven by a pinion on the mainspring arbor and the adjustable pallet. Fig. 9 shows the functioning quite clearly. The cam is concealed under the pierced cock, bottom left, and is shaped with a 'stop' projection which replaces the uncut portion of the cam-carring wheel in the stackfreed. (See p. 53.) As the cam revolves it causes the pinion on the bottom of the arbor carried by the curved arm to engage with the rack connected with the pallet arbor, decreasing the angle of incidence of the upper pallet and to a certain degree, that of the lower pallet also, in this way shortening the period of contact, resulting in a shorter period of oscillation as the force of the un-

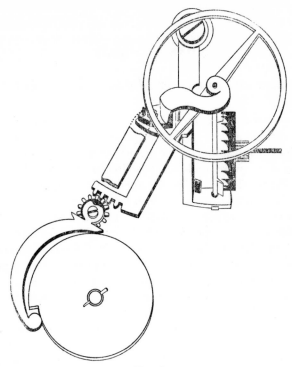

FIG. 9

coiling spring decreases, giving an equalising effect to the power transmitted to the train, as in the case of the fusee. Top right in *Plate 7b* is a dial for the months of the year, each month being represented by its zodiacal sign.

CHAPTER THREE

Lantern and Bracket or Mantel Clocks 1600-1735

THIS period has been chosen for the first stage in the description of both portable clocks, i.e. bracket or mantel clocks, and long-case or grandfather clocks, because during these years were made all those important inventions which have influenced the clocks we are considering, viz. domestic clocks. They were: the pendulum in 1657; the anchor escapement in 1671; the rack and snail striking method in 1676, which in its turn made repeating clocks possible; the illuminated night clock, first made about 1670-80; the equation clock in 1695; the dead-beat escapement in 1715; the mercury pendulum and the grid-iron pendulum about 1726.[1]

All changes in the design of domestic clock movements after this were modifications of existing ideas; nothing fundamental was introduced. The inventions introducing fundamental changes took place in the design of chronometers and precision time-keepers with which we are not here concerned. It would be interesting to carry this study further and to embrace all methods of time-keeping, but limitations of space do not allow.

The early clocks we have seen illustrated in Chapters I and II were either designed for hanging on the wall or for placing on a table. On the Continent the table clock gained considerably in favour during the early part of the seventeenth century, while in England we were only just beginning to think of making anything but heavy turret clocks.

In the latter years of the sixteenth century a few, very few, makers were working in England, such as Bartholomew Newsam and Nicholas Vallin; some of them appear to have made watches only, at least only their watches have survived to come down to us. The names of Michael Nowen, Randolf Bull and David Ramsay come to mind. This last was clockmaker to James I, who came to London and was to become the first Master of the Clockmakers' Company in 1631.

[1] See Appendix II.

Very few examples exist of the productions of these early workers in London, either British born or of foreign origin. One which the author found a few years ago is seen in *Plate 8*. It is a table clock signed by N. Vallin, whose name we have just mentioned and dates about 1600. It was found and still is in the Museum in Banff, Scotland, in a section devoted to the work and memory of James Ferguson, the eminent eighteenth-century astronomer and horologist, who started life as a humble shepherd lad in the district, and whose name will be seen engraved on the base cover.

Mr. C. B. Drover has made an extensive research into the biography of Nicholas Vallin, who was the son of John Vallin, a Fleming who emigrated to London about 1580. John died in 1603, perhaps of the plague and Nicholas also died of the plague a few months later. That he helped his father is shown by the passage in John's will which indicates that he makes bequests to his son Nicholas in consideration of the way he helped him to earn his living.

This clock is probably one of the most untouched pieces of Vallin's work extant; we see from the back plate that the ratchet wheel for setting up the mainspring is missing, as is also under the top plate a pinion of eight leaves that should engage with a wheel of sixty-four teeth which carrying the hour hand. This combined with the sixteen turns on the fusee, would give two revolutions to the hand every twenty-four hours.

The balluster pillars, used in their logical position are interesting; we shall see later how, when clocks were made to stand up vertically, in the early examples the pillars are still of the balluster type with the base pinned through the back plate although their position is now horizontal and their shape has lost all functional meaning.

The pinion carried on the hand arbor, seen on the top of *Plate 8b* gears in a 2:1 ratio with the wheel carrying the globe, giving a 24-hour period of rotation. This pinion is undoubtedly original and proves that the clock was always intended to carry a globe. Was this an early attempt to 'find the longitude'? The present globe and the engraving of its dial are both about 1830, but the fact that the clock carried a rotating globe seems to have interested the restoration savant John Desagulier, a well-known figure in the Royal Society at that time; he appears to have acquired it in 1719. The scientific interest in the clock is further indicated by its passing to Benjamin Franklin in 1757, thirteen years after Desaugliers died. Benjamin Franklin and James Ferguson are known to have been friends; as Franklin is known to have been in London in 1766, it is presumed that he gave the clock to Ferguson in that year. Kenneth McCulloch was Ferguson's assistant. Who G. W. was we do not know. Henderson, in his *Life of Ferguson*, writes that Andrew Reid, a close friend of Ferguson's, shortly before his (Reid's) death, gave a curious clock to McCulloch, which showed the motion of the earth by the rotation of a globe. We can, therefore, assume that the clock had a globe at that time. Ferguson died in 1776 and McCulloch apparently had the clock in 1774. If the clock did not always have a globe, there would be nothing to distinguish it from many other table clocks of the period, and it would not have had this particular interest to its many scientific possessors. The dial for the globe is engraved I to XII twice over, once clockwise and once anti-clockwise, so that readings were given both east and west of the meridian.

Prior to the seventeenth century, when the English evolved their own style known as the lantern clock, sometimes miscalled the Cromwellian clock, very few domestic clocks were made in England. These 'Cromwellian' clocks were first made in the reign of James I and continued to be made until the reign of Queen Anne, and even later in the provinces.

In the previous chapter it was mentioned that the early clockmakers were either blacksmiths or locksmiths as long as they were working entirely in wrought iron; but when brass was introduced this involved a different technique, that of casting at temperatures considerably lower than that of iron. Just how the change came about is not recorded, but we know that in 1628–29 there were a sufficient number of clockmakers, working in or within ten miles of London, to seek affiliation with the blacksmiths as a separate craft, but without success, and the following year on February 23rd, 1629–30, between fifty and sixty clockmakers petitioned King Charles I for incorporation as a Company, which was granted in 1631.

Plate 9a shows an early English 'transitional' clock of date about 1600–10. The wrought-iron decorated corner posts and the iron top and bottom plates remain, but front and back are faced with brass sheet, on to the former of which is engraved the hour circle, a fairly narrow ring, with 'dumpy' numerals. This is a sign of early work. The side plates have not yet appeared. The wheels are already of brass and the pinions of wrought iron; their different colours can be distinguished in the photograph. The crown wheel is also of brass, the pallet arbor and the pallets will be of wrought iron. The balance wheel is clearly seen under the bell, which is supported by four arms, at the end of each of which is a small pin, which is in turn sprung into a hole drilled in the finial to receive it.

Metal screws were already in use in clocks on the Continent about 1500; they are here making their appearance in England; in the top plate, just above the shield with the monogram, which in turn is seen above the xii, can be seen the square-headed top of an early screw; the finials and feet too are screwed into the pillars, keeping the top and bottom plates in place.

The going train is in front, the striking train behind; the locking plate or count wheel can faintly be seen among the shadows concealing the back plate.

The hand should be noted, a somewhat clumsy, wrought-iron hand with an 'arrow-head' point, heavy central boss and a medium-length tail; the word tail is used here because, with the general heavy construction of the clock, a counterpoise to the hand would not be of any practical use. In later years, when clock movements become works of exact precision, second and minute hands do have a counterpoise, or else the wheels driving them are cut out to provide a true balance in all positions. It will be noticed that there is an absence of the frets in the front and sides which will appear on later models.

The general shape and lay-out became standardised and was practically the only shape of clock made in England for sixty years. Square, going train in front, striking train behind. The similarity to lantern design of the period is shown by the second illustration on *Plate 9*, which is of a silver lantern, taken by King Christian IV of Denmark on his journey to the North Cape late in the sixteenth century. This is now in the Rosenborg Castle Museum near Copenhagen. English country lanterns of this period also bear the same general shape, if less ornate in design.

Plate 9 shows two more examples of lantern clocks, *9c* being

by William Selwood, who worked at 'Ye Marmade' in Loth-
bury. The side door has been removed for the purpose of
photography. The date of this clock is about 1620; the somewhat heavy chapter ring, an early indication, is still there; the
hand is still of wrought iron, but the 'curls' each side of the
arrow-head show signs of rather better finish than that of the
preceding example. The hour numerals are still 'dumpy'. By
the way, the term *chapter ring* or *hour ring*, which is so often used,
comes, no doubt, from the monastic chapters or offices which
took place at each hour of the day and night.

The centre of the dial is engraved all over, a style that persisted in lantern clocks so long as they were made. Sometimes
the maker's name and address were included, but very often,
as in the Selwood clock, they were engraved at the bottom of
the fret placed over the dial. This detail in the photograph has
been lost in reproduction. Regulation was effected by increasing
or decreasing the going train weight by adding or removing lead
shot. An original weight, sheathed in copper, with a cup on top
for the lead, is seen in the illustration.

There is a definite progression in the design of the frets. The
type illustrated, an heraldic shape, is early in the progression;
the arms of the original owner have been roughly scratched on
it. Later crossed dolphins were adopted (*Plate 11a*) passing
eventually to a more nondescript design (*Plate 9d*).

The chapter ring has a circle divided into quarter-hours and
the marks are enclosed, as are the hour numerals, in a narrow
double circle. Later clocks have only a single circle. The half-
hour mark, a star at the end of a line, is also seen in the preceding example. If these half-hour marks be followed, it will be
noticed that they tend to become more elaborate, developing
into a fleur-de-lis *motif* and then gradually reverting to simplicity, until they eventually disappear, together with all other
markings on the dial, except for the bare numerals. It took
nearly a hundred years after the establishment of the minute
hand as a general practice for all quarter-hour, half-hour and
other intermediary marks to disappear as useless, so hard does
habit and tradition die.

The long slender feet with sharp-edged decorative 'ridges'
seen in *9c*, as opposed to the more rounded 'bosses' of *11a*, are
indicative of Charles I's time. The bell, as before, is supported

by four arms, each having a pin at its terminal for springing into the finials. There is a semi-circular suspension hoop for passing over a hook on the wall, as well as two distance pieces which project from the back plate. *Plate 9d* shows a rather later example of lantern clock, dating about 1715. Here we have a slightly wider chapter ring, the hour numerals somewhat larger, but still only one hand and only quarter-hour divisions marked; no minute hand yet. The half-hour marks are the diamond shape usually associated with clocks made by George Graham, as indeed this one is. This example is interesting in as much as it shows the habit of taking one's one and only clock with one on journeys. Very possibly this clock belonged to some wealthy man who had town and country residences, and the clock went with him, back and forth. From the stout nature of the oak travelling case and its somewhat coarse construction, one would judge that this was made at the country seat of the owner. The slot in the upper frame holding the driving and alarm weights, to take the finial surmounting the bell is interesting, indicating that Graham did not make this especially as a travelling clock, or he would surely have omitted this unnecessary decoration. The hollowing out of places to receive the loops of the weights, the forward curve of the bell and the boss of the hand arbor indicate the care taken to prevent all movement during transit. The fret is a very late type, indeed this clock is a very late London example, but it cannot be before 1713, as Graham only succeeded Tompion in that year. Before that date he would have no right to put his name on any clock without that of Tompion as well.

Here we will introduce an Italian clock in the English lantern style by Camerini and dated 1656 (*Plate 10a*). It will be noted that it is fitted with a pendulum and that the date is a year earlier than Huygens' invention. This clock, which was bought by the Science Museum, London, at the Webster sale in 1954, has been the subject of much controversy as to whether the pendulum is original or a conversion. The top plate does not contain any filled or unused holes that would have been necessary for a balance or foliot used in connexion with a vertical crown wheel; if any conversion from balance to pendulum has been made, then the whole top plate would have had to be renewed. A recent close examination of the clock at the Science

E

Museum resulted in the opinion being expressed that the top plate was original.

Professor Morpurgo has recently made extensive researches into early Italian horology and in his recently published *L'Orologio e il Penduolo* he shows two more Camerini clocks with pendulums, one dated 1652 and the other undated. He also shows sketches of pendulums and escapements taken from manuscripts of the sixteenth and early seventeenth centuries. He has kindly allowed the author to choose one or two for inclusion in this book (*Plate 10*). Fig 3 shows one of Leonardo's sketches for a pendulum and verge escapement, about 1485; probably designed as a storer of energy. *Plate 10b* shows a drawing which contains the germ of the idea of the anchor escapement. This is from a MS dated about 1524 by Benevuto della Volpasia, who was the son of a Florentine friend of Leonardo.

The other two drawings appear in a MS *Questo Benedetto Pendolo* of the early seventeenth century. The one seems somewhat far-fetched in its idea, but the other is a verge escapement with a reversed crown wheel, just as one finds the only two known signed pieces of Johann Treffler (one is in the Museum at Kassel), and who is reputed to have made a pendulum clock for Archduke Ferdinand II of Tuscany in the 1650's before the Huygens invention, and who also is said to have had knowledge of Galileo's pendulum.

While there is no evidence that these sketches were of pendulums actually applied to clocks, we must concede that Italian thought had been very active with the idea of pendulum control, so that the genuineness of Camerini's clocks now appears much more probable than was the case, say, ten years ago. Had Camerini any idea that the pendulum achieved isochronism? There is no indication in the documents that this was so. This property had been noted, but not broadcast, by Galileo, but it still remained for Huygens to provide the theoretical proof.

After the pendulum had been invented, lantern clocks continued to be made in large numbers fitted with a pendulum hanging down the back, the going train in front and the striking train behind, as before, square in shape, although there was now no necessity for this since we have no longer to accommodate a circular balance wheel. Clocks could be, and were, made 'flat' in shape, as we shall soon see.

The next two illustrations (*Plate 11*) show a passing fancy in lantern clock design which lasted only ten or twenty years in the last quarter of the seventeenth century. These are no exception to our generalisation that the going train is in front and the striking train behind, but the pendulum is placed between the two trains. This prevented a pear-shaped bob being used; it would have taken up too much depth. The pendulum bob is made, therefore, from a piece of sheet brass and takes the form of an anchor, the flukes of which appear in the wings as the pendulum swings from side to side. Not many of these clocks survive today. The date of our example is 1675–80; it is an alarm clock, and the disk for the setting of the alarm is seen in the middle of the dial. The chapter ring is still wider and pro-trudes still further beyond the corner pillars, so much so that it has to be flattened out top and bottom to fit between the top and bottom plates. This overlap of the chapter ring gets still more pronounced later, these clocks getting the name 'sheeps-head', though why one cannot imagine, unless it be the sup-posed likeness to a sheep's curved horns on each side of a narrow face.

But to return to our particular specimen. The hand is getting progressively lighter in design, the spade head is developing and the shank is much thinner, and it is still fixed by a simple pin through a hole in the hour-hand arbor; tightening washers, or collets, are not yet used, although they are already common in better-quality clocks of this date. The fleur-de-lis *motif* for the half-hour mark is becoming more pronounced and there is only a single circle surrounding the hour numerals. The frets are of the dolphin type.

What we have said about frets is only a very rough guide to dates. These frets varied very much and early styles were often copied in later years. The chapter ring, style of engraving of the hour numerals and the details of the intermediate marks, also the design of the hand, provided that it is original, are surer guides to the date of these lantern clocks.

Lantern clocks were *always* weight-driven and consequently had to hang on the wall; they are one of the most popular types for modern reproductions. These, normally, have a dirty 'stale mustardy' colour achieved in the attempt to make modern brass look old; the hands are invariably stamped from a sheet, and they always have minute hands, as it is not much use making a modern clock without; whereas genuine lantern clocks would not be made originally with two hands. The engraving, as a rule, is crude and heavy and they are *always* spring-driven. Sometimes one gets a genuine old housing containing a modern movement. In this case there will be two hands and the winding holes for the spring movement will have been cut in the dial of the clock. The novice should look out for these points; he should also remember that clocks with their original balance wheel or foliot are very rare indeed, and while it is not impossible that he find one, the odds are very much against him.

In England the lantern clock was the forerunner of both the long-case and mantel or bracket clock. (These latter two terms are used indiscriminately.) On the Continent the long-case clock made its first appearance about the same time as the lantern clock in England, as we shall see later.

The table clock was a very usual style on the Continent for domestic clocks in the sixteenth and seventeenth centuries; it took many forms: square, rectangular, round; sometimes embellished with figures or animals that performed at the striking of the hour. Its basic construction was a top plate and a bottom plate; the distance pillars holding them together were usually shaped and often ornate. Continental practice tended to a greater degree of ornamentation than English. Actually table clocks by English makers are very rare.

The dial plate is placed over the top plate of the movement, and since these all have to be spring-driven, as they stand on the table, the spring barrel often offers another surface for decoration with engraving. A German table clock of the latter half of the seventeenth century is shown in *Plate 11c*. This is of gilded brass, finely chased, with figures of Venus and Cupid on the dial. The bell was placed either under the movement, as in the example illustrated, or above it, in which case the dial and hand were placed above the bell, which would be in a domed housing. The thought and care put into the whole clock, the elaborate engraving on the cock protecting the balance wheel, the engraved hammer-head shaped like an eagle's, make one sigh for the times when men worked for the glory of their craft. The maker is Christian Caroli of Koenigsberg.

The year spring-driven clock made by Tompion in the late 1690's for King William III and now in Lord Mostyn's possession, is well known. It has, however, a forerunner, a clock in the Brunswick Museum made by Johannes Buschmann of Augsburg in 1651–2. This is illustrated in *Plate 12*. This early pre-pendulum clock shows the hours on the main dial and the quarters on a subsidiary dial below. The phases of the moon are shown by a revolving globe and its age in days on the small horizontal dial just below it. The master mainspring (*Plate 12c*) is housed in the base, on the one side of which is a dial divided into 365 days, the numbering being at intervals of 5 days up to 100, starting again 5, 10, etc. up to 200 and again starting at 300 to 365 (*Plate 12b*). On the other side of the case at the base is another annular calendar dial with the days of the year and indicating the fixed feasts of the church. At the back in the upper part is a day of the week dial with deities.

Once a day the rack seen in *Plate 12c* is released and governed by the four-bladed fly; it winds up a subsidiary spring in the upper part of the movement. This principle of the remontoire had already been practised by Jobst Burgi about 1595. The force transmitted to the train from the secondary spring wound daily, would be much more even than that that could be transmitted from the big year spring. The chain attached to the housing of the subsidiary spring can be seen in *Plate 12d*.

While Buschmann aimed at a going period of one year, it is understood that he did not quite attain his objective; here Tompion, half a century later, had better success.

We have already seen one example of pre-pendulum effort at accurate time-keeping, the cross-beat escapement. *Plate 13* shows a clock which embodies both this and a falling ball. The latter, in this case, is only decorative and has nothing to do with the driving mechanism of the clock; it was merely designed to give an impression of perpetual motion.

This clock is by Johann Georg Meyer of Munich, date about 1660. It has dials on all four sides, those for the fourth side being held by runners passing into the slots seen at the top and bottom of the inside left of the case (*Plate 13d.*) The case is tortoiseshell veneered, with embossed silver mounts. It shows about everything that it is possible to embody in a single piece. The dial on the right *Plate 13a* shows the hour and minute (it is pre-pendulum but its cross-beat escapement makes it worthwhile to have a minute hand), the phases of the moon and its age. The dial on the left in this view is seen enlarged in *Plate 13c*. In the picture showing the other two dials, that on the right gives the hour, minute, day of the week only. The dial on the left gives the hour and minute, the minute hand is scarcely visible, a thin blued steel hand almost coinciding with the gilt hand with the sun's effigy. The minutes are all individually marked on the bevelled ring immediately outside the roman numerals. The position of the sun and moon in the ecliptic can be read off this dial; where the sun and moon hands cross the circle of the zodiac as it revolves once a year around the inner space of the hour circle, show this. There is also an annual calendar dial. The four subsidiary dials probably give the Italian hours starting at sunset and the Babylonian starting at sunrise and possibly golden number and solar cycle.

Taking the view into the movement (*Plate 13d*) top right, can seen a locking plate for grande sonnerie striking, there being four notches for each hour, the quarters would be struck on another train with its own locking plate. The position of this locking plate is indicated on the 'Back Plate Dial' (*Plate 13c*), top left, the indicating hand is missing. There would also seem to be a switch over to 'dutch striking', where the hour is repeated or anticipated at the half-hour on a different toned bell. The dial for this, complete with hand, is seen below that of the grand sonnerie. The dial on the right may be a minute hand connected with the minute hand on the opposite dial; it will be noted that it is travelling anti-clockwise.

The original cross-beats with cherubs heads painted on them are still there, but the clock has been converted to pendulum with verge escapement, the crutch for the pendulum is seen right at the top. The gilt hour hand with the effigy of the sun and the steel minute hand are to be read off an hour ring engraved on the glass of the door. In the centre is an alarm setting disk. As already mentioned, the ball rolling down the spiral is purely decorative, as is the armillary sphere on the top.

The relationship between the English lantern clock and the Continental Gothic clock is seen in the example illustrated in

Plate 14 which shows a clock of mid-sixteenth-century date indicating the hours, quarters and phases and age of the moon. This influence on design persisted for some time as is evidenced by the late seventeenth-century Italian example of a weight-driven wall clock by Jo. Baptiste Albertis, dated 1685. These examples all have metal cases, indeed all English lantern clocks have metal cases, wood was not introduced for cases in England till after the invention of the pendulum in 1657. Wood was, however, used for cases on the Continent a century earlier. *Plate 4b* shows a wooden base housing the movement for a 'Flagellation' clock of the early seventeenth century. In the Kuensthistorisches Museum in Vienna there is a clock with a painted wooden case as early as 1560–70.

In considering lantern clocks, we have passed from the period of the balance wheel to that of the early days of the pendulum, which, as already stated, has enabled 'flat' instead of 'square' clocks to be made. We will now embark on a series of spring-driven pendulum clocks and follow their progression from the early efforts up to, in this part, the first third of the eighteenth century, during which period all the main improvements had been invented. After this all efforts were concentrated on 'finding the longitude', on improving escapements and the development of chronometers, on finding the means to simplify their construction and consequently their cost, and at the same time on bringing their construction within the capability of a greater number of makers.

In this connexion Arnold, Earnshaw, Mudge and Dent stand out, Earnshaw's work having, perhaps, the most lasting influence; but their efforts are not of a nature to be included in a popular non-technical book.

Since the pendulum came from Holland we go to Holland for our first examples. *Plate 14c* shows a most delightful small clock of early Dutch design known as 'Haagsche Klokjes', or Hague clocks, since they were first made by Salomon Coster of The Hague, who was the original licensee of Huygens. The date would be about 1660. It is quite small, made to hang on the wall, the bevelled edge of the door being veneered in tortoise, shell, following very closely the lines of wall mirrors of the period of the Restoration. Taking first the dial – the word dial, by the way, is derived from the Latin *dies*, a day, medieval

Latin *dialis*. A *diale* was as much land as could be ploughed in a day, according to the *New Century Dictionary*. The term dial was used in early times to denote a watch as well as a sundial:

> 'And then he drew a dial from his poke [pocket];
> And looking at it with lack-lustre eye,
> Says very wisely, "It's ten o'clock;
> Thus we may see," quoth he, "how the world wags."'
> *As You Like It*
> 'Then my dial goes not true.'
> *All's Well that Ends Well*

Just in what order Shakespeare wrote his plays is not known. Many have tried to set them out in chronological order and have failed, but for our purpose the period 1590–1610 covers the years of issue of the bulk of his plays. Although at the end of the sixteenth century and the beginning of the seventeenth century England was lagging behind in clockmaking and many of her efforts were crude and clumsy, there were working in London watchmakers who, judging from specimens of their work to be seen in the British Museum, the Museum of the Clockmakers' Company, and other collections, were producing watches that were equal in craftsmanship and decorative design to anything that contemporary makers on the Continent could produce. The names of David Ramsay, Michael Nowen, Thomas Nixon, Richard Masterton, Isaac Symms, Samson Shelton, Edward East, John Willow, and Nicholas Walter all appear on English watches of this period.

To return, however, to our quotations, the expression 'how the world wags' would seem to indicate a reference to the balance wheel of a watch, and 'my dial goes not true' can scarcely refer to a sundial which, once fixed, always records truly. A pocket sundial would only record incorrectly if incorrectly held by the owner and the expression 'goes' would scarcely have been used. We can conclude therefore that Shakespeare was alluding to watches and not to sundials.

It was the reference to the dial of our early Dutch clock that betrayed us into transgressing into the dissertation on the word *dial*; let us now return to the clock. The dial plate, as was customary at that period on the Continent, is covered with velvet, usually black, but sometimes, as in this instance, plum-coloured. The chapter ring is of solid silver, the hand gilded

brass and finely engraved. The small silver shield hanging
below the dial bears the maker's name, *J. Bernard van Stryp,
fecit Anvers*. This shield can be lifted up and the pendulum bob
reached with the finger through a hole covered by the shield to
set it in motion, if need be.

Since there is only one hand, the quarter-hours are marked
on the inner edge of the chapter ring, and there is an ingenious
and rather unique method of approximating the minutes by
engraving on the outer edge of the chapter ring six inverted Vs
between each hour, the distance between their apexes indicating
ten-minute intervals.

The illustration (*Plate 14d*) shows the movement of this interesting and charming little clock. This type of box housing, with
the whole movement swinging forward, was very generally
adopted in Holland, even when clock cases were designed to
stand on the mantel and not to hang on the wall as in this case.

It will be recalled that we dealt with the build-up of the table
clock, and this and some of the following examples show how
conservatism in design remains when the function of the design
has eased. The early type of baluster pillar would be quite
natural and functional if the movement were turned over to
the left in a horizontal position instead of vertical, as would be
the case with a table clock, but it is some years before the
baluster pillar disappears and a pillar with a centrally turned
boss appears. In conformity with table-clock construction, the
pillars are neatly riveted into the front plate of this clock, which
would be the visible bottom plate in a table clock, and protrude
through the back plate, and are there pinned, an untidy finish,
which in a table clock would have been hidden under the dial.
As we shall see, makers gradually awoke to this point after some
years of somnolence, and the pillars become neatly riveted into
the back plates and are pinned behind the front plates.

This little clock is only a timepiece; hence there is only one
winding hole. The pendulum is suspended by a silken thread,
the usual Continental practice, and is actuated by a crutch
affixed to the end of the pallet arbor.

Bearing down on each side of the pendulum suspension will
be noted two curved arms. Huygens discovered that a pendulum, in order to beat truly, should not swing the exact arc of a
circle, but in what he termed a cycloidal curve – i.e. the line

traced by a point on the circumference of a circle which is rolling along a straight line. This gives a slightly more U-shaped line than the pure arc of a circle. He therefore tried to give the pendulum this more upward swing at the end of its traverse by guiding it by these specially designed curves; this was possible since he adopted the silk-thread suspension. The trouble was that the correction introduced more errors than it overcame, and so had to be abandoned some few years later. The rectification came with the anchor escapement, with its small arc of swing as compared with the verge (Figs 6 and 1). By limiting the swing to a few degrees the cycloidal curve and the true arc of a circle are practically the same. It is remarkable that Huygens never adopted the anchor escapement in any of his experimental clocks, although it was invented nearly a quarter of a century before his death.

This clock is probably one of the oldest pendulum clocks in existence today.

Three of the clocks shown on *Plate 15* are English, and of about the same date as the two Dutch clocks, around 1660, but before we go into the details of the clock let us consider what we know about their maker, Edward East.

There has been a good deal of confusion as to his life-span. This was brought about by a claim made by a Dr. Williamson, in a book entitled *Behind my Library Door*, to identify a Quaker named Edward East with the clockmaker. This Edward East was buried in 1701, having died 'of age'; but he was only eighty-four at the time of his death, which would have made the year of his birth 1617. Yet East the clockmaker was elected in 1631 an original member of the Court of Assistants of the Clockmakers' Company, which in modern language would be termed the Council or Board of the Company – manifestly impossible for a boy of fourteen. Thus Britten and Baillie have been led to surmise that there may have been two men of the same name working during the period 1631 to 1693 when Edward East was still alive and associated with the Company, as its records show.

The recent discovery (by the author) of Edward East's will shows the claim for the Quaker buried in 1701 to be false. East made his will in 1688 and it was proved in February 1696 –7, so that he was ninety-four when he died, records in the parish of Southill in Bedfordshire showing his baptism on August 22nd, 1602. It is a strange coincidence that he should have been born within three miles of Northill, Bedfordshire, where thirty-six years later Tompion was born, and it is an interesting speculation whether the success of East had any influence on the young Tompion in deciding him to come up to London to establish himself.

In his will he describes himself as 'Watchmaker, Citizen and Goldsmith of London'. The Goldsmiths' Company records show that he was the son of John East, of Southill, Beds, and that he was apprenticed to Richard Rogers on March 27th, 1618, at the age of sixteen years; for a period of eight years, being made free of the Company in 1627. Thus he had been a master-goldsmith for four years when he was elected, at the age of twenty-nine, the junior member of the Court of Assistants of the Clockmakers' Company. He was Warden of the Company in 1638 and 1639, and Master in 1645 and 1652.

He was watchmaker to King Charles I and, according to Atkins and Overall in their *History of the Clockmakers' Company*, Charles II, when Prince of Wales, would play tennis, the stakes being an 'Edwardus East' – i.e. a watch by East. The Prince must have been quite a boy when he did this, as he was born only in 1630 and was sent to the Scilly Isles in 1646 and later that year to Paris. He remained abroad then until after his father's execution, and when he did return he, of course, did not come to London. East would appear to have held his Court appointment until King Charles' execution. Sir Thomas Herbert's memoirs of the last two years of the reign refer to an incident when he, Herbert, oversleeping, failed to call the King in time, upon which the King remarked, 'Herbert, you have not observed the command I gave you last night. Well, I will order you for the future; you shall have a gold alarm watch, which as there may be cause shall awake you; write to the Earl of Pembroke to send me such a one presently.' The Earl immediately sent to Mr. East, his watchmaker in Fleet Street, about it.

In 1671, when the clockmakers were applying for a coat of arms, the application was made in the names of the Master, the Wardens and several named Assistants, and 'also Edward East, the only person now living of those mentioned in the said Letters Patent of Incorporation'.

In 1654 Henry Jones, who was probably then fourteen years of age, was apprenticed to him. When Jones was Master in 1692 we have the following entries in the records of the Company: ' 1692, October 20. Mr. Henry Jones, the present Master this day acquainted the Court that Mr. Edward East formerly Master was pleased to give £100 now in his lifetime to this Company for the benefit of the poor. And Mr. Jones after the charitable example of his said Master having promised to give one hundred pounds more for the benefit of the poor likewise in such manner as shall be hereafter appointed and declared by the said Mr. East and Mr Jones. . . .'

' 1693 June 20th. Mr. Edward East gave the £100.'

' 1693 July 18. Mr. Henry Jones did give the £100 promised.'

It is thus clear that the one and the same Edward East was referred to up to this date, and according to our reckoning he must have been ninety, and wishing 'to make a gift in his lifetime'.

Having thus dealt with our Master's life-history, let us return to these examples of his craft. The delicate little clock (*Plate 15a*) is probably one of the earliest departures from lantern clock tradition in England and to be put in a wooden case. Dealing first with the case, this is of ebony veneered on oak, and takes the classic 'portico' type so much favoured by the early masters in the third quarter of the seventeenth century. The two three-quarter Corinthian columns and the two quarter columns at the back have beautifully built-up capitals of acanthus leaves, brass gilt. The little glass-fronted side door (on the side not seen in the photograph) is hinged to open with a little key. The object of this is not very clear. It might be to allow access to the pendulum bob at the back if the clock stopped, but this clock is unusual inasmuch as the movement fits so tightly in the case that it cannot be withdrawn through the door, either front or back. The whole of the top pediment lifts off and the clock is withdrawn upwards. When the top is removed it is easy to touch the pendulum rod with the finger and to set it in motion. Possibly, being a very early case, it was designed for the side door to open as was usual in lantern clock practice, it only being asertained later that it was necessary to have a movable top.

The movement extends inside the case only to the bottom

of the front door; in order to maintain a balanced design, the casemaker has been obliged to introduce a deep base; this contains a drawer for keeping the key, one of the prettiest pieces of cabinet-work imaginable. The early gilded claw-and-ball feet are interesting. The door at the back is of solid wood and the back plate plain; glass back doors and engraved back plates came later.

Dealing with the dial, we have a change from the engraved dials of the lantern clocks we have so far been considering and from the Dutch velvet-covered dial. In England the plain gilt dial found favour in the early clocks. This is matted all over, an art that seems to have been entirely lost; it is finely gilt. In some of the very early clocks a Tudor rose or similar design is engraved around the central hole through which the hand arbor passes. The corner decorations or 'spandrels', have not yet appeared. Spandrel is an architectural term used to denote the three-cornered space with one flat and two curved sides to be found between the apexes of a series of archways in a colonnade.

The chapter ring is of solid silver and slightly chamfered towards the centre, giving a nice effect of delicacy. The methods of depositing silver from its salts on to brass was not yet practised. The quarter-hours are marked on the inside of the chapter ring, although since there is a minute hand this is no longer necessary, but custom and tradition die hard, as we shall see in several cases. Quarter-hour marks continued, in some cases, up to 1740–50, although minute hands were usual from 1660 onwards. While some early clocks with minute hands have every minute numbered (*Plate 17a*), this particular example has the numbering every five minutes, the figures being placed within the minute circle. If these numberings are followed, it will be found that the figures get progressively larger, first within the minute circle, and later on the outside.

The hour hand is now a very delicate development from the crude arrow-head that we had on our early lantern clocks and the true 'spade' hand has appeared; the minute hand has good proportions and is stout enough to fulfil its functions. The minute hand has, perhaps, to stand more handling than any other part of a clock. The hands 'fit' the dial exactly, each one terminating at its respective marking, hour or minute. When the hands do not fit they are usually later replacements. The hands are still fixed with a simple pin through the arbor. Lantern clock practice is still found in this clock, inasmuch as when the dial is removed the motion work between the dial and front plate falls away. Later practice was to keep this in position by means of a bridge screwed to the front plate.

The winding squares, placed in a high, very high, location, between the x and ii, is an early sign. These winding squares gradually get lower as times goes on, till they reach viii and iiii, when they rise again to ix and iii, at which position they appear to stabilise during the last quarter of the eighteenth century. Both trains of this clock wind left-handed. Right-handed winding had not yet become standardised. Later, if a clock winds left-handed it is usually a sign that it is a month movement.

In *Plate 37a* is seen a dial with the squares very low. This is an exceptional piece in which the positioning is for reasons connected with the case. The winding is effected through idler wheels.

Another indication that the clock (*Plate 15a*) is a very early departure from standard lantern clock practice is that the fusees have only fourteen grooves instead of sixteen; thus the going period is exactly seven days. The advantage of the extra day's going had not yet been appreciated. Sunday after lunch is clock-winding time at home, and this one has to be 'caught' before two o'clock or else the hour hand covers one winding square and the clock stops before it is clear. Prior to this date lantern clocks were, almost without exception, made to go for thirty hours only; indeed some very early ones, such as the Selwood shown in *Plate 9c* go only twelve hours for a six-foot drop.

The back plate, as is consonant with a solid door, is quite plain, except for the maker's name and the slight decoration on the pendulum cock and locking plate (*Plate 42c*). The flowing style in which the name is engraved is very pleasing. It will be noted that the baluster pillars and the pinning of the pillars behind the back plate, table clock practice, still persist.

Two other clocks (*Plate 15*), are other examples of the work of Edward East. In one we have again the 'architectural' type of case, ebony veneered on oak. The centre of the dial is now matted, but the corners are plain and spandrels have appeared.

This form of cherub head is one of the earliest. The chapter ring is still narrow and the hour figures 'dumpy'. The five-minute notation remains small within the minute ring. The hour hand remains the same but the minute hand is becoming more ornate – bayonet-shaped. A collet has now appeared; this is rather earlier than one would expect. On the other hand, the minute hand is of a style rather later than the rest of the clock. Possibly about two hundred and fifty years ago the minute hand was broken, and a 'modern' one of the time fitted and the collet added at the same time. The winding squares are a little lower and a calendar wheel has been added. The door at the back of this clock is also of solid wood and the back plate plain.

The third clock by Edward East, illustrated, has an interesting history. It belongs to the Huddleston family of Hutton John, near Penrith, Cumberland, and is reputed to have been given to an ancestor, Father Huddleston, who was at the Court of Catherine of Braganza, by James II. Father Huddleston is reputed to have brought Charles II into the Roman Faith on his deathbed. The clock, which is 2 feet high, is probably a little earlier than that we have just been considering. Originally it wound from the back, the change having been made when it was converted to anchor escapement and the bell replaced by a gong. The engraving on the dial is by the same hand as that on the dial of the Hilderson clock shortly to be described. As with the clock (*Plate 15a*), the going period is exactly seven days.

The fourth clock (*Plate 15*) has been introduced to illustrate the anticipation on the Continent, both of the use of wood for cases and their design. It shows a clock by Jobst Burgi, made in Prague in the first decade of the seventeenth century.

Plate 16 shows another clock of very similar design, which most people at first sight would attribute to Edward East, but, as a matter of fact, it is made by a certain John Hilderson. We find no record of his entry into the Clockmakers' Company, but we find records of apprentices bound to him. His name is sometimes spelt Hillersden. The plain severity of the lines of this case, again ebony on oak, are most pleasing. The dial is held against the front of the case by two small wooden pegs that have to be inserted, behind the dial plate, into two holes drilled into the top of the framework of the case, a most awkward proceeding. But the main features of the clock are its striking arrangement and the engraving of the dial; this is illustrated again in the section on dials (*Plate 37c*).

It will be noted that the chapter ring is widening and that the minute ring and the numerals within it are, proportionately, a little wider. The chapter ring is no longer solid silver, but consists of a thin silver plate sweated on to a thicker brass backing. Solid silver was often used, after the deposition of silver had been practised, in very high-class clocks; also silver spandrels and case decorations, as we shall see later.

Reverting to the striking arrangement, to which reference has already been made, this is quite unique; the clock has what is termed 'Dutch striking'. In the early days of clocks they were very expensive and could be afforded only by the very wealthy. They were usually placed in the rooms of large mansions where it was not easy to read the time across the room. For this reason quarter-striking and quarter-chiming clocks had already been made, especially on the Continent, for a hundred years or so already. But this system did not indicate to the listener the hour, only that it was one, two, or three quarters past an uncertain hour. A system of repeating the hour at the half-hour was introduced by the Dutch – presumably since it is so called – but the author has not been able to ascertain just when this system was first used.

The general rule was to have two bells and two hammers. When the hour had struck, during the next half-hour, the striking mechanism was transferred, or 'pumped' as it is termed, over to the hammer acting upon the smaller, higher-pitched bell, which is struck at the half-hour, and back again for the striking of the hour on the bigger bell. Thus we have two bells and two hammers; but in the clock in question we have the two bells, but only one hammer. The actuating mechanism is seen in *Plate 16b*. The minute-hand wheel is geared into another having the same number of teeth, and which therefore revolves once an hour with the minute hand. On to this second wheel are fixed two humps, one on each side of the wheel and 180° distant. The bells (the smaller is hidden behind the larger but can be seen in the illustration of the back plate, *Plate 42d*) are mounted on to the left hand of the two upright columns, the right-hand one being merely to provide the upper pivot. Attached to the lower end of the bell-supporting column is a bent arm forked at the end and straddling the wheel carrying the two humps; in the illustration one of the humps can be seen entering the fork. As the wheel turns, the hump presses the forked arm outwards to the left and turns the bell-supporting column to the right, bringing the larger bell in front of the hammer. Conversely, as the wheel with the hump turns round 180°, the hump on the other side turns the bell column to the left and brings the smaller bell before the hammer.

In Dutch, German, Swedish and some other languages the quarters of the hour are expressed in terms of the next coming hour; thus while we say a quarter-past six, half-past six and a quarter to seven, in these languages they say a quarter seven, half seven and three-quarters seven, and the clock can be set to strike either the number of the hour just past or that of the next succeeding hour, according to the custom of the country.

The disadvantage of Dutch striking is that it needs more power as, during an eight-day going period, there are 2496 hammer blows to be made against 1298 for a clock striking the hours only, or 1440 for a clock striking only one at the half-hour. Later, to overcome this difficulty of telling the exact hour in a large and often poorly lit apartment, a full system of striking was introduced, when the hour was repeated at each quarter together with one, two, or three blows on a higher-pitched bell to indicate the quarter. This required a great deal of power, was expensive to produce and appears only in the most exceptional clocks, mostly made for royalty. One of the earliest was given by Charles II to one of his mistresses, Barbara Villiers, Countess of Castlemain. She was the mother of the first Duke of Grafton and the case and dial are still in the Grafton family, though the movement was taken out by B. L. Vulliamy. In his time he did irreparable damage to many valuable clocks by putting movements of his own design behind their dials. He considered his movements superior to those of any other maker and had a complete disregard for tradition or history, a fact we much lament today. The movement is in possession of the Institute of Civil Engineers, to whom Vulliamy presented it.

Reverting to our Hilderson clock, we still have the table clock design persisting in the baluster pillars neatly riveted into

F

the front plate and pinned behind the back plate (*Plates 16b* and *42d*). Incidentally, the two trains wind inwards; that is, the going train on the right winds to the left and the striking train on the left winds to the right. Standardisation has not yet come.

Our next stage in the progression of design is a lovely clock by William Knottesford in an olive-wood case (*Plate 16c*). The use of cross-sections of branches to produce the 'oyster-shell' effect should be noted. The pediment top to the case has disappeared and a flat top takes its place, later to pass into the dome-shaped 'basket' type. We also get in this clock the twisted 'barley-sugar' columns, still with the fine acanthus-leaf capitals of the Corinthian column. The door at the back is glazed, although the decorated back plate has not yet appeared. In the top of the case is a little drawer to hold the key; in this position this is quite an unusual feature.

The matting in the centre of the dial is very fine, the corners remaining plain under the early cherub-head spandrels. The hour ring remains relatively narrow, but the minute spaces are deeper and the half-hour marks are becoming bolder. The hands, which are similar to the last example, are fixed under a collet. There is a seconds dial, an unusual feature in a spring-driven bracket clock, because the pendulum rarely beats a simple fraction of a second; thus although the second hand may revolve once a minute, the hand will not indicate one second at each advance. The winding squares are covered, which indicates that the clock has maintaining power; that is, on opening the shutters an auxiliary pressure is brought to bear on the train which causes it to continue its forward motion for the short period during which winding nullifies the force of the spring. Actually, winding only takes a few seconds, but it is usual for the maintaining power to operate for two or three minutes. When the period of maintaining is finished, the shutters automatically drop again into position, so that the clock cannot be wound again until the maintaining power has been brought into operation. While the idea was good in theory, in practice it was a useless elaboration in a verge clock, since the errors in time-keeping inherent in the design of these clocks was far more than the few seconds lost while winding. By the time this clock was made the anchor escapement with the seconds pendulum and dial had made its appearance, and it is probable that the maker, or possibly the man who ordered the clock, wanted all the latest details incorporated in his clock, irrespective of whether they were really effective or no. The clock has also a calendar dial, showing the day of the month through the aperture in the bottom of the dial. This would have to be adjusted by hand at the end of the short months.

When we turn to the back of this clock we notice that the distance pillars have now a turned central boss as well as turned bosses at each end and that they are neatly riveted into the back plate and pinned into the front plate. We have left the table clock practice, never to return to it. The signature has passed from the back plate to the bottom of the front plate. Later it will rise to within the dial itself. The movement is held in position on the seat board by two small swivelling hooks catching each corner; this is not found in later cases.

The illustrations on *Plate 17* show the stage next in progression, known as the 'basket top'. This description will be better appreciated if the succeeding illustrations with their decorative metal plaques or entirely metal baskets are consulted. In the earliest form, here illustrated, the basket is relatively flat, and in point of overall height above the door very little different from the William Knottesford clock we have just been considering. A fret, better to allow the escape of the sound of the bells, has appeared in front, but not yet at the sides. The case, as was still the fashion of the time, is ebony veneered on oak. On each side of the door frame are modifications of the cherub spandrel design. It will be noted that, while that on the right is fixed with a pin top and bottom, that on the left slides in a groove at the bottom and swivels about the pin at the top, thus exposing the keyhole of the door. This is a feature employed exclusively by Joseph Knibb, the maker of this clock. The reader should also note that a handle has appeared. Clocks were expensive; there would be only one in the house and this would be carried from room to room, hence the handle. Handles were a regular feature until the third quarter of the eighteenth century, when clocks became sufficiently inexpensive to have several in the house.

Turning to the maker of this clock, there were several members of the Knibb family who were clockmakers. Samuel would seem to have been of one generation. He was born, according to

Dr. Beeson to whom I am indebted for many of the details of the Knibb family given here, at Claydon in Oxfordshire, coming later to London in 1663. He died in 1674. There is a clock by him in the Guildhall Museum, of which the dial is engraved by the same hand as that which executed the dial of the Hilderson clock we have just considered (*Plate 37c*). The date would be around 1665–70, and therefore during the period when Samuel Knibb was working in London.

Joseph, who was the most renowned member of the family, was also born at Claydon; he was a cousin of Samuel. He started working in Oxford, as is shown by examples of his work signed Joseph Knibb, Oxon, *fecit*. In 1670 he entered the Clockmakers' Company and remained in London until 1697, when he retired to Hanslope in Oxfordshire. Here he seems to have done a little work, as occasionally examples signed Joseph Knibb, Hanslope appear. He was buried at Newport Pagnell in Buckinghamshire, about five miles distant, on December 14th, 1711.

Joseph's brother John worked with him while he was in Oxford, and seems to have continued a fairly close collaboration after Joseph came to London, the one helping the other out if they were short of a particular type of movement at any given time. John remained in Oxford and acquired local eminence, having been Mayor of the city in 1698 and again in 1710. Joseph would have been a small boy when King Charles set up his government in Oxford in 1644–46.

There are two members of a younger generation, according to the records of the Clockmakers' Company. Peter was apprenticed to Joseph Knibb about 1670 and was made free of the Company on November 5th, 1677. Edward Knibb was apprenticed on December 5th, 1693, also to Joseph Knibb, and young Joseph, who was the son of John, was apprenticed to Martin Jackson on June 5th, 1710. Neither of these two last appear to have proceeded to acquire the Freedom of the Company. When a son is apprenticed to his father it is usual for this fact to be recorded. We have no evidence that Edward was the son of Joseph. Peter was George's son,

Joseph is, however, the outstanding member of the family. His best work can compare with that of Tompion and Quare, but he had not the creative ability of Tompion. He devised a quarter-striking Grande Sonnerie on a locking plate, but the size of the clock limited the striking up to six, when it recommenced at one (*Plate 43a*). (The size of Georg Meyer's clock, (*Plate 13d*), enabled him to have this system striking for the full twelve hours.) He also introduced into this country what is known as 'Roman Striking'. In order to save power by reducing the number of blows of the hammer necessary during one winding, he caused the hours to be struck on two bells, one deeper toned than the other. The deeper-toned bell represented the v in the roman numeral system, four being represented as IV on the dial, instead of IIII as is usual in chapter rings (*Plate 18c*). I, II and III were struck on the high-pitched bell, IV, one high one deep, IX, one high two deep, XII was two deep and two high. This meant only 60 blows a day instead of 156, or 480 for an eight-day movement instead of 1248. This system did not find general adoption and only a few of Knibb's clocks with it have survived; they are consequently much sought after by collectors.

It is thought that Knibb specially developed a connexion with Italy. Good Knibb clocks have been found there, and the Roman Striking is another indication. Further, Knibb may well have got the idea of night clocks from Italy, where they were reasonably common in the latter part of the seventeenth century. Not many night clocks of this period have survived, but whereas three or four are known to the author by Knibb, he knows only one each by one of the Fromanteels, East and Henry Jones. These were all examples made in the last years of their respective careers. More about these clocks will be found in the chapter on night clocks.

Returning to the clock illustrated, the dial is very fine and unusual inasmuch as it is a skeleton. Joseph Knibb, and occasionally other makers, made some of their better clocks with this type of dial. It must have been a good deal more expensive to produce as the matting of the dial alone covers an area nearly twice as large as with an ordinary full chapter ring, to which must be added the cost of cutting out the numerals, quarter-hour and minute rings, a very delicate operation. Each minute is numbered, as previously mentioned, an early indication. Special attention should be paid to the hands, how the hour hand is of relatively heavy metal, yet, through chamfering,

given a delightful appearance of lightness. Even the collet
securing the hands is decorated. The clock is a repeating movement.

Our next illustration is an elaboration of the basket type due
to the insertion of frets between the basket proper and the case.
It is an alarm clock, the disk for setting the alarm being in the
centre and the winding square for the alarm top right. The
maker, Thomas Tompion, did not intend that his client should
oversleep by reason of not hearing the alarm, for not only have
frets appeared at the side of the case at the top, but the side
panels are openwork and lined with silk. It is only a timepiece –
that is, it does not strike the hours. We see this as there is only
one winding square for the going train. Tompion towards the
middle of his career numbered his clocks and watches. This
clock is early in the clock series of numbers, No. 15, date about
1685.

As is always the case with Tompion, the finish of every detail
is exquisite; all the frets are cast, hand-finished and chased.
Tompion usually favoured simplicity both in dial and case, and
the gilt frets in this case are, therefore, somewhat unusual. The
clear-cut lines of the dial should be noted, the hour hand is a
typical 'Tompion' hand, the half-hour marks are simple and
clear. Here we have the five-minute numbers, still small,
appearing outside the minute ring.

Of Tompion there has been more written than of any other
clockmaker. He was, without doubt, the leading craftsman of
his day and did more than any other to raise the standard of
English clockmaking at the end of the seventeenth century.
Biographical details have been flogged to death in these past
few years, probably because Tompion is a name to be conjured
with in the auction room in these post-war years, where his
clocks are so often being bought up for fabulous sums by those
who are wealthy but are without any knowledge or appreciation
of their possessions. They simply buy a Tompion as they would
buy a Reynolds or a Rembrandt, not that they could distinguish
the style of one painter from that of the other, but as a means of
capital investment. So writing up Tompion is 'good business'
today, and if it creates a still greater demand for his clocks and
Mr. X's clock goes up in value, the appreciation is all tax-free
in these days of heavy taxation. As far as Mr. X is concerned, he

would not have minded if his money had been employed in buying anything, as long as he could see an equal appreciation in capital values. These particular gentry are making the market impossible for the genuine clock-lover, who knows and appreciates what he is acquiring.

Tompion, who never married, was the son of a Bedfordshire blacksmith, and his father was churchwarden at the local church. Statements have been made that he was a Quaker, but Dr. Raistrick, in his book *Quakers in Science and Industry*, admits that Tompion's name does not appear in their records and that there is no evidence on this point. When he came to London is not known, but he is assumed to have trained as a blacksmith and to have been apprenticed to that trade outside London. He did not enter the Clockmakers' Company till 1671, when he was thirty-one, at which time he was admitted as a brother – that is to say, as a fully qualified craftsman. He is described as a maker of 'Grete Clocks' – i.e. turret clocks. He must have rapidly established himself as a worker in brass, for about 1674–75 he made a fine astronomical clock, the only one known by him and now in the Fitzwilliam Museum in Cambridge, and in 1676 he was commissioned by Sir Jonas Moore to make two clocks for the use of the first Astronomer Royal, John Flamsteed, in Greenwich Observatory. These two were year movements, and the author inclines to the view that they were the first year movements ever to be made in England. They also had two seconds pendulums approximately 14 feet in length; here again they were probably the first of their kind to be made.

It has always been supposed that the pendulums of these two clocks hung down in the stair-well under the floor behind the clocks.[1] Now that the Observatory has left, the Ministry of Works is restoring the original buildings and the 'Octagon Room' to the state in which they were when first built, in John Flamsteed's day. A replica of one of Tompion's clocks has been made and put in position. In doing this it was discovered that the floor mentioned was intact and had never been disturbed. On the other hand, the beams above the clock position had been hollowed out to allow for a pendulum rod and the passage of a weight suspended above the clock. Thus it is seen that Tompion took advantage of Hooke's experiment of 1669, when

[1] See Appendix II.

he demonstrated that a freely suspended pendulum of 14 feet beating two seconds, with a heavy bob, could be kept in motion by a pin fixed on to the rim of a watch balance.

All Tompion's work is of excellent finish, but the movements and cases of some of his finest examples are superb. He was Master of the Clockmakers' Company in 1704; he died in 1713 and was buried in Westminster Abbey; and therefore could not have been a Quaker at the time of his death. If indeed he joined the movement only to secede, he could not have been a very good Quaker.

Tompion was an exquisite craftsman and an ingenious designer of complicated clocks but, except in so far as better timekeeping is inherent in good workmanship, Tompion made no contribution to the improvement of timekeeping as did Graham, Harrison, Earnshaw and others whose inventions and improvements are still in use today in high-grade clocks; whereas Tompion's products are merely collector's pieces. This cult for a name has had the regrettable result that we have recently lost to the States one of the finest examples of Tompion's clocks and cases. A few years ago we were gratified to learn that this clock had been bought back from the States, but this importation put the clock in a category which did not need a special export licence, and it has now returned to the States at a very much enhanced figure, to the great regret of all except those directly concerned in the transaction.

Plate 17c shows a metallic basket clock and from this illustration the description is better understood. In this case we are fortunate in having a clock with silver mountings, from the hallmark on which we can get the exact date of this specimen, 1698. The maker is Joseph Windmills, a maker of repute, who was Master of the Company in 1702. In this dial we still have the early cherub-head spandrels; these were retained much later in bracket clocks than in long-case clocks, since, as we shall see when dealing with this type later, the dials of the latter gradually became larger and consequently required larger spandrels, which were too big for bracket clocks of the same years.

The chapter ring has become much wider and the five-minute figures are much larger and have appeared outside the minute ring. The half-hour marks are more ornate and in addition to the inner circle for the quarter-hours there have appeared little +'s for the half-quarters between the five-minute marks. The winding holes are ringed, a fashion more usual in long-case clocks for a few years than in bracket clocks. The hands, both hour and minute, have become more ornate. A slot in which swings a false bob has also appeared, enabling the clock to be started without tipping or having to turn it round and open the back. In the photograph the pendulum is fixed in its carrying hook and the false bob is just seen on the extreme left of the slot. Another clock on *Plate 17* illustrates a somewhat excessive exuberance in decoration and is known as a double basket. With the exception of the design of the hour hand, the two dials are very similar. The coming of finials on the corners of the case should be noted. The maker is John Shaw of Holborne. Here again the pendulum has been fixed in its carrying hook, in this case to leave clear the back plate of the slot carrying the maker's name. The false bob here is on the extreme right.

Plate 18 shows a rather elaborate basket clock by Samuel Watson; its plain wooden basket-top tones down the somewhat heavy ornamentation of the sides and the ornate side panels. Particular attention should be paid to the fine handle. The back plate of this clock is shown in *Plate 43c*. The faceted bob as a means of more exact regulation should be noted.

Samuel Watson is a maker who in the past has not received sufficient attention or recognition from horological writers since our early friends, Smith and Derham, who were loud in his praises. They record a famous astronomical clock made by him to the order of King Charles II, who however died before it was finished in 1690, when Queen Mary II honoured her uncle's order and took delivery of the clock for £1000. No description of it had appeared in any standard horological work until the author rediscovered it in 1942 in Windsor Castle and described it fully in the *Horological Journal* for December of that year. Watson was the leading astronomical clockmaker of his day, in this branch surpassing Tompion, who is only known to have made one astronomical clock. The clock we have just referred to was ordered by King Charles II after he had already taken delivery of a more simple one in 1682 for which he paid £215. Watson also made two astronomical clocks for Sir Isaac Newton. One is constructed on the Ptolemaic principle – that is, with the earth fixed and the sun and planets revolving around it. This is in the possession of the Clockmakers' Company. Another, in the possession of the author, made about 1695 – i.e. after the publication of the *Principia* – is on the Newtonian (Copernican) principle of the fixed sun, with the universe revolving around it. This latter clock is probably the first to be made in England embodying Newton's principles. This book is not the place for the illustration and discussion of complicated astronomical clocks; the author hopes one day to write another book dealing with the more unusual phases of seventeenth- and eighteenth-century horology, if he can find a publisher who thinks that there are sufficient readers interested in the subject. The purpose of the present comments is to bring Watson's name more fully into the position it deserves in the horological world.

We will stop our chronological progression for a moment and take a step a year or two backwards to examine three clocks included for the specific points they illustrate. It will be noted that all three have the five-minute numbers within the minute ring and that they are therefore, presumably, a little earlier than the last example considered. *Plate 18b* shows a clock by Knibb where he has attempted to have the *grande sonnerie* striking referred to earlier – i.e. striking the full hour and the quarter each quarter of an hour. There are three trains: going, hour-striking and quarter-striking. To strike the hour four times an hour instead of once requires 5192 blows of the hammer in 8 days instead of 1248. The spring driving the hour strike has to be much stronger to provide the necessary power. Knibb did not feel quite equal to this at this time, so he only provides for the hour to be repeated up to six, dividing the day into four parts of six hours as far as striking is concerned. He left it to the listener to decide in which quarter of the day he is by 'the Hexercisin' 'hof 'is brain – that is, assumin' that 'e's got any,' as our friend Private Willis in *Iolanthe* ruminated in Palace Yard as he watched the M.P.s pass into the House while he stood as sentry at the entrance gates. In this way Knibb 'gets away' with 384 blows a week instead of the 1248 required for a normal clock to strike the hours only. He can therefore do with much less power in his modified *grande sonnerie* than in an ordinary striking clock and yet tell the exact hour every quarter to the listener, who has only to make a very simple mental effort during two six-hour periods, in one of which he will almost certainly be asleep. The back plate of this clock is seen in *Plate 43a*. From this it will be seen that it would not be easy to incorporate the much larger locking plate necessary to provide for *grande sonnerie* striking over the twelve hours.

In *Plate 18c* we have another Knibb idea to reduce the power needed for striking – the Roman striking already referred to on page 79. It will be noted that the four is shown as IV and not IIII. The clean Knibb hands should be noted; otherwise there is little to comment on this clock, beyond the remarks already made in connexion with previous clocks. The fourth clock on this page shows one of the many attempts to get good time-keeping at sea. The clock is suspended from a ball-and-socket joint, and under the base is a ring to which a cord could be attached to limit movement.

'Finding the longitude' was a problem which beset all mariners, and the English in particular as a maritime nation, from the earliest times until the last quarter of the eighteenth century, when as already mentioned it was solved by John Harrison and later brought into the realm of economic possibility by Earnshaw and Arnold. At the time we are considering, watches did not have the isochronous balance spring; it was only just being invented, let alone perfected, so that they were far inferior to clocks in time-keeping.

Some travelling clocks were made with balance-wheel movements at this time, but they were for land travellers whose determination of their whereabouts did not depend on the accuracy of their timepieces. The most accurate clocks of the day were weight-driven pendulum clocks. The weight is an ideal driving force; it is constant in application and needs no adjustment. Many were the varied efforts made to find a suitable method of keeping time at sea with pendulum clocks. All failed, of course, because the solution of the problem did not lie in that direction; but it was to take many years of weary searching to discover this.

In examining this clock we find that the chapter ring is much broader in proportion to its diameter than in the other examples, giving a much heavier appearance to the dial; the hands, while good, are not so well finished as Knibbs'. The

decoration of the day of the month aperture, an early appearance of this feature, makes it too heavy in relation to the small
matted surface of the centre of the dial. The back plate of this
clock is seen on *Plate 43d*.

The maker of this clock is Daniel Quare. He was one of the
leading makers of the latter half of the seventeenth century and
the first half of the eighteenth. He entered the Clockmakers'
Company as a brother in 1671 and was Master in 1708. He was
a Quaker and a stout defender of his religious beliefs, several
times fined or punished for non-compliance with different
ordinances that conflicted with his conscience. He was clockmaker to King William III and, as will be seen later, he appears
to have moved in the diplomatic circle of his time, which probably accounts for the relatively frequent appearance of his
clocks on the Continent. The *Friends' Quarterly Examiner* of 1900
gives full details of Quare's career. He was one of the petitioners
to James II in 1686 for liberty of conscience, which petitions of
Nonconformists James tried, a couple of years later to bring in,
to cover, under the guise of general religious freedom, the
emancipation for his Roman co-religionists, which he knew he
could not get by direct appeals.

Quare's progress in the social circle can be followed by the
ascending degree of those attending the marriages of his various
children. In 1705 Anne Quare married John Falconer, and the
envoys of Venice, Florence, Hanover, Portugal, Sweden, Prussia
and Denmark were present. In 1712 both a son and a daughter
were married, the guests including the Earl of Orrery, the
Duke of Argyll, the Venetian Ambassador, the Compte de
Briançon, etc. But in 1715 when his daughter Elizabeth married Silvanus Bevan, besides the Countess of Brocklinborough,
the Count and Countess of Guicord, Francis de Fleurs and
many others, Sarah, Duchess of Marlborough, was present.
The Prince and Princess of Wales and all the 'High Quality'
were only prevented from attending the wedding by an Act of
Parliament which forbade the attendance at dissenting places
of worship. The Princess of Wales attended the reception.

Quare refused a pension of £300 a year as watchmaker to
King George I, because his conscience forbade him to take the
oath; nevertheless he was given access to the palace.

Quare also invented the repeating watch, but he had a rival

claimant, Dr. Barlow, who about 1676 invented the rack-and-snail system of striking for clocks and so made repeating clocks possible. According to William Derham, about 1687 (towards the end of King James' reign), the two rivals submitted their claims to the King in Council, the King giving the award to Quare, whose watch repeated the hour and quarter with one push of a lever, whereas Barlow's needed two separate levers for hour and quarter.

Plate 19 introduces a maker well worthy of being, if not put into the front rank, at any rate being placed at the top of the second flight, Peter Garon. The clock in a tortoiseshell veneer basket case was recently found on the Continent; it is *grande sonnerie*. The date is the first decade of the eighteenth century; it will be noted that the decoration around the calendar date has spread to the lower winding hole and the false bob aperture, also that the other two winding holes are ringed. Garon may have been a good clockmaker, but he does not seem to have been a good man of business, for Baillie records that he was adjudged bankrupt in 1709 and the final record of him in the Company's records is that he was insolvent.

The illustration (*Plate 19b*) shows a reversion to the plain wooden basket. The clock is by Tompion and is one of his more 'ordinary' productions. Nevertheless it has elegance of proportion, simple and clean-cut lines, and altogether is a very pleasing piece. The reader is immediately struck by an innovation in the design by the introduction of the two subsidiary dials at the top. That on the right is a simple lever which prevents the striking train from functioning (now that we have the rack-and-snail, described below, we can shut the strike off at will without upsetting the sequence) and so renders the clock silent during the night hours if so desired. It is a repeating clock, and so we can imagine its original owner taking it up by the handle and carrying it up to his bedroom, divesting himself of his full-bottomed periwig, full-skirted coat, flowered silken waistcoat, knee-breeches and red-heeled shoes, putting on his nightshirt and drawing on his nightcap. He then places the clock on a table beside his bed where he can easily reach the repeat pull cord by passing his hand through the bed curtains. He snuffs the light and pulls the curtains of the four-poster and settles down to sleep, only to be told by his wife in the morning that his snoring was far worse than any hourly striking of the clock could have been. The repeating cord, for which he sleepily groped during the night, is clearly seen in the picture. As will be seen from *Plate 44b*, these clocks were generally so arranged that the repeat could be actuated from either side.

We have heretofore only considered the locking-plate type of striking, where the count wheel, independent of the hour-hand arbor, is released each hour and continued to turn, allowing the clock to strike the necessary number of hours, after which an arm falls into a groove and locks the plate until it is released by the lifting of the arm just prior to the next hour. In this way, only a continuous sequence of the hours can be struck (*Plates 42c* and *d* and *43a*). About 1676, according to Wm. Derham, a Dr. Barlow invented the striking system known as the rack-and-snail. In this case a stepped wheel is fixed to the hour-hand arbor, the hour hand being only a tight friction fitted on the arbor, so that for adjustment it can be moved around the arbor without setting the going train in motion. As the hour wheel turns once in each twelve hours, each step, which comprises one-twelfth of the circumference at that point, remains in position to receive the rack tail in the same position for the whole of that hour. This regulates the number of teeth that the gathering pallet can collect, and so the number of blows that can be struck before the striking cuts out. Thus, however often the repeat cord is pulled during any hour, the same number of blows is achieved.

Thus with the locking plate you have to set the plate to the hour by releasing the detent of the striking train with the finger until the number of blows struck corresponds to the hour on the dial, but with the rack-and-snail, if the strike gets out, and this is very rarely so, the hour hand can be pushed round until stroke and dial agree.

The function of the strike-silent dial led us into this dissertation on repeating and striking mechanisms. Reverting to the clock being described, the subsidiary dial on the left is what is generally referred to as the 'rise and fall' regulator; it is for altering the length of the pendulum. We have seen how on the Continent the earliest pendulums were supported independently by a silken cord from a cock on the back plate and were actuated by a crutch fixed to the escape pallet arbor, while in

England the pendulum rod was affixed direct to the escape pallet arbor.

As related in Chapter One, the anchor escapement, actuated by a crutch with its pendulum carrying the heavy lenticular bob, suspended by a thin spring strip passing through a cock on the back plate, came into use in the early sixteen-seventies. Towards the end of the decade Tompion appears to have combined anchor-escapement practice with verge movements; that is to say, he suspended his verge-movement pendulums from a spring and actuated them through a crutch. This necessitated a heavier bob, which would take up much too much depth if made ball- or pear-shaped as have been the bobs we have heretofore seen; so a flat lenticular bob had to be used as with the anchor escapement. This introduced a complication; the bob had to swing parallel with the back plate so that any adjustment could not be less than one half-turn of 180 degrees. But this might be too much, so the bob was made a loose sliding fit on the rod, the bottom of which was threaded to take a 'rating' nut placed underneath, which could be screwed round any desired amount and so raise or lower the bob as in an ordinary grandfather clock. This again had the inconvenience that the whole clock had to be turned round and the back door opened to get at the rating nut, so Tompion introduced the rack-and-lever principle of regulation from the front. The central arbor of the left-hand dial carries a toothed rack which gears into the end of a lever from which the pendulum is suspended (*Plate 44b*), the steel spring suspension being free to move through the cheeks of the cock. Thus very fine adjustments could be made to the pendulum length with the minimum of effort. It may here be noted that although the anchor escapement was readily and generally recognised as much superior to the verge in time-keeping properties, verge escapements were general for all mantel or bracket clocks until the latter half of the eighteenth century, because the clocks were carried from room to room and the verge escapement did not need anything like the same exact levelling that is required by the anchor. Thus, until clocks were cheap enough to have several in the house and there was no longer any necessity to move them from room to room, the anchor escapement did not become popular for this type of clock.

Reverting to our Tompion clock, it will be noticed that the cherub spandrels and all elaborations of them have gone and we now have a female head as the central point of a more or less indefinite design. Tompion's escutcheons are different from those of Knibb. The signature has now appeared above the chapter ring, between the two subsidiary dials. This was adopted by Tompion and his successor Graham, but was not very much used by other makers. The hour hand should be compared with that of *Plate 17b*; it will be seen that both are elaborations of the plain spade *motif* of *Plate 15*, but this hand has developed the design still further than in *Plate 17b*.

Following on this Tompion, we have a real bracket clock – i.e. a clock standing on the original bracket made for it – a product of the hands of George Graham (*Plate 19c*). In pursuance of our custom, since we are dealing with another of the great clockmakers of his day, we will give a few biographical notes on this maker before considering in detail the clock he has made.

For the past seventy-five years George Graham, the horologist, has been identified with a child, George, born on July 20th, 1673, and registered by the Society of Friends as being the son of George Graham, of Rigg, in Cumberland.

The author finds, however, that the Grahams of Rigg also registered the births of Hannah in 1677, another George in 1708, and six more children between 1715 and 1724. The burial registers mention Elizabeth, wife of George in 1708. Surely this indicates that by 1707 George of 1673 has succeeded his father and married. His wife dies soon after his own first-born, George, is born; he marries again and raises a second family.

Clearly this George Graham never came to London.

The Apprenticeship Indentures of Graham to Henry Aske, July 2nd, 1688, read: 'George Graham, sonne of George Graham, late of ffordlande in the County of Cumberland, Husbandman, deceased'. Here we have Graham's own declaration of his origin, and the Friends burial registers confirm the burial of George Graham, of Foordlands, on October 20th, 1679.

The horologist was buried in Westminster Abbey, beside Tompion, and the Abbey burial records give his age as seventy-eight in 1751, which makes him born in 1673, so that he was fourteen or fifteen when apprenticed.

There is no record in the Society of Friends books that Graham ever attended any London Meeting House. He was not apprenticed to a Quaker. When made Free in 1695, he was free to affirm; but there is no record that he did not take the oath. He did not marry a Quakeress. He entered Tompion's employ in 1696 and later married his niece. Burial in Westminster Abbey would not be open to a Quaker. Thus we have no evidence that he practised the Quaker faith after the age of five or six years. Indeed all the evidence goes to show that he did not.

But Quaker or no Quaker, a man whose reputation has come down the ages as 'Honest George Graham' must have been a fine character.

He was Warden of the Clockmakers' Company 1719–21 and Master in 1722. On Tompion's death in 1713, he succeeded to his business.

Graham is best remembered in horology for his two inventions which are today still widely employed, viz. the dead-beat escapement and the mercury pendulum (Fig. 7 and *Plate 26c*).

He was also a maker of astronomical instruments for Greenwich and other observatories and the inventor of the cylinder escapement for watches. He was a Fellow of the Royal Society and communicated several important papers to it.

Reverting to our illustration, we see that the basket has had an addition on top, giving what is termed the 'inverted-bell'-shaped case. Still ebony veneered on oak, the bracket repeats the *motif* in a reversed form. The bracket contains a drawer to hold the key.

In the main the dial is very little different from the Tompion we have just been discussing, except that the half-hour *motif* based on a fleur-de-lis is gone and a diamond has taken its place. Graham favoured this mark, others used it also, but not often to denote the half-hours. The marking of the eighth-hours between the five-minute marks has also gone. The spandrels, while still based on a female head, are becoming less elaborate in design; the hour hand, while remaining on the basic spade design, is becoming more pointed.

Also on this plate we have an interesting clock by Joseph Antram, who was Clockmaker to King George I. Its date must be before 1723, for in that year Antram died. In this case the

a

arch has been used to accommodate a calendar dial showing the day of the month, the month of the year and the day of the week. The two subsidiary dials are, left for rise and fall pendulum regulation and on the right a strike/silent arrangement which allows for the clock to strike the hour only, hours and quarters on one bell, or to chime the quarters on six bells or to cut out the striking altogether. The clock has very historical associations. George I married, as Prince of Brunswick-Luneberg, Sophia Dorothea of Celle. It was a marriage of convenience and suited neither party. George neglected his wife and she sought consolation elsewhere, although there is no evidence that she was actually unfaithful. In the event she was divorced and sent to the castle of Ahlden and known henceforth as the Duchess of Ahlden. There she was kept prisoner till her death in 1727. She never came to England and was a queen who was never crowned. The clock we are illustrating would seem to have belonged to her; on the front plate is scratched 'Sophie Dorothea geb. 15.9.1666 zu Celle gest. 13.11.1726 zu Ahlden. vermaehlte 21.11.1682 mit Georg Ludwig, spaeter Georg I von England. geb. 7.6.1660 gest . . . 21/22.6.1727.' rest of inscription illegible. (Note: some of the days of the month given do not tally exactly with English histories.) Translated: Sophie Dorothea born 15.9.1666 at Celle, died 13.11.1726 at Ahlen. married 21.11.1682 to George Lewis, later George I of England. born 7.6.1660 died 21/22.6.1727. George I died in his coach on his way to Osnabruck, in Germany.

CHAPTER FOUR

Long-Case Clocks 1660–1735

W E will now leave for a while the bracket clock and follow the development of the long-case clock. This, in England, only started after the invention and the adoption of the pendulum. Concurrently with the early long-case clocks which stand on the ground, there was a limited movement to have wooden-cased clocks hanging on the wall. One such clock is illustrated in *Plate 20b*. It is a very fine eight-day striking movement by Edward East and is a good example of the change-over from 'square' to 'flat' clocks mentioned in the last chapter. It is in an ebony-veneered case with the hood sliding up along grooves in the back board, as was common practice in the early long-case clocks. These were short by later standards, only six feet to six feet six inches high. As the clocks got taller they were too tall conveniently to have the hood sliding up, so the hoods were made to slide forward and to come off instead of sliding up, and finally they were fitted with an opening door, as in a bracket clock.

Except for the two pineapple pendants, which are believed to be later additions, and the apron concealing the lock to the hood, the overall design follows very closely mantel-clock practice of the period. The three flaming-urn decorations on top are the start of a vogue for the decoration of the top of long-case clocks that was to persist for nearly two hundred years. The columns, it will be noted, are only three-quarter columns, being let into the framework of the hood; the Corinthian capitals should be compared with those on the early East mantel clock shown in *Plate 15a*. The date of this clock is a little later than the mantel clock; engraved spandrels have appeared, the hands are slightly more elaborate, it has maintaining power and a calendar dial. The winding squares are here in the 'low' early position as compared with those in the 'high' position in *Plate 15a*. As with lantern clocks, there is no back door to reveal a back plate. The clock is therefore signed on the front plate, in this case outside the chapter ring, the words Edward East appearing between viii and vii, and London between v and iv. The weights, as is always the case with weights of this period, are brass-encased.

The clock illustrated (*Plate 20a*) is an example of a short pendulum movement originally made to stand on a bracket hanging on the wall. It was later encased, either to exclude dust, or more likely because Mistress James, the wife of the President of Queens' College, Cambridge, from 1675–1717, to which college this clock was presented by the maker Edward East in 1664, wanted something more in keeping with the fashions of the time. At that time, anchor escapement, to which system this clock has been converted, and long-case clocks were becoming 'all the rage', and Mistress James did not want to be left behind in the race. It would seem that the job was given to a local joiner, about 1685–90, who had no knowledge of contemporary clock-case design, and he just boxed it in in oak to harmonise with the panelling of the room in which it stood. The minute hand was probably added at the time when the conversion to a seconds pendulum anchor escapement was made – perhaps about 1685–90. The 'bar' across the dial is an engraved plate reading *To Queenes Colledg Cambridg The Guift of Edward East Clock-maker to King Charles the second 1664*. This plate was evidently originally placed on the apron of the bracket supporting the clock, but when it was encased it was riveted on to the top of the beautifully engraved dial, quite spoiling the proportions. It is a great pity that it was not affixed to the door of the hood, or in some other place on the case. The engraving is by the same hand, both as regards lettering and design, as that on the author's clock illustrated in *Plates 37c* and *42d*. The similiarity of design shown in the illustration of the dial of this clock in *Plate 37* and the dial of the author's clock in *Plate 37* should be noted.

It will be recollected that we said earlier that in England the long case only came into use after the invention of the pendulum, but on the Continent there are examples half a century earlier, one of which is illustrated in the Frontispiece. This fine anonymous three-train clock is of date about 1600, stands about 8 feet high, is fitted with automata and is finely painted and gilded.

The overhanging scallop shell supporting the platform for the Jacks to circulate and strike the quarter bells, is most pleasing. Above in the next tier, Christ and Death will appear alternately with the hours, a favourite, if gruesome, reminder of the frailty of life, very popular at the time. Surmounting the whole is a cock that will crow, again a reminder of the frailty of man in recalling St. Peter's denial of Our Lord. This cock will flap its wings and crow, probably every twelve hours, the hours being struck by Jacks on the big bell at the top.

In the arch of the dial we have the phases of the moon and its age (incidentally this arched dial appears nearly a century before it makes its appearance in England, see *Plate 25a*). The hand with the reproduction of the human hand will indicate mean time, the idea was that this was the hand of God controlling men's lives; that with the sun will revolve once a year and will show its position in the zodiac, the symbol for each sign being painted in the twelve 'gothic' shaped divisions in the centre of the dial. Within them in the centre are the numbers 1 to 16 twice over, the tail of the sun hand passes before these to indicate the hours of daylight, and by subtraction from twenty-four, those of darkness for the month in question. The hand with the lunar effigy will revolve once in a lunation and will show the position of the moon in the zodiac at any time. The two subsidiary dials show left, the day of the week and right the quarter-hour. A really fine piece of work.

Plate 20d shows a good example of 'how not to do it'. Here is a very nice clock of the third quarter of the seventeenth century, utterly ruined in an attempt, some two hundred years ago to modernise it. 'Keeping up with the Joneses' is no new idea. The clock, by Henry Jones, has had the very attractive narrow panelled case, following the cabinet practice of the period, utterly spoilt by additions to increase its height. The insert between the hood and pediment and the addition of a double plinth and feet, of a style a hundred years later than the clock, quite ruin its appearance, and proportions.

Our next illustration (*Plate 21*) is of the historic clock ordered by King's College, Cambridge, at Michaelmas 1670 from William Clement. Mr. Saltmarsh, archivist of the college, has kindly supplied me with the following facts from the college records. A clock was evidently in existence before 1670 under the care of one Wardell. During the Michaelmas term of that year, William Clement visited Cambridge to inspect the clock and was paid £1 10s. for his expenses. He evidently recommended a new clock and would naturally be keen to introduce his new invention of the anchor escapement, as being an infinitely better time-keeping proposition than the verge or very possibly foliot balance on the old clock. The college contracted with him to supply a new clock for £40 and eventually paid in all £42. The clock appears to have been finished and installed before Michaelmas 1671, because all payment entries are in the accounts for the year ending on that date, and that date is marked on the clock.

The following are the actual entries in the College Mundum Book:

Custus Ecclesie
Term. Nat. 1670
    Sol. Wardell pro supravisione Horologii pro Anno
        ultime elapso   0.6.8
    Et pro reparando Horologio   0.3.0

Expensae Necessariae
Term. Mic.
    Sol. Gulielmo Clement pro expensis Itineris ad viden-
        dum Horologium   1.10.0

Reparaciones Novi Templi
    Sol. Gulielmo Clement in partem 40ll pro Horologio
        novo secundum Articulos in Manibus Mri Drake
        depositos   5.0.0
    Sol. Gulielmo Clement in plenum pro Horologio novo
        Secundum Articulos   35.0.0
    Et eidem ultra Articulos ex Conssesu Mri Prepositi et
        Seniorum   2.0.0

From which we see that the keeper Wardell was paid 6s. 8d. per annum for maintenance, and in addition, in this year, he was paid 3s. for repairs. Next comes the payment to Clement for his journey expenses to view the old clock and to make his recommendations, during which visit he appears to have contracted to supply a new clock for £40. Who was the Master Drake in whose hands the contract was deposited we do not know. A Mr. Drake was among the original subscribers to the Clockmakers'

Company in 1631, and in 1656 we find John Drake a signatory to a petition to the Lord Mayor and Aldermen in a dispute between the Clockmakers and the Blacksmiths. The researches of Dr. Penfold have disclosed that Clement was an anchor smith in Rotherhithe, south of the Thames, who moved north when he joined the Clockmakers Company in 1670. This discovery strengthens the claim for Clement to be the inventor of the anchor escapement.

Then come the two payments totalling the £40 of the contract and in addition a payment of £2 for some reason unknown.

From the illustration it is seen that the Master has signed his work + GVLIELMVS + + CLEMENT LONDINI + + FECIT 1671 +, and the foregoing history proves that this date is correct. It will be noted that the flukes of the anchor are riveted on to the curved base, a proof that this part of the escapement is original. Had it been replaced a hundred years or so later, the anchor would have been made in one piece.

The present escape wheel and the pendulum with its double suspension spring and wooden rod are later replacements, but the new brass escape wheel would have to follow the pattern of the original one in order to work with the original anchor. One or two of the other wheels in the train are also of brass and therefore not original; these changes may have been made when the clock passed to St. Giles' Church. One thing is certain; the clock has always had a recoil escapement; it has never been converted from a verge.

The little central dial records when the clock passed from King's College, Cambridge, to St. Giles' Church at Cambridge, in 1819.

In this clock we have the Genesis of all long-case clocks, and derived from this clock we have nearly all the regulators and observatory clocks for two and a quarter centuries, and for many of them for a further fifty years. The dead-beat escapement and refinements thereof were only made possible by improvements of the principle demonstrated by Clement in this clock.

In Chapter One we have traced the arguments for and against Clement and Hooke as inventors of the anchor escapement, and the author submits that there is no evidence at all in favour of Hooke. This is gradually finding wider acceptance; there are a few who obstinately cling to the older idea, but none can produce any evidence. That Hooke's experiment with the small arc 14-foot pendulum was due to the anchor escapement, has definitely been exploded.

Ponder on this clock carefully, as it introduced an improvement in time-keeping as important as that of the pendulum itself, and let us give honour to the *real* contriver of the royal pendulum, as Smith says.

Just when the long-case clock started is a matter for conjecture. Some of the earliest known have very narrow trunks, only wide enough to take the weights of clocks with verge escapements and bob pendulums. The author inclines to the view that it was the anchor escapement with its narrow arc of swing that so thoroughly established the long case, but no invention, however revolutionary and improving, sweeps the board at once. Some makers, such as Fromanteel, who introduced the verge escapement with the pendulum into England and who would naturally be predisposed to it, still continued to make verge escapement movements with short pendulum and encase them in the new and rapidly becoming fashionable long case.

If this be true, we do not get any long cases before 1671–72. It has generally been accepted that the desire to see the weights enclosed led to the placing of short bob movements in a long case some time in the sixteen-sixties, but the author knows no real basis for this. Certainly the enclosing of lantern clocks from time to time was, in the writer's opinion, a result of the introduction of the long case and a desire to 'modernise' an existing possession; not, as has sometimes been asserted, a precursor to it.

In *Plate 22* we have four early long-case clocks by Johannes and Ahasuerus Fromanteel, Edward East and Joseph Windmills respectively. The Johannes Fromanteel has a short pendulum with a verge movement, that by Ahasuerus an anchor escapement with seconds pendulum. These early cases follow the mantel-clock tradition of ebony veneered on oak, slide-up hoods, and have 'spoon' locking devices for the door. This is a hinged hook with a broad tail, rather like the handle of a spoon, which, hanging down below the hood inside the case, has the tail pressed backwards when the door is shut, bringing the hook forward to engage the lower framework of the hood and preventing its being raised until the door is again unlocked and opened, thus ensuring no meddling with the hands by unauthorised persons.

The general style of the cases, with their panelled doors, and, in the case of Ahasuerus, panelled base, is in conformity with cabinet-making trends of the period. The higher base, supported on a deeper plinth resulting in a shorter trunk, gives better proportions to the Ahasuerus clock than to the Johannes, and is one of the reasons for dating this clock a little later than the other. A 'swag' or decorative ornament has appeared on each case, one on the top of the door, the other on the pediment. These swags more often appear on early long-case clocks than on mantel clocks and, in any event, disappear about 1690. It will be noted that the moulding at the junction of the hood and the case is convex in form; this style continued until around 1700 when it took a concave shape, which shape has so continued ever since.

Except for the fact that, being a short pendulum movement, it has no seconds dial, there is nothing special about the Johannes Fromanteel clock that has not already been dealt with in the chapter on mantel clocks. For, as has already been stated, at this period, in outward appearance, the long-case clock of the day was simply a mantel clock placed upon a trunk and base; it was quite small, had a dial only about ten inches square and stood about six feet to six feet six inches tall.

The dial of the Ahasuerus Fromanteel is very interesting, and for many years it proved an enigma to experts. It will be noted that there is no xii; a ◇ takes its place. The minute ring is a loose friction fit, as are also the seconds ring and the ring in the lower part of the dial. The dial of this clock is illustrated in *Plate 37b*, and it will be fully discussed in the chapter dealing with dials and back plates. Otherwise the chapter ring, hands, spandrels and matted centre are all true to type of the period.

The other two small long-case clocks with ten-inch dials are approximately six feet high. That on the left is by Edward East and incorporates two interesting innovations. Firstly, the case is veneered in walnut. We are breaking away from the black case only to return to it relatively rarely during the next fifty years, and never thereafter, in spite of the fact that when questioned by her husband, who in 1675 had gone to London to buy a clock, as to whether she would prefer olive wood, walnut-tree wood or ebony, the young wife replies (as quoted by Symonds): 'My dearest Soùle; as for the pandolome case, I think black suits anything.' The second innovation is the 'lantern' or glass aperture let into the door at the level of the pendulum bob so that its motion may be clearly seen through it. The seconds hand is now making its regular appearance but the design of the hands and the width of the chapter ring have not changed much. The other clock shows the next stage of development, the abandonment of the portico top and the adoption of a decorative case, a development more in harmony with the taste for elaborate cabinets at this period. The height is up to six feet six inches, and the hood is now flat-topped. The door is veneered with 'oyster pieces', i.e. cross-sections cut from the boughs of trees, often laburnum, and displays a geometrical design in ebony and holly, offset by an ebony edging to the door. The maker is Joseph Windmills, one of the best makers in the second flight. He entered the Clockmakers' Company in 1671 and was Master in 1702. It will be noted that with the departure of ebony we also have the departure of the gilded capitals.

Plate 23 shows clocks which illustrate the steady trend to increase in size, and since proportions must be maintained, this increase is all round: in height, size of dial, width and depth. On to the flat top of the hood has been added a cresting, to which was added originally, but which has since been lost, a central finial, probably a wooden ball; the socket to receive the peg on which it would be set is still there. The case is veneered with walnut and has inset marquetry panels of flowers, with, in addition on the centre panel, a bird. The general style of this design is reminiscent of the Dutch floral painting of the period and gives credence to the theory that the earliest marquetry panels were imported from Holland. Very little information exists as to the early history of English clock cases; it would seem evident that the earliest cases were the product of the general cabinet-maker's workshop, but as clocks in wooden cases became more universal in production there seems no doubt that clock-case makers established themselves as a separate trade, or at any rate as a specialised branch of cabinet-making. In a list of clockmakers from 1631 to 1732 the name of Richard

Blundell occurs as a case maker. Blundell was admitted as a Brother on July 3rd, 1682 – that is to say that he was already free of some other company, possibly the Woodworkers'. On April 3rd, 1682, Blundell was arraigned for exercising the craft, not having been admitted, and was served with a writ. The result was that on May 1st 'Richard Blundell paid his fine, and promised to take his Freedome the next Quarter Court'. From the date of his admission we gather that he did so.

There is a certain school of thought that maintains that, since no examples of early development efforts in marquetry cases have come down to us, there was not any production in England, and that all these marquetry cases were imported from Holland. On the other hand, there were many foreign craftsmen living and working in London who could have produced these panels locally. The author has not had the opportunity of studying closely case construction and developments, and does not feel qualified in any way to be dogmatic on this subject. He will, therefore, content himself with following the developments in the finished examples rather than delve into the details of origin of production.

Marquetry passed through many stages in English clock cases and was popular from about 1680 to 1720, except with Tompion and Graham, who rarely used it. It will not be possible in this small book to deal with all the phases of marquetry design, but an attempt will be made to show the main developments from which they sprang. We had in *Plate 22d* an example of the early geometrical pattern, which is really inlay instead of marquetry proper. This was followed by a more complicated type of inlay involving flowers, birds and figures (*Plate 23a*). In these designs stained wood and often stained bone or ivory were inlaid. Later came more intricate designs of conventional beasts and scrolls (*Plate 24b*), to be succeeded by what the author describes as Persian carpet designs (not illustrated), and finally in very small arabesque patterns, sometimes known as seaweed marquetry.

Reverting to the clock with the cresting in *Plate 23*, it will be noted that the glass lantern referred to in *Plate 22c* has appeared in the base of the case. This indicates that the clock has an approximately 61-inch pendulum beating $1\frac{1}{4}$-seconds instead of the usual 1 second. When William Clement, who was the maker of this clock, invented the anchor escapement the vastly superior time-keeping properties achieved with the 39-inch 1-second pendulum were recognised to be due not only to the design of the escapement and greater freedom of the pendulum, but also to the fact that the slower the pendulum motion the less the cumulative effect of any slight error. Clement, therefore, tried out a $1\frac{1}{4}$-seconds pendulum and was copied by others. Occasionally one finds a genuine $1\frac{1}{4}$-seconds pendulum clock; on account of their rarity they are much more valuable than a 1-second clock of exactly the same style by the same maker. It is an easy matter for an unscrupulous person to substitute an escape wheel of twenty-four teeth for the standard wheel of thirty teeth and to fit a $1\frac{1}{4}$-seconds pendulum, but unless the clock was originally designed for a $1\frac{1}{4}$-seconds beat the seconds ring will have each 5-seconds interval divided into five instead of four. Further, if the case was originally made for a 1-second movement there will be no door in the base of the case, nor will a lantern have been fitted into the door in the base. The provision of a lantern is by no means universal in original $1\frac{1}{4}$-seconds clocks. After all, the object of the lantern is to allow the swing of the pendulum to be seen, and this cannot be achieved with the lantern in the base unless one stands very far back or else performs contortions close up. If the case be of marquetry or other type of inlay it is almost certain that a lantern cannot be added without impinging on the design employed. In our case we see the marquetry pattern nicely designed around the lantern. In other words, more care should be exercised in the purchase of a $1\frac{1}{4}$-seconds clock than in the case of an ordinary 1-second clock. The author does not know of any $1\frac{1}{4}$-seconds clocks later than 1710–20 and can only recollect seeing one dating later than 1700.

The second illustration of this clock shows the clock with the hood removed. This hood, undoubtedly, originally slid up; there are joins in the back board where the original grooves ran. It now pulls forward. In order to obviate the necessity for kneeling on the ground in order to reach a rating nut below the pendulum bob, Clement fits a micrometer screw adjustment above the pendulum suspension. He was very fond of this type of adjustment and it is felt that we can claim originality for him although the Ahasuerus Fromanteel clock shown in *Plate*

22a has a similar device. The dial of the Clement clock is shown in *Plate 38d*.

In the other illustration in *Plate 23* we continue our growth upward and as a result the case is slightly wider and deeper. The clock is another 1¼-seconds clock, this time by John Clowes.

It has just been said that, for all practical purposes, 1¼-seconds clocks were not made after 1700, but in the search after better time-keeping efforts were made to minimise the cumulative effect of slight errors by increasing still further the length of the pendulum, thus reducing its frequency. Tompion made two clocks in 1676 for Greenwich Observatory with 14-feet 2-seconds pendulums, each with a year movement, thus practically cutting out losses in accurate time-keeping due to winding, in spite of maintaining devices. These two clocks are thought to be the first year movements he made. Hooke, in 1669, experimented with a 14-feet pendulum with about a 2-seconds beat which he reported to have an 'excursion of half an inch or less' and with its weight of 3 lb. to be 'moved by the sole force of a pocket watch'. This would seem to indicate a light impulse to keep a free pendulum swinging. But the whip of these long pendulums counteracted the advantages gained from their length and they died a natural death. It has recently been discovered that in installing the two one-year clocks at Greenwich, Tompion adopted this method of a free pendulum suspended above the clock with the crutch engaging below the bob. Two-seconds pendulums are now only found in some turret clocks, where a sufficiently stiff pendulum rod can be used.

But to revert to our John Clowes clock, a small flat dome has appeared on the top of the hood; this dome will gradually get higher. The author inclines to the view that the majority of flat-topped square-hooded clocks existing today started life with domes which have been discarded either for reasons of space or taste. The case we are considering is veneered with very nicely figured walnut. The hour hand is becoming more elaborate; it will be noticed that the seconds hand in these early clocks has no tail or counterpose. There are glass panels in the hood, as has been the case with practically all these long-case clocks illustrated so far. One school of thought says that London makers put in these glass side panels and that provincial makers did not. The author has not had sufficient experience of the multitudinous provincial makers of the latter half of the eighteenth century to be dogmatic on this point, but it is interesting and worth putting to the test.

The clock (*Plate 24a*) embodies both earlier and later features; later inasmuch as the dome is higher, it also has had three finials on the top, and the bases for the two side ones remain. The dial has now been increased to twelve inches, at which size it remained for seventy-five years, and the overall height is eight feet four inches. It will be noticed that this is the first example we have had of the arabic five-minute figures appearing outside the minute ring. The cherub-head spandrels are now much more ornate, as is also the hour hand. Winding squares are ringed, and the seconds hand arbor is also heavily ringed, which in the author's opinion is a mistake, because it makes the seconds dial too fussy. The date aperture is decorated. All these are later points than in any long-case clock we have so far discussed. What is jumping back fifteen to twenty years is the inlaid case, which really should precede *Plate 23a*, but, as Bernard Shaw says, 'You never can tell'. The inlay is of coloured woods and stained bone in the form of flowers, with a helmeted warrior's figure, a most unusual *motif*, as the focal point of the design. The whole is on a black ground, probably pear-wood ebonised, which gives it a mournful appearance, quite different from the plain black cases with their gilt mounts that we have seen in the earliest examples. It is not a clock that appeals to the author; it is very nearly top-heavy, if not quite. The maker is Christopher Gould, a maker of renown, who was admitted to the Company in 1682 and died in 1718, but who never occupied the Master's chair.

The William Osborne clock on *Plate 24b* gives a fine specimen of the heyday of English marquetry and illustrates an example of beginner's luck. As an impecunious newly-wed a year or so after the First World War, the author was unable to satisfy his desire for a grandfather clock at the inflated prices for antiques then ruling, but in the early thirties prices had come tumbling down, and having been lent Britten by a friend he proceeded to be somewhat selective in his search. Eventually the clock on the left was selected and, as times were very bad, a price a good deal below the marked price was agreed upon. This figure happened to agree roughly with the yearly income from a small

legacy bequeathed by a recently departed aunt and the first
year's income was so allocated. Thus 'Aunt Louie's Tombstone'
came into the family. Having had the clock about three years,
when wandering down Piccadilly one day the author saw
Macquoid's *Age of Walnut* open in a shop-window showing a
coloured illustration of a clock case in the Victoria and Albert
Museum which seemed familiar. The official photograph of this
case was procured, from which it was seen that the two cases are
'part' and 'counterpart' of the same marquetry pattern. To
find two such cases is very rare indeed, except where a pair of
clocks might have been made for some family and have remained in the possession of that family ever since.

When only two woods are used there are just the part and
counterpart, but when more woods are used, and in this case
about six different woods are in use, there are as many counter-
parts as there are different woods.

The date of this clock is about 1705-10. The dial is illustrated
in *Plate 39a*. The chapter ring is broadening and consequently
the hour numerals are elongating. The spandrels have passed
into the next stage of progression, and two cherubs are complete
instead of heads only, supporting a crown surmounted by a
cross. This design was frequently found in the furniture of the
day, on the stretchers of chairs or on chair backs. It is also to
be found on the door furniture in Hampton Court Palace. The
hands are more ornate and very fine, the date aperture is
decorated and the winding holes are ringed with slight ringing
around the seconds-hand arbor – altogether a very pleasing dial
and case.

The third illustration on this plate is a small example of
early lacquer-work – a lady's boudoir clock of Queen Anne's
time. It is a small thirty-hour timepiece with a six-inch dial.
The trunk of the case is only six inches wide and the height six
feet. The maker is John Drury of London and the date about
1710. Being a timepiece, it will have only one weight; there
would scarcely be room for two in so narrow a case. It has a
short-bob verge movement. If the dial be examined closely it
will be seen that the hour hand has a slight counterpoise indicating that it originally belonged to a one-handed clock. This
is confirmed by the absence of minute markings on the minute
ring. The addition of the minute hand was probably made soon

after it was taken into use. Another feature is the late employ-
ment of the early cherub-head spandrel which went out of use
in long-case clocks twenty to twenty-five years earlier, but, as
previously mentioned in Chapter Two, they are found in these
smaller dials because they are much smaller than the actual
spandrels in current use at the time. The lacquer is in the best
Chinese style, the bird of paradise at the top and the weeping
willow towards the bottom of the case being particularly finely
executed. Those interested in lacquer and its method of production should visit the Russell Coates Museum on the East
Cliff at Bournemouth, where there is a very fine series illustrating all the manifold stages in the production of lacquer objects.

These dainty little Queen Anne clocks are very rare and
consequently much sought after; the drawback is that they
have almost invariably thirty-hour movements and this severely
restricts their value. If you have one of these clocks the author's
advice would be to have it in the main living-room of the
house, where it is handy to be wound up each night, as he does
with the little gem illustrated in *Plate 31c*, which is also only
thirty-hour; or else have it in some position that you pass on the
way to bed. Human nature is so naturally lazy that the zeal of
possession soon wears off and it becomes just too much trouble
to go into a room specially to wind a clock every evening, even
if you *do* remember it.

To find clocks in Royal possession that have been there ever
since they were made is not very rare, but to find a clock of the
seventeenth or eighteenth century that is still in the family is
much rarer, and to find that the original invoice has been preserved is much rarer still. Such an example is to be seen in the
last clock illustrated on this Plate. It is an eight-day clock by
George Graham, No. 681, sold in 1728. From the invoice (Fig.
10) it will be seen that the clock cost 16 guineas, packing and
carriage 12 shillings. An accompanying note says that in Mr.
Clay's ledger for 1728 there is an entry for the payment of
£17. 9s. 0d, possibly 1 shilling tip to the carrier included.

The clock does not have Graham's dead-beat escapement,
only an ordinary anchor, it is a walnut case and is about eight
foot overall, including the flaming urn finial. The hands,
unfortunately, have been broken and have been replaced in the
early nineteenth century by a very ordinary pair.

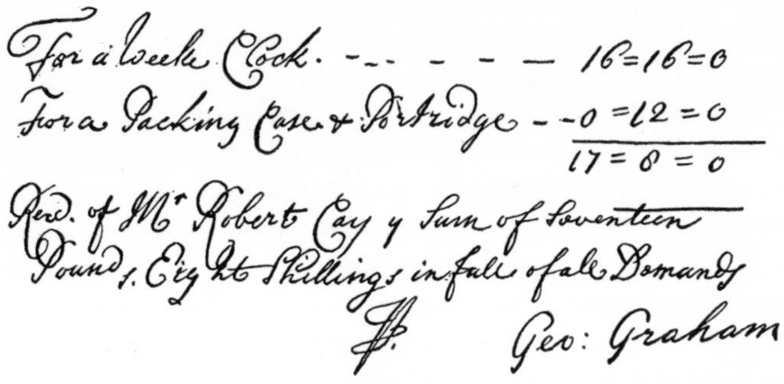

For a Weeke Clock. -.. - - - — *16 = 16 = 0*
For a Packing Case & Portridge - -*0 = 12 = 0*
                                    17 = 8 = 0

Recd. of Mr. Robert Cay y Sum of Seventeen
Pound, Eight Shillings in full of all Demands
                        Geo: Graham

FIG. 10

The next two illustrations (*Plate 25*) are interesting inasmuch as they show the 'birth' in England of the arched dial and case so familiar in later clocks from 1715-20 onwards. An example by Tompion, presented by him to the City of Bath in 1710, is frequently cited as the start of arched dials and cases, but the magnificent arched case of the Tompion clock on the left is fifteen years earlier. And as we have seen, the arch appeared on the Continent nearly a century earlier. The second clock is by Richard Street of London and is actually dated 1708, and shows that these early arches were not confined to Tompion, although the author feels that there is some connexion between Tompion and Street that has not yet been discovered. Examples of Street's work are sometimes so 'Tompionesque'.

There is a great deal to say about these two clocks, so let us begin our detailed examination. The Tompion clock is a year equation movement and was made for King William III about 1695. The difference between mean and solar days, giving rise to the equation of time, has been explained in Chapter One. The beautiful lines of the finely figured walnut-veneered case are at once apparent. It will be noticed that the arch has been introduced to show on the annual calendar ring the zodiacal circle indicating the position of the sun in the ecliptic as well as the day of the month and the month of the year; it should be noted that its introduction is purely functional in origin, not decorative. The door of the trunk, which is decorated at the corners with little spandrels, has a Gothic-shaped lantern which is placed lower than in other examples; that is because the escapement – an anchor escapement – is

H

placed below the movement proper. One arm of the anchor can be seen in *Plate 25c*. The winding square, covered by the plate of the maintaining power lever, is situated at the upper XII. The pendulum bob shows so clearly in the photograph because it swings in front of the heavy slab-shaped weight necessary to drive a year movement. As has previously been recorded, Tompion's first year movements were made in 1676 for Greenwich Observatory and had two seconds pendulums, which were not very satisfactory. Here, to get sufficient drop for the weight for a year's running within the compass of a clock eight feet high, Tompion arranges for the hour hand to revolve once in twenty-four hours, and the minute hand once in two hours. The minutes are numbered every five *between* the hour numerals and the minute ring on the fixed dial and outside the minute ring on the mobile minute circle showing the equation. The dial is shown separately in *Plate 38c*. Now, it was explained in Chapter One that for two reasons there was a daily difference between mean and solar time; this difference is irregular both in amount and direction. The variation lies between mean time being about sixteen minutes fast on the sun around November 4th and its being about fourteen minutes slow on the sun around February 12th. But the rate of change is not a simple progression between these two extremes, as the mean and solar days are equal at four irregular times during the year, around April 16th, June 14th, September 1st and December 25th. Further, the variations in the length of the days falling between any two of the four days of equality just cited are themselves irregular, so that any simple circular motion is ruled out. The difference between mean and solar days had been known to astronomers for hundreds of years, but it never entered into the daily lives of the people until the invention of the anchor escapement made time-keeping sufficiently accurate that errors of a minute or so a day became noticeable. Before the pendulum was invented, errors up to half an hour a day were common, and even after its invention, and its use with the verge escapement, its time-recording was not very reliable.

Many efforts were made between 1670 and 1695 to find some way of recording the equation, but they were all based on wheel work and were not successful. The problem was finally solved by the invention of the 'equation kidney' which is seen in *Plate 25d*. This is rotated once a year by the clock's ordinary movement. Bearing against its edge is a compensated rocker arm, clearly visible in the illustration. This rocker arm terminates in a toothed rack, seen on Plate *25c*. As the kidney revolves about its axis, the pin on the rocker arm bearing against its edge will approach towards or recede from the centre of revolution, giving a corresponding backwards or forwards movement to the toothed rack, which in turn engages in the toothed wheel carrying the outer and moving minute circle (*Plate 38c*). The outline of this cam is so calculated that the moving circle advances or recedes the necessary amount each day in relation to the fixed minute ring, thus giving the daily difference, plus or minus, as between mean and solar time. Later a third hand was fitted on to the central arbor instead of the mobile minute ring, thus giving a clear and direct reading (*Plate 38b*).

The first equation table calculated for use in the correction of clocks was probably that made by Christian Huygens, the Dutch mathematician and astronomer, and published in his *Horologium Oscillatorum* in 1673. The date of the calculation is not known, but records show that it must have been before February 15th, 1662, thus very soon after his invention of the pendulum in 1657. These tables were presented before the Royal Society on May 10th, 1669, i.e. before the invention of the anchor escapement, which, by the way, Huygens never used. John Flamsteed, who was later to become the first Astronomer Royal, compiled tables in 1666. In 1668 John Smith, whose writings have already been mentioned, published a little book on the *Unequality of Natural Time* embodying an equation table. Tompion and possibly others had tables printed for them and sometimes stuck them inside the doors of long-case clocks.

All these tables, however, were only a means of enabling a check to be kept by the owner of a clock on the true time-keeping of his clock when compared with a sundial; they did nothing towards the solution of the problem of the direct recording of the equation. Heretofore Joseph Williamson, a London clockmaker, has been regarded as the inventor of the kidney on the strength of a letter written by him in 1719, to the Royal Society, i.e. about a quarter of a century after the event, in which he claims to have made all the equation clocks with equation movements that had been made in England up to that

date, his first being about six years before 1700. He writes:
'So that I think I may justly claim the greatest right to this
contrivance of making clocks to go with Apparent time and I
have never yet heard of any such clock sold in England, but
what was of my own making, though I have made them so
long.' It will be noticed that he does not claim the invention,
only the making. That his claim is not correct is shown by the
Tompion clock here illustrated, which bears the inscription
Tho: Tompion London Inventit, indicating it as a first production
of this type. There are four more Tompion equation clocks
known to the author, and there may possibly be more.

Now Williamson worked for Quare, and all Quare equation
clocks have the equation work quite separate from the clock
movement proper, driving the former by means of a long connecting rod and endless worm. It would be, therefore, quite
feasible for two individuals to have worked on these clocks and
united their work. In all the Tompion equation clocks known
to the author the equation work is integral with the movement
and must have been the work of one man only. The date of the
Tompion clock illustrated is *ca.* 1695. Huygens, in his last
recorded letter, dated March 4th, 1695 (he died in June 1695),
writes to his brother in London: 'You will have spoken to him
[Tompion], I take it, of my newly invented Clock of which I
am going to make a description and demonstration. I have had
it adapted to an old clock with a three-foot pendulum which
also shows the hour without need for the equation of time. . . .
The Barometers of the Quaker [Quare] are in Alance's book,
but perhaps he has made improvements.'

It would seem that Huygens died before he made any description or demonstration; but here we have a definite reference
to a direct recording of the equation coupled with Tompion's
name and with a less direct reference to Quare, in the very
year that the Buckingham Palace clock has been quite independently dated by the late Mr. Percy Webster, the greatest
expert on old English clocks we have ever had.

An equation clock by Huygens was bequeathed to Leyden
University by A. J. Royer, a great-nephew of Huygens, in 1809;
this has since been lost, and Professor Vollgraff, the erudite
editor of the *Œuvres Complètes de Christian Huygens*, takes the
line that this clock was, probably, not an equation clock. He

assumes that Royer had not sufficient horological and astronomical knowledge to know an equation clock when he saw one
and was confusing the equation clock with a seconds clock made
for Huygens by Thuret of Paris (the French 'Tompion') which
is now in the University Museum. The writer submits that since
in that same museum there is Huygen's planetarium, or Orrery,
which bears an inscription to the effect that Royer restored it
with his own hands, Royer certainly would know an equation
clock when he saw one; furthermore, by 1809 equation clocks
were no longer novelties, they were fairly common. It seems,
therefore, to the author that we should accept the evidence
recorded by the only man who is known to have seen and
handled the missing clock and not brush it aside as a mistake.
Vollgraff assumes the new clock referred to by Huygens in his
letter of March 1695 to be a clock made by Huygens in 1693
with an isochronous balance, designed to be tested in his efforts
to 'find the longitude'; but, however successful this might be
from a time-keeping point of view, accurate equation tables
would be a necessity, yet Huygens says that his clock has no
need for the equation of time, i.e. it records it automatically.
Again, Huygens writes that he is going to make a description
and demonstration, yet the clock of 1693 is fully described in
Huygens' notes. Further, Huygens was a man of prolific inventions; would an invention of 1693, on which he had been working since 1683, still be his new invention of 1695? It would seem
probable that Huygens died before even the prototype of his
clock was made, hence we have no claim from him to the invention. When Vollgraff made his assumptions the coincidence
of the letter from Huygens with the appearance of the first
clocks to be made embodying the equation kidney had not
been established; this was first done by the author in an article
in the *Horological Journal* in December 1943, which, owing to
war conditions, would not have had circulation in Holland.

If Williamson were really the inventor it is funny that a man
who could make the intricate calculation to establish the shape
of the kidney should not have sent his invention into the world
under his own name, instead of letting Quare get all the credit,
as far as he was concerned. If he were the inventor and had an
arrangement with Quare it does not seem very commercial that
Quare should agree to pass it on post haste to his chief rival,

Tompion; for Williamson never mentions Tompion in the letter he wrote to the Royal Society.

We have seen from the date of Huygens' equation tables that he had had this problem of the equation before him since soon after the invention of the pendulum. The author submits that he had the type of brain to calculate the kidney and that Tompion, Quare and Williamson were more mechanically than mathematically creative.

Equation clocks by Williamson are known in which he places the equation kidney directly under the pendulum suspension and so modifies the length of the pendulum day by day, with the result that the hands of the clock show 'sun time' directly, and there is no indication of mean time. Such a clock could then be compared directly with a sundial for checking purposes. Clocks of this type have been signed *Joseph Williamson, Inventit,* and the author maintains that this claim to invention, as well as Tompion's already mentioned, refers to the method of applying the kidney and not to the invention of the kidney itself. There are three methods, so far; Quare-Williamson had the equation dial separate from the meantime dial, Tompion integrates it into the dial and Williamson gives a direct reading of the equation.

All this diversion and digression introduced because the case of the clock happened to be the first known with an arched hood! The author hopes that the lay reader has not been too bored with the development of a rather abstruse theory (at any rate he can skip it if he wants to); but it is his weakness to try to delve into the past and elucidate such of the mysteries of early English horology as still remain to be solved and to apportion credit where it is due, although in this case there is no great benefit to horology, as was the case of the anchor escapement. An equation clock is really only a glorified toy, and good equation tables were just as effective.

The second clock on *Plate 25* is another early example of the use of the arched case. It is rather a case of 'arches above them, arches below them, arches all round them,' but it is very historic and deserves inclusion. As mentioned above, it is by Richard Street, who was Junior Warden in the Clockmakers' Company in 1715, and is dated 1708. The clock was presented by Sir Isaac Newton to the Observatory at Trinity College,

Cambridge, where he had spent so many years as a Fellow and where his *Principia* was written. The dial illustrated in *Plate 39b* bears the following inscribed plate: 'Collegio St. Trinitatus Cantab. ISAACUS NEWTON Equis Auratus Dato D.' The term of eulogy *Auratus* was applied to anyone who had attained an outstanding position in his profession or calling – The Gilding of refined Gold. Thus we have the arum lily, believed to be the most perfect of its kind, giving rise to the expression of today of 'gilding the lily' as trying to improve perfection.

In connexion with our particular clock, the following letter among the records of Trinity College is interesting.

Letter from Roger Cotes in Cambridge to his Honoured Uncle, Professor Cotes; dated February 10th, 1708.

'I have lately been in London, I found y^r letter at Cambridge upon my return. The occasion of my going thither was partly to view a large brass sextant of 5 foot radius (y^t had been making for us & is now finished) before it should be sent down. Whilst I was in town Sir Isaac Newton gave order for ye makeing of a Pendulum Clock which he designs as a present to our new Observatory. The sextant will cost the College 150£ & I believe Sr. Isaac's Clock can cost him no less than 50£.'

This is an interesting commentary on the cost of a clock that runs one month between windings.

The lay-out is very like the Tompion. The escapement is below the movement and the winding square high up, just below the XII. In both cases there is maintaining power. The spandrels are of no particular period or fashion; they have evidently been designed especially for this clock. The dial in the upper arch is a dummy to balance that below the dial in which the seconds hand is affixed direct on to the escapement arbor. The calendar is of the ordinary variety and has to be adjusted by hand for the short months. The pendulum rod is tubular and has a heavy cast-iron and gilded bob; this is thought to be a late eighteenth-century alteration; the columns of the hood and the spires are of gilded wood. The case is ebony veneered on oak.

Plate 26 shows two very beautiful examples of burr walnut cases, both the work of the finest masters of their day, Quare and Graham respectively. That on the left is a three-month movement by Daniel Quare, the details of whose history have already been given in Chapter Three. In point of chronological

sequence it is rather earlier than our last illustration of the
Street clock. This Quare clock would date the later half of the
last decade of the seventeenth century; its height, seven feet
six inches, eleven-inch dial, ringed winding holes and later type
of cherub spandrel would all confirm this. Furthermore, the
convex moulding below the hood is a pretty safe indication of
'before 1700'. Just when the change from convex to concave
took place cannot, like all changes of course, be determined with
exactitude; it was probably gradual, but it was more quickly
established than most changes. The cutting of the base panel
veneer into two horizontally is unusual and, in the author's
opinion, detrimental to the overall lines of the clock. It may
well be that this line is more marked in the photograph than is
apparent to the eye; these details are often more pronounced in
photographs, especially when a filter is used.

The other clock on this plate is by George Graham and is of
date 1715–20. It must be after 1713, because Graham did not
succeed Tompion until the latter's death in that year. This
clock, in the author's opinion, comes very near to perfection for
simple and effective design, proportions and legibility; the dial
is separately illustrated in Plate 39d. It probably had some
ornamental finial on top originally, and this is all that is lacking
to complete the harmony. We are progressing in our overall
height, with a twelve-inch dial, and we have an overall height
of just over eight feet. This height is, in part, achieved by the
double plinth.

Especially pleasing is the large diameter and narrow width
of the seconds dial permitting the long and delicate seconds
hand. It will be noticed that the dial is as large as is possible to
fit in between the chapter ring and the hand arbor. The ringed
winding squares have gone, the hour hand is much more
elongated and is establishing a 'Graham' pattern. The quarter-
hour marks on the inside of the chapter ring have given place
to half-hour marks only. The half-hour 'lozenge' has now gone.

All Graham's work is characterised by simplicity of line and
design; you never find a Graham clock in a marquetry or
highly decorated case; this is probably due to the influence of
Tompion; also quite possibly to his Quaker father's influence
during his early formative years, till he was five or six.

We now say good-bye to the square hood and very nearly

to the square-topped door to the trunk that goes with it. For a while square-topped doors were fitted to cases with arched hoods, but it was soon considered that an arched door 'went' better with an arched hood and it was universally adopted. Personally, the writer likes the square door with the arched hood.

One more clock by Graham is shown on this plate (*Plate 26c*), being an early mahogany case; few, very few, cases were made in mahogany prior to 1760 and these are usually of solid mahogany, as is the case with the clock illustrated. Later mahogany cases were almost invariably veneered. The author owns a clock of about the same date as this Graham, which also has a solid mahogany case. The dial of his clock is illustrated in *Plate 40c*. In this Graham clock we have another example of simplicity of design; the door originally had a glass panel, no doubt to show to all and sundry the newly invented mercury pendulum fitted to the clock, for this is a very early type of this pendulum invented by Graham in 1726 and still in use today in high-grade clocks. A later owner has removed the glass door panel and substituted a mahogany panel.

Graham found out, more or less accidentally, in 1721, that mercury had an expansion rate that was exceptional, as explained in Chapter One. He read his paper on his mercury pendulum before the Royal Society in 1726, and the present clock is about 1730. The period of going is one month. The dial is very similar to that in the previous plate. There are still half-hour divisions on the inner edge of the chapter ring, although these will probably get lost in block reproduction, and in both cases the seconds dial is as large as can be accommodated, but now the seconds hand is compensated, which detracts from its delicacy, but which is necessary to help to reduce friction. The longer the going period of a clock, the greater the number of wheels in the train that are needed and the greater the necessity to eliminate all possible causes of friction. The third hand is to show the equation of time. When the first Tompion equation clock was considered it was seen to have a second movable minutes ring mounted on a toothed wheel and actuated by a rack; here Graham has a third hand fitted as a tight friction fit on the main arbor. Thus we get direct visible reading of the equation, the hand bearing the effigy of the sun indicating solar time.

The introduction of a concentric equation hand involves much complicated gearing. As we have seen, when there is a separate dial to record the equation, the difference can be shown by a follower arm on the equation kidney actuating a rack and pinion recording on a separate dial or minute ring; but in the case we are considering, both hands have to record on the same fixed dial. Joseph Williamson was the first to do this, employing a true differential gear such as we find in motor cars today, but he used two dials back to back. In the example we are considering there is a complicated system of epicyclic gearing actuated from the equation kidney to give the effect of the equation to the third hand. Any clock with a concentric equation hand is well worthy of further study and investigation. They are very rare.

Many clocks of this period had year calendar disks on which were engraved, daily or at intervals, the daily difference due to the equation. This clock has such a calendar disk in the arch, which revolves once a year and shows the day, the month, the equation, the position of the sun in the ecliptic and the rising and the setting of the sun. This calendar disk in the clock is not the original. In September 1752 the adjustment from the Julian to the Gregorian calendar was made in England, when the calendar was advanced eleven days, leading to riots among the ignorant, who thought that they were being deprived of eleven days of life and rioted under the slogan, 'Give us back our eleven days!'

This adjustment, of course, put out all previous calendar and astronomical dials, and from the style of the engraving of the present dial it is evident that a new one was made soon after the adjustment mentioned above. At the same time the dial was 'modernised' by the substitution of spandrels of the style in fashion in the middle seventeen-fifties, thus explaining how these relatively late spandrels appear on this early clock. It is only a timepiece; the second winding hole will be for the setting of the equation hand.

The last illustration of clocks in this chapter in *Plate 26d* is of a clock dated about 1735, which is in a dark walnut case, interesting inasmuch as it has a glass mirror panel in the door, which consequently is of quite different construction to that of an ordinary clock-case door. It is of the same type as the door of a bookcase or wardrobe. A similar type of construction is seen in the Graham clock on this plate.

The production of flint or crystal glass was a London speciality in the Restoration period and in the century that followed it. The location of the works was at Vauxhall, on the Surrey bank of the Thames. The Duke of Buckingham is reported to have established a works at Vauxhall about 1670, employing Venetian workmen. The nobility of those days had no less an eye to the main chance than is assumed natural today. Buckingham, no doubt, sought and obtained a monopoly for the production of flint glass, in which the distinguishing feature is the introduction of lead. The relatively large numbers of mirrors of the Restoration period that have survived to come down to us are indicative of their popularity at that time. They are also found in bookcase doors and in bureau doors of the Queen Anne period.

A glass plate with mirror surface three and a half feet long would be quite a technical achievement at the time this clock was made, before the introduction of rolls for the rolling of hot glass. At the bottom of the right-hand corner can be seen the slightly different reflection of the bevelled edge of the panel; all these old original panels when bevelled, and they usually are, can be distinguished by the somewhat irregular edge of the bevel as opposed to the strictly regular edge of the modern machine-cut mirror.

In the *Present State of England*, written in 1683, it is stated that 'flint glass plates for looking glasses and coach windows were made about 1673 in Lambeth by the encouragement of the Duke of Buckingham'. The author also read recently, somewhere, he cannot now recall just where, how My Lady X, driving in her coach, wished to bow to an acquaintance passing in another coach, forgot that she had had her coach windows fitted with the new glass, which was so clear that she pushed her head through it.

The maker of this clock is Anthony Hebert, who entered the Clockmakers' Company in 1725. The arch is purely decorative, the arch of the dial-plate being engraved with a nondescript design centring around a woman's head. The quarter-hour marks are still here, and the ringing of the winding holes and the decoration around the calendar date aperture, which latter will no doubt be lost in reproduction, are late in their appearance. The spandrels are of a type of two cupids supporting a crown surmounted by a cross (*Plate 39a*).

Thus, as was the case with bracket clocks, we come to the close of the period where, horologically interesting, developments have taken place in domestic clocks. From now on, movements are more or less standardised and the main interest assumes a furnishing aspect. In movements the chief development towards the latter part of the eighteenth century was the introduction of more complicated musical mechanisms and often extravagant automata.

Bracket or Mantel Clocks 1735-1835

W E are now entering a period of definitely plain clock
dials, not that they are any the worse for that. Indeed
many, one might almost say most, are very pleasing
and very legible at a distance, which is a great asset; after all,
that is their chief function. Not so always with the later long-
case dials, as we shall see in Chapter Five, which deals with
them; some of these are so cluttered up with ornamentation that
they become the very height of illegibility.

We are arriving at the time when clockmakers began to make
their dials round, instead of square or rectangular; although,
as we shall see, the arched dial still persisted for many years,
side by side with the round dial. In *Plate 27a*, the door is edged
with brass and a brass bezel encircles the glass. The whole front
of the clock still opens, although it would only be necessary for
the bezel-mounted glass to open; that came later. The dial is
silvered and no longer has an applied chapter ring. The
quarter-hour divisions have gone, but their erstwhile presence
is remembered by a single circle that will persist for many
years, until we finally bury this relic of single-handed lantern-
clock practice about a hundred and fifty years after it started,
and about a hundred years after it ceased to have any meaning.
The five-minute numerals are still there and will remain there
on and off for some time. The hour hand is becoming plainer
and will continue to get more and more simple. The minute
hand has the characteristics of the mid-eighteenth century.
The winding squares are rising again to the ix and the iii,
where they will remain stationary, indicating a standardisation
in the lay-out of the trains and fusees. We still have a carrying
handle and the escapement is still verge. Clocks are not yet
cheap enough to have them all over the house.

It will be noted that we have passed to the 'True Bell' style
and the top is convex instead of concave. The case is pearwood,

ebonised, and the door has not the brass beading around the edge, but against this we have the clock fitted with brass pineapple finials, a type of decoration which died very hard; in fact for many purposes it has never died; it is used in architectural design still today. It had its origin in the commemoration of the introduction of the pineapple into England in Charles II's reign. There is a picture of the gardener at Hampton Court presenting the first pineapple to the King. The movement is a verge, but for the rest the description applied to the clock on the left will apply equally to this clock, except that it has a strike-silent mechanism, the end of the lever operating this can be seen by the forty-five minute mark, conveniently placed so that the door need only be partly opened to silence the strike when the clock was taken upstairs to the bedroom. There is no trace of the maker, George Hodgson, in any London records. It sometimes happened that an apprentice or journeyman would make a clock privately for one of his master's customers and inscribe it with a fictitious name in order to escape detection.

The Plate shows two more English bell-topped clocks; that by Stennet shows at a glance that it is a good movement; the general careful finish is at once apparent. The case is ebonised pearwood. It is rather an enigma. So far the 'going' has been too good for us, everything has proceeded in an orderly chronological fashion, but this comes to 'put a spanner in the works' of all our theories. It should come in the 1780–90 period, but Benjamin Stennet did not become free of the Clockmakers until 1808 and it does not give the impression of a first effort. It is a case of the resuscitation of earlier styles a quarter of a century later (such cases are by no means unheard of), or Stennet may have had it to overhaul at some time or possibly to fit a new movement and at that time replaced the original silvered half-hoop with one bearing his name. This also was by no means an uncommon practice. Probably it is the case of the late appearance of an earlier design; at any rate, whatever its history may or may not have been, it is a very fine clock.

It is a reversion to type in another way, the chapter ring being again superimposed and the centre of the dial matted and gilt. It has a seconds dial, most unusual for a bracket clock, and it has a half-seconds dead beat escapement with a wooden pendulum rod to minimise the effect of changes of temperature. The reversal of the usual arrangement by placing the subsidiary dials in the base of the case instead of in the arch is interesting. The dial on the left is a calendar dial and that on the right for the strike-silent lever. Just at the right of the xii the light catches the end of the lever for regulation. The spandrels are of the 1770–90 period.

The clock by Metcalfe on this plate is also of ebonised pearwood, with a plain painted dial and verge escapement, a simple straightforward piece. The inner circle below the hour numerals has gone, as have also the five-minute markings. The hands, which are of gilded brass, have become much lighter and are of the openwork pattern favoured in the Regency period. It will be noted that it is signed in French.

The fourth clock on this Plate has been included to illustrate yet another case of Continental anticipation of English clock design. It is a 'true bell' case made by Elias Kreitmeyer of Friedberg about 1710. It was formerly in the Town Hall of Vienna and is now in the Vienna Clock Museum. The case is in the style of Boulle, the famous seventeenth-century cabinet maker, who worked for Louis XIV. It is a three train-clock and it will be noticed that the dial still retains the pre-pendulum habit of recording the quarters with the minutes only marked in a subsidiary manner, both these markings being on the inside of the hour ring. The subsidiary dials are left, the month of the year with its sign of the zodiac and its number of days, and right, the age and phase of the moon and the day of the month.

Here in *Plate 28* we interpose a type of clock that was very popular for forty or fifty years from about 1760, known as 'balloon' clocks. They were made in all sizes and in all kinds of wood, often with a Sheraton type of shell inlaid in the lower part. Not infrequently they had their own wall-brackets. Small balloon clocks up to, say, ten inches in height are very much sought after in these days of small flats. The clock on the right is of an elaborated balloon type showing marked French influence with its black ebonised case, and brass gilt mountings and feet. The dial is an early example of enamelling; the inevitable chips, which sooner or later disfigure all enamel dials, sad to say, can be seen by both winding holes. The hands are of the serpentine type and are correct for the period. It has a recoil escapement and a pull repeater on two bells. Repeating clocks remained in vogue until the invention of friction matches in 1827. The maker is Thomas Brass of Guildford, who was working from some time prior to 1767 up to 1784.

The other balloon clock on this plate is a pure balloon in a mahogany case with narrow brass inlay, the whole having a very warm and pleasing tone. This clock is dated 1796 and is pretty well at the other end of the span of years during which these clocks were made; this is reflected in the style of the dial. The heavy copying in paint of the old superimposed chapter ring as seen in the photo on the right is gone; the dial will compare with those in the later plates of this chapter. The hands are delightful. Unfortunately the clock is anonymous.

In the flat inverted bell clock (*Plate 28c*) we go back a few years to about 1775. The reversion to the inverted bell is interesting. This is a very nice clock by Justin Vulliamy, the first of a long line of noted makers who came to London from Switzerland. This is still a verge movement – the false bob can be seen in the top of the arch – but since it swings above the escapement arbor the shape of the slot is in the inverse to that shown in other clocks (*Plate 17*). This arrangement allows the curved slot to be tucked in very nicely under the arch. The dial is beautifully enamelled, but here again, unfortunately, there there are signs of chipping round the winding holes. The dial is delightfully clear and the hands are most pleasing. Unfortunately the photographer, who in this case happened to be the author, slipped up in not moving the hour hand from in front of the winding square. The subsidiary dials are for pendulum regulation on the left and for strike-silent on the right. The case is ebony on oak. The spandrels, although nicely finished, are of the uninteresting late eighteenth-century type. The back plate of this clock is seen in Plate *44c*.

The fourth clock on this plate introduces another very prolific type of case, the 'arched' case. There are broken arch, shallow broken arch, deep broken arch, broken arch decorated passing to the plain arch, plain arch decorated, etc. All of these will not be illustrated, but a sufficient number will be shown to enable the reader to visualise the remainder.

This clock is another of the author's lucky finds. It is a deep broken-arch type, which is not lacquered but is decorated with coloured and varnished prints of flowers, after the style of

'Vernis Martin'. These prints are interspersed with latticed traceries in gold. It is a real 'lady's' clock, and the author has never seen another quite like it. When the doors, back and front, are opened they are seen to be decorated on the insides as well; more simply, of course. The whole of the inside of the case is also coloured. The maker is Henry Fish of the Royal Exchange, London, a son of Henri Poisson, a Huguenot refugee who worked in London about 1695–1720. Henry Fish died in 1774.

As will be seen from the slit with the false bob and the light pendulum, it is a verge movement. The subsidiary dials are the usual, pendulum regulation and strike-silent. The rise-and-fall arm, which is worked by an eccentric cam, a much cheaper form than the rack-and-pinion, passes behind the dial to fit on to one end of a movable arbor which, passing through the front and back plates, transmits the movement to the second arm fixed to the other end of the arbor, which, in turn, carries the pendulum suspension.

Here again we have a late retention of the matted and gilt dial centre with superimposed silvered chapter ring. All these details are essential to the harmony of the conception of this clock, with its delicate warm tones derived from the colouring of the flowers and the painting of the case. A silvered dial, such as we have just seen, or the new fashioned enamel dial would be quite out of place. Altogether a very pleasing piece.

Plate 29a shows an example of the shallow broken-arch type, of date 1780–1800. The case is ebonised with brass bezel and brass-filled spandrels. This retention of an earlier style leads the eye away from the enamelled dial, which is, however, delightfully clear. Minutes are now represented by dots only, and the hands show an elegance of design combined with sufficient boldness to assure easy reading. The five-minute numerals have disappeared, the hands are Regency and always remind the author of the delicate ironwork of balconies and verandas of this period.

From now on there is no definite style of hands by which a clock can be dated to within a few years, each maker, it seems, having followed his own fancy. The reader will notice that the hands in every clock in the remainder of this chapter are different from all the others.

The carrying handle is still there, although this clock has an anchor recoil escapement and will need much more care when moved from place to place. The handle is probably only a relic of the past and will not be intended for daily use.

This plate shows the coming of the plain arch. A very broad generalisation in handles – and, like all generalisations, directly you have made it you can start to pick holes in it – is that when the arch is broken the handles will be on top, but when you get the plain arch and later chamfer tops which followed it, and the Gothic style lancet clocks, there are two handles, one on each side.

This plain arch clock is by Edward Baker, London, who was working between 1785 and 1821. It is also in a mahogany case with brass inlay and feet. The dial is painted and the hands again different from the previous examples.

The third clock on this plate brings us a further step in our progression; it is a chamfer-top clock in mahogany with brass inlay, it is anonymous, but very pleasing in appearance. Its back plate is shown in *Plate 44d*, from which it will be seen that a coiled-wire gong has been introduced instead of a bell, giving a deeper, richer tone. The case is light mahogany with brass inlay, the hands are particularly attractive; the hour hand is fractionally too long, but there is no doubt that they are original.

Plate 29d illustrates what is known as the lancet-type, Gothic style, in harmony with the newly established Gothic revival. This by Hawkins of Southampton is quite pleasing; it has a cream-painted dial and a milled bezel to the glass instead of the ordinary pressed one. This milled bezel is more expensive and indicates that more than usual care has been put into the clock. The ebony inlay in the mahogany case is very restrained and pleasing. The hands are dainty but not very practical; note how the minute hand gets lost in the III.

And so we come to what may be called the end of ordered progression in clock design. After this date case design, like the hands already referred to, was very much a case of individualism, frequently striving after effect and trying to be different, often with disastrous results. One could illustrate as many variations in bracket clocks between 1830 and 1860 as there are illustrations in this book; but the Victorian era is not renowned for its good taste in artistic design.

Before, however, we finally leave bracket clocks, let us look at a few made towards the end of the eighteenth century for export to China and the Far East. From the very elaborate examples illustrated, it would seem that this was a very lucrative luxury trade. Indeed, from the fact that at the time of the Boxer Rebellion in 1900 there were over six hundred clocks in the Hall of the Imperial Palace alone, it would seem that there was plenty of scope for trade; the only proviso would seem to be the make everything move that can move and to decorate every possible inch of space. Unfortunately most of these pieces are unsigned; the names of James Cox and Francis Maquire are associated with this market, but there must have been many others.

Plate 30a shows a very fine example; it strikes the hour and the quarters and is musical. At each hour the lotus flower in the centre emerges from the square housing and the petals unfold, as in the illustration. When the hour has struck, the lotus flower on the top, seen with petals folded, opens and the petals turn upright and the blossom is open, so that there is always one blossom open and one shut. The lotus flowers are set with paste in various colours. The *appliqué* ornamentation is of gilt brass. The base of the bodywork appears to be plain black steelwork until closely examined, when it is seen that it is very finely engraved all over. Besides the opening and shutting of the lotus flowers, the glass rods in the base turn, giving the impression of a waterfall.

In *Plate 30b* the clock surmounts a large case containing a musical train which is released by the clock at set intervals. Here we have three stages of twisted glass rods that turn at the hour giving the effect of a cascading waterfall. The first tier is supported by palm trees with outspread foliage; surrounding the glass rods is a series of figures, alternately fat and lean, possibly some Chinese lore that escapes the author. The two swans, apparently nesting on the top of two somewhat fantastic palm trees, seem to have followed, or set the fashion of today for the ladies frequent 'hair-do'. The second tier, decorated with figures of children has still fewer glass rods simulating the source of the waterfall. The dial represents a sunflower and is flanked by female figures.

Plate 30c is still more elaborate. It is again a three train musical clock with a centre seconds hand. The minute hand is missing. The whole supported on gilt lions, each with a taper holder on its head. The corner columns are in imitation of lapis lazuli. The *appliqué* ornamentation is gilt brass and all the floral decoration is set with multi-coloured paste. At the hour the glass rods, including the four at the upper corners, turn with the usual waterfall effect, a procession passes through the aperture under the dial and a group revolves in the circular opening in the top tier.

The last illustration (*Plate 30d*) is more restrained and more pleasing to the western taste. Again three train and musical. At the hour the spiral at the top, which is set with red and green paste, opens out and revolves; the 'jewelled' disk below the dial also revolves. The case is decorated in coloured translucent enamel on an ultramarine base. The dial and circle below surrounds are set with red and white paste. The hands are solid gold.

After this digression into oriental splendour, we will leave bracket clocks and return to more sober western styles in the later long-case clocks.

CHAPTER SIX

Long-Case Clocks and Regulators 1735-1835

As was the case with bracket clocks, during the earlier part of this period there were some mechanically interesting pieces, followed later by an increase in the number of musical clocks and those showing mechanical automata; the simplest form of this last was a ship's effigy in the arch of the dial attached to the top of the pendulum rod (rather in the manner of the false bob in the verge escapement), which rocked 'in the waves' as the pendulum swung. This developed later into moving figures, a man or two men sawing, revolving windmills; in fact anything that could be driven by a straight-forward wheel motion or cranked from a pin set eccentrically in the wheel surface. None of these automatic figures is illustrated, limitations of space do not permit, but they are all only adjuncts to the prevailing style of clock; they usually appear after 1770–75 and do not call for any departure from the general trend of design which we are now going to discuss.

In *Plate 31a* we have a fine astronomical clock by Thomas Budgen of Croydon. Croydon lies just on the fringe of the ten-mile radius of London to which the jurisdiction of the Clock-makers' Company extended. William Budgen, possibly a son, was made free of the Clockmakers' Company in 1750 and there-fore seems to have recognised that the authority of the Company extended to his town; there is no mention of Thomas in the Company's records. Croydon is sufficiently near London for the case to have the clean London lines, and it was probably made in the City and sent out to Croydon. It is of finely figured walnut; in Chapter Four we had examples in these arch-topped doors of the trunk being outlined in a banding of cross-grained veneer. Here we have a fine inlaid line of holly or laburnum or other light-coloured wood within the frame of the door itself and also forming two spandrels on the trunk above the door.

It will be noted that the hour hand goes round only once in twenty-four hours and that the minute hand revolves once an hour; owing to the position of the seconds dial the minutes between four minutes to and four minutes past the hour have to be approximated. The hands, it will be noted, do not fit. They are not of a style of the period of the rest of the clock, but rather belong to the end of the eighteenth century, at which period they were probably renewed.

This clock has a very pleasing arched-type top, unencumbered by any superstructure; probably at one time the arch between the door top and the top of the hood had a fret, but in the course of time this has become broken and the space has been filled in with a piece of plain veneer, cut running with the grain of the wood instead of across it, as is the case with the veneer in the rest of the case. The introduction of a double plinth with the corresponding reduction in the depth of the base panel tends to give a rather squat appearance to the base, but this is probably more noticeable in the photograph than in the original. The dial is illustrated in *Plate 40d* and will be dealt with in the section dealing with dials.

The second clock on this plate, by Charles Coulon, shows another well-proportioned case in walnut veneer; this time the clock has the flat-topped finish to the hood, which very probably was originally surmounted by a dome as in *Plate 26b*. We have again the fine banding in the door and in the spandrels above, giving a pleasing touch of lightness to the case. The dial is clear; it will be seen that the inner markings on the chapter ring for the quarter-hours, or as we have seen in the case of the Graham clock in Plate *26b* the half-hours, have quite disappeared, never to reappear. The most we shall have in future is a simple circle at the base of the hour numerals on painted or enamelled dials, this being the survivor of the inner edge of the applied chapter ring, as seen in the illustration (*Plate 28b*), but very often not even that. After all, why should it be there? It serves no useful purpose. The spandrels are no longer designed around a female head and the dolphins have disappeared from those in the arch. They are now composed of purely conventional design, but are quite interesting. Later in the century they tend to become less full and to give a skimpy appearance. The hands are rather clumsy and really not worthy of the clock. The design is correct, but they could, with advantage, have been more delicately finished. The author suspects an accident and replacement by unskilled hands; they are too much out of harmony with the finish of the rest of the clock. The arch is purely decorative, conforming to fashion, and has a strike-silent lever in it.

Next in chronological order is the clock illustrated in *Plate 31c* which shows the author's largest and smallest long-cast clocks. (He is not the proud owner of a year clock, which would have needed a still higher case against which to make the comparison.) The larger is a fine month-equation movement by Graham's successors, Colley and Preist, housed in a dark walnut-veneered case. The inlaid banding and the spandrels above the door are there, but as they are not in such a contrasting colour they do not show up so well in the photograph.

Graham died in November 1751, aged seventy-eight; this clock has a year calendar disk made out in the new style which was adopted in September 1752. It has a dead beat escapement and has all the signs of Graham's handiwork; it was probably among his stock when he died and was taken over by Colley when succeeding to the business. The dial has that clearness of finish and simplicity that marked Graham's work (*Plates 19c* and *26b*). This dial is shown again in Plate *38b*.

That traders often had long to wait for their money in those days is shown by two letters in the author's possession written by Colley to a customer, Mr. Cyrill Wycke of Hockwold, near Brann, in Norfolk, for whom he was making a quarter-chiming musical long-case clock. It was to be a large clock, fourteen inches dial with arch, these larger dials being fashionable in the latter half of the eighteenth century. It was to play 'The Smirking Man', 'Willy's ye lad for me', 'Ally Croaker' and 'The Lass of Patie's Mill'. In the arch were to be two subsidiary dials, one for pendulum regulation and the other for silencing either all strike, chime and music, or the hours and music, or the quarter chimes. There was also a day of the month dial showing through an aperture.

The first letter reads:

SIR,

I have been in hopes of seeing you in London before this and likewise settled ye account of the clock case; I think it and ye packing case come to fourteen Pounds which is a great deal of Money for a Tradesman to be out of for two Years together and as your coming is so uncertain I shou'd take it as a favour if you would Please to let me have Ten Pounds on Acct. thereof which would greatly oblige Sir,

Your most hum^ble Servt,

LONDON, *Sept.* 8, 1759.　　　　　　　　　　　　　THO^s COLLEY.

The outside of the letter is endorsed: *Colley, Watchmaker, Sept. 8, 1759, rec^d· 10th. 4d.*

It is interesting to see that as late as 1759 clockmakers were still being called watchmakers, that a letter took two days to get to Norfolk and that the charge was 4d. The second letter is more satisfactory to Mr. Colley; he gets his £10.

SIR,

I rec^d yours with ye bill enclosed of Ten Pounds which I Receive in part of Payment for your New Clock I am making for you; I have herewith sent you a sketch of ye Dial Plate of ye Clock and I believe 3 weeks hence will do for your determination as I can forward part of ye clock without tho' I am a little afraid I shan't have time to get it completed before you come to Town.

I am S^r

Your most oblig'd hum^ble Servt

LONDON, *Octo^r* 6, 1759.　　　　　　　　　　　　　THOS. COLLEY.

The outside is endorsed: *Colley, Watchmaker, Oct. 6, 1759, recd. 8th (4d). D-al Pl-te- Cl-ck. £10 (Pd).*

The other little clock shown on *Plate 31c* is evidently the work of a craftsman making a little piece as a hobby for the love of his craft. It is a little thirty-hour movement with a plain brass dial, dated on the front plate, by means of a punch, June 15th, 1817. It is signed Sanders, Brinkworth. There is a village of that name in Wiltshire, but the author has not yet had time to search local records to find if any entries exist. Just the name Sanders, without any Christian name or even initials, leaves a pretty wide field.

There is another Brinkworth, a small railway junction in South Australia, so presumably a Wiltshireman went out to Australia in years past and founded a settlement named after his native village. However, the object of this book is to discuss clocks, not to give geography lessons, so we will return to the 'Grand-Baby,' or 'Baby' as it is popularly known in the

author's household. It is cased in mahogany, with beautifully
reeded columns having turned Doric capitals and bases, with
quarter columns inset each side of the trunk. The door is edged
with laburnum and ebony domino banding, and the base is
decorated with two lines of the same. The trunk could, with
advantage, have been a little longer and the base correspondingly shorter. Its overall height is two feet eleven inches. All
lady visitors 'fall' for this little pet, which stands on its own
bracket on the library wall. The library is the family's main
living-room, so the author practises what he preaches in having
a thirty-hour movement in a place where it is handy for winding
each evening before going to bed.

Plate 32 shows two clocks of the 'hollowed pediment' type;
this type ran concurrently with the curled pediment 'Chippendale' style seen in this plate, for sixty years or so. While the
terms Chippendale, Adam and Sheraton are often applied to
clock cases, these really only incorporate some features in the
style of one, and frequently more than one, of these cabinet-
makers. These were, in fact, cabinet-makers, and the basic
structure of the pieces they designed was quite different to that
necessary for a clock case; their typical designs would not have
been practical. The clock on the left is by George Margetts of
London; it is astronomical, a type in which Margetts specialised. This is a very high-grade clock and as a result has a very
high-grade case. It is of mahogany, and in fact practically all
cases from now onwards will be of mahogany. The use of any
other wood was exceptional, although towards 1800 oak was
sometimes used, rarely in London, more frequently in the
provinces. An innovation which will be maintained from now
onwards is the chamfering of the corners of the trunk and the
frequent insertion of quarter columns, or their reeding. The
plain arch top to the door has now given way to the broken
arch; from now onwards makers will let their fancy play with
the shape of the door in the trunk. The flaming lamp *motif* of
the finials is a revival of a style of a hundred years earlier.

The clock, by John Benson of Whitehaven, in Cumberland, is
rather an enigma. It is a very fine clock, yet nothing is known
of its maker. Neither Baillie nor Britten list him, and it seems
peculiar that nothing else should have survived of a man of such
capabilities. The case bears every stamp of being London

made; it has open frets at the side of the hood for one thing, and this, if our theory is correct, rules the provinces out. It has such a close resemblance to the other clock illustrated on this plate that the two may well be by the same hand. The name of the maker is on a plate let in behind the main dial plate, immediately below the lunar dial in the arch; this is seen more clearly in the plate showing the dial in detail (*Plate 41b*). It is quite possible that the man who supplied the clock bought it in London and then had his own nameplate inserted. If so, this is a pity. It is a very fine clock with perfect lines, whoever made it, but London-made clocks usually fetch better prices than those made in the country.

It differs from the other clock in this plate in the more elaborate Corinthian columns to the hood, the quarter columns to the trunk and, what is most unusual, quarter columns in the base. The author is never very keen on anything light in colour in the base of a clock, such as the gilded column capitals and bases in this case; they take the eye too easily from the dial, but this, no doubt, is a matter of individual taste. From the three winding holes it will be noted that it is a quarter-chiming and musical clock.

The other two illustrations on this plate are of the 'Chippendale' type of case as portrayed by provincial makers. That in *Plate 32d* is a British-made clock by Philip Lloyd, Bristol (not an ancestor). The proportions are good, but it is a pity that the dial, which reflects a London style of thirty years earlier, is all of brass, a feature often found in provincial clocks but not often in London-made, except in cheap thirty-hour movements. The lack of contrast of a silvered chapter ring makes the dial flat and dull. It could easily have been re-silvered.

In the arch is a lunar dial with two rings of marking, the inner 1 to $29\frac{1}{2}$ giving the age of the moon and the outer from 6.30 to 6.30 twice over. This is a tidal dial, the outer circumference of this dial being marked HIGH WATER AT BRISTOL KEY. At new and full moon high water at Bristol is at approximately 6.30, and this lunar disk, which revolves once in two months, indicates, e.g. 6.30 A.M., high tide at new moon on the first day of a lunation, gradually changing the time daily till at full moon at $14\frac{3}{4}$ days 6.30 P.M. is reached, and finally at the end of the lunation we come back to 6.30 A.M. The moon's effigy then disappears behind the dial for the second month and a second effigy appears in the upper half of the arch. The dial is only suitable for Bristol. In all the tidal clocks the author has seen made for Bristol the word *quay* is always spelt *key*, nor has he found the word *key* or *quay* on any tidal dials except those made for Bristol, although he has made a special study of this type of dial. The reason may be that Bristol is the only port where shipping came right up the river into the city streets in the centre of the town.

This clock has Corinthian columns with gilded capitals and bases, but these are not carried on in the trunk; the chamfered edge is simply reeded. The trunk door is decorated and has a base panel to match.

The fourth clock on this plate is another mahogany-cased provincial clock, this time with only a lunar dial, since as the maker, Thomas Brown, was in Birmingham there was obviously no need for a tidal dial. The dial is silvered all over and engraved in the centre. Towards the end of the eighteenth century engraved dials were fairly frequent, but in the majority of cases this engraving only had the effect of making the dial less legible. There are two subsidiary dials, seconds the upper and calendar dial the lower. Instead of having only a small aperture, through which only one date could be seen, the fashion arose for a semicircular opening as seen, the uppermost mark being that of the current day; since only every fifth day was numbered, a smaller diameter disk could be used.

Regarding the case, the quarter columns on the trunk have an ivory inlay at their base, distracting the eye from the dial. The base corners are now chamfered and carved, presumably to add to the importance of the piece, but in the author's view making the case too ornate.

Plate 33a shows a Liverpool clock by Rigby, presumably Henry, who died in 1787. Others, James and Joseph, do not appear in the records till 1813 and 1821, too late for this piece. This has lunar and tidal dial combined, this time for Liverpool, where high tide at new and full moon is about eleven o'clock. In this case the moon's effigy is painted on the same dial as the days of the moon's age and the time of high tide, the whole revolving as one dial; the reading for the day for the lunar dial is taken from the high point. The outer edge of the arch is inscribed *The moon is appointed for Seasons*. Again we have the engraved dial centre. There is a compensated centre seconds hand of the whole diameter of the inside of the chapter ring, also a calendar hand, which in the photo is hidden behind the minute hand; four hands on one dial is too much for easy reading.

The mahogany case has double columns to the hood, and at the trunk the Doric columns have been fashioned in the round, but do not go the full length of the trunk, which is a pity. The panelling at the bottom of the door and the high bases to the columns are an unfortunate experiment.

The quoins on the chamfered base corners seem a Lancastrian detail; the writer has only seen this on Lancastrian-made cases, two by Barker of Wigan, which he has particularly in mind, and another by Coats, illustrated by Ceszinsky and Webster, also a Wigan maker.

Plate 33b shows another clock made to show high tide at Bristol Key, by Thomas Bruton of Bristol. It is a very good quality clock in a finely figured case of kingwood. The radial star parquetry design in the centre of the pillar formation of the case is interesting. Its whole design is reminiscent of the equation clock presented to the City of Bath by Thomas Tompion in 1710. The dial records the usual seconds and date besides the moon's phase and tidal details; it is silvered with an applied and silvered chapter ring. The centre is again embellished with unnecessary engraving; nevertheless a very handsome piece.

The remaining two clocks on *Plate 33* are two types of pedestal clock; *Plate 33c* illustrates a clock in the Adam style made by Finney of Liverpool. It is unusual in that it has a year movement in that very small case; less that six feet high. The dial is interesting and will be described later. The other clock is an anonymous piece in the Empire style, recording quite simply hours and minutes.

These pieces obviously need setting in a room furnished in a corresponding style, when they will harmonise and look very well. It will be noticed that in *Plate 33d* the door of the trunk is hinged on the left as one faces the clock.

Plate 34a and *b* shows two clocks which, towards the end of the eighteenth and in the early nineteenth century, were increasingly made; very plain and simple designs both for dial and case, but with movements made with much more care than had been usual for the average long-case clock up to this time. Almost invariably they will have Graham's dead beat escapement and prove themselves really sound time-keepers. That on the left is a striking movement by Josiah Emery of London, who was noted for the all-round high standard of his movements. It is in a plain oak case; all the money has gone into the movement. The silvered dial is a little late for the retention of the inner line at the base of the hour numerals and the numbered minute ring is in contradiction to the brass openwork hands; nevertheless they are certainly original.

The other timepiece, by Ross & Peckham of London, is essentially simple and utilitarian. In its plain mahogany case and severe dial it seems to say, 'My function is to record time accurately, that's all'. It has Graham's dead beat escapement and a wooden pendulum rod to minimise as far as possible temperature compensation errors; but it has no maintaining power.

Plate 34c and *d* shows two more of the later type of case in vogue towards the turn of the nineteenth century. Both are provincial clocks, that on the left is anonymous and shows the adoption of the Gothic-shaped door. The columns to the hood and down the trunks which are of the multiple perpendicular style, give a link with ecclesiastical architecture. These columns, as in *Plate 33a*, do not extend the whole length of the door, but there is no corresponding panelling at the base of the door, so that these shorter columns do not so much detract from the length of the trunk on the whole design of the case. The heavily carved and scrolled pediment is surmounted by a carved taurus topped by a ball and spire to match the sides. The base should have an octagonal-shaped moulding, but this appears to have been broken off, only the glue marks remaining.

Both these provincial clocks have solid side panels to their hoods, thus maintaining our theory that this is a feature of provincial clocks.

The illustration on the right is of a 'Yorkshire clock'. This type of clock was not confined to Yorkshire, but is found all over the North Midlands. The clock case is broadening, dials are increasing from twelve to fourteen inches, with a corresponding increase in width, but without any increase in height;

indeed clocks are already high enough, seven feet six to eight feet six is tall enough for any clock in domestic use. The particular clock illustrated is about as nice an example of the type as the author has seen; it still retains a degree of elegance. Generally these Yorkshire clocks remind him of Mr. Jorrocks in their relation of width to height. Our clock is the work of an unknown maker at Otley, in Yorkshire, Chippendale's birthplace, and there is a trace of both Chippendale and Sheraton in its design. The case is of richly figured mahogany inlaid with satinwood. The small door is a feature of these Yorkshire clocks; this the author avers is a mistake, as it tends to increase the air of 'stumpiness' they already have by reason of their large width-to-height proportions. The turned hood columns are another feature to be found in country clocks from now on; columns are just columns to the country maker. He has no appreciation of the elegance of the proportions of the classic designs, and turned columns are cheaper to make. The feet are too light, but again this is a fault to be found in nearly all these clocks. The painted dial is, in this case, of exceptionally good finish.

REGULATORS

All the long-case clocks we have so far considered in this chapter have been for domestic use, nearly all being fitted with the ordinary recoil anchor escapement; only one or two have had, exceptionally, Graham's dead beat escapement. In the next two plates will be illustrated some regulators, i.e. clocks made specially for use in observatories for astronomical observations.

The clock illustrated in *Plate 35a* and *b* is very historic. It was made by John Shelton of Shoe Lane, London. Shelton, of whom too little has been heard in the past, was born in Clerkenwell, London, in 1702. He was apprenticed very young, at the age of ten years, to Henry Stanbury in 1712, and was admitted to the Clockmakers' Company in 1720. He was one of the original Liverymen at the creation of the Livery in 1766. He worked for Graham in the making of clocks for astronomical use, and there, no doubt, received the training that made him capable of making high-grade regulators later. There is still at

Greenwich Observatory a regulator, the work of Shelton, which for many years served as their transit clock. Besides this there are three others known to survive: one at Armagh Observatory in Northern Ireland, one in the Museum of the History of Science in Oxford, and one, that illustrated, owned by the Royal Society, London, by whose permission it is reproduced. It has had a most notable history.

In the latter part of the seventeenth century Christian Huygens had perceived that because of the rotation of the earth an object must weigh less at the Equator than at the poles. About the same time, Richer of Paris had shown that a pendulum clock regulated in France ran slow when tested in Cayenne, in French Guiana. Newton also found that 'the variation of gravity in different latitudes depended not only on the centrifugal force, but also upon the figure (shape) of the earth'.

In the latter half of the eighteenth century a great deal of attention was paid to this problem of establishing the earth's shape by sending clocks to different places and noting their different rates of going as compared with the same clock going at Greenwich.

On December 23rd, 1760, the Royal Society paid Shelton £34. 16s. 6d. for the clock we are illustrating. We find that in June 1761 it is in St. Helena, and according to a report dated June 30th, 1761, it had been used for gravitational experiments and also in connexion with the Transit of Venus on June 5th of that year. On November 28th, 1761, it was sent to the Cape of Good Hope for gravity experiments and returned to St. Helena on December 31st of that year. In 1762 it was returned to England and reported working at Greenwich on June 17th, 1762. In 1763 the Commissioners of Longitude were sending an expedition to Barbados to test John Harrison's chronometer; the Royal Society loaned the Shelton clock to them on August 18th, 1763. It was used in experiments in Barbados from November 10th, 1763, to October 8th, 1764. On November 11th, 1764, Maskelyne, then Astronomer Royal, announced that the Royal Society would sponsor the measurement of one degree of latitude in Pennsylvania and that they had offered the use of the clock that had been sent to St. Helena and to Barbados. It was shipped in the good ship *Ellis*, Sam Richardson Egdon, Master. This ship it appears was wrecked, but the clock suffered no damage beyond the breaking of the pendulum suspension. On December 11th, 1766, it was set up in 'Mr. Harland's field' until it was dismantled for return to England on February 28th, 1767, sailing on May 26th of that year.

On November 19th, 1767, it was reported again set up at Greenwich ready for the ensuing Transit of Venus. Later we find it going in the *Endeavour*, Lieutenant James Cook (later the famous Captain Cook), on an expedition to the South Seas. In a report dated September 15th, 1769, from Fort Venus, Royal Bay, King George Island (now Tahiti), details were given of the observation of Venus. In 1774 Maskelyne took the clock to Perthshire, where he measured the deflection of a plumb-line caused by the attraction of the mountain Schiehallion. In 1815 Lieutenant Parry made a voyage to the Arctic. The reports from this expedition stated that the clocks used for the pendulum experiments were the property of the Royal Society, and the same as had accompanied Captain Cook round the world; they were made by Shelton.

The clock was specially prepared for travelling by securing the pendulum at its point of suspension and also by fixing the bob rigidly by means of two pieces of shaped wood encasing it and screwed firmly to the back of the case. In the photograph the holes in the back board necessitated by this proceeding are clearly visible, thus proving this to be the same clock as that of which we have been following the travels. The correct position for the upper edge of the pendulum bob on the pendulum rod to ensure a recorded rate of going at Greenwich was scratched on by Maskelyne before the clock left Greenwich; this mark, made one hundred and ninety years ago, is still there and today records the correct position for the bob.

Plate 35c and *d* shows a regulator made by the famous John Arnold, his No. 1 made for Greenwich. He made two, No. 1 and No. 2. In 1774, £84. 16s. was certified for payment to Arnold, and an inventory dated December 14th, 1774, includes an 'Astronomical clock by Arnold with ruby pallets' in both the Quadrant Room and the Great Room. Greenwich does not seem to have used the Arnold clocks very regularly; the main transit clock was made by Shelton under Graham's observation in 1748 and taken into use in 1750. Presumably the Arnold regulators did not offer any advantage over the clocks then in use. The dial shows the hours through the slot below the centre, the minutes on the main dial, and in the subsidiary dial the seconds.

Arnold, however, did not make his reputation with regulators, his main claim to fame being his work on improved and simplified chronometer escapements after Harrison had primarily solved the problem of 'the longitude'. In 1764, when he was twenty-eight, he made the smallest repeating watch ever attempted. It was set in a finger-ring and was presented by him to King George III, who was so pleased that he gave him 500 guineas for it. This brought him before the public, who were ready to appreciate his extraordinary skill in fine workmanship and finish. The King also gave him £100 to enable him to experiment with the improvements to chronometers.

The heavy compensated grid-iron pendulum, made after Harrison's principles, is clearly seen, as are also the holes in the back of the case where the clock has been bolted to the wall at different times. To ensure accurate time-keeping it is essential that a clock be kept absolutely rigid.

Plate 36a shows one more English regulator by Barwise, London. This may be either John Barwise, who was working in St. Dunstan's Lane 1790-1820, or his successors, Barwise & Sons, in the same road. Again, its direct simplicity proclaims its purpose; the minute hand is compensated; the two slots show one the hour and the other the day of the month. It has a peculiar grid-iron pendulum consisting of three bars only, two of brass and one of steel.

Plate 36b shows a very graceful Vienna Regulator by Gluecksstein, about 1830. It is an eight-day, quarter-striking piece with a lunar dial in a fire-gilt case, as opposed to the very severely designed English regulators, which are always only timepieces and destined only for severely practical uses. These decorative domestic pieces were in great favour in Austria in the early part of the nineteenth century, their elegance matching the general elegance of that country at that time. The design shows distinct French influence, the dial especially being reminiscent of Breguet.

The final illustration in this chapter, *Plate 36c*, shows what is popularly known as an 'Act of Parliament Clock'; just how

K

this name became fixed on to this type it is hard to say. In 1797 a tax of five shillings per annum was levied on any clock or watch, whether public or private. In some of Rowlandson's drawings of the period are depicted Tavern scenes showing this type of clock on the wall. It may well be that large dial clocks were exhibited in public places to offset the loss of the watch or clock privately owned, and it has been assumed that these clocks originated for this purpose. The Act was repealed next year as it caused such unemployment in the horological industry, so that many clocks of this type could not have been made during that short period. The fact is that, whilst we have known for a long time that the style dated from at least 1760, there hangs in the Vestry of St. Mary's church, Bury St. Edmunds, a clock of this type made by George Graham. This clock is numbered 575; now Graham was a partner of Tompion until the latter's death in 1713, and the highest known Tompion & Graham number is 556. Graham carried on with the numbering when he succeeded to the business, so that 575 is most likely about 1715, or eighty-two years before the Act of Parliament which is supposed to have given rise to the appellation.

CHAPTER SEVEN

Dials and Back Plates

THE decoration of clock dials, as well as their housings, was always a favourite means for the craftsman to express his love for his handiwork and the degree of veneration in which he held his patron. Some sixteenth-century pieces are housed in structures which are works of art in themselves; worthy housings for the wonderful mechanisms they contained, which were held in awe by the uninitiated masses of that day.

The desire to decorate as a finish to the design and as an expression of the degree of importance of the piece continued when clocks became more general in domestic use; but, as we have seen in perusing the pages of the preceding chapters, decoration gradually gave way to simplicity and functional design, till at the beginning of the nineteenth century all the grace and effect in clock design was the function of line, pure and simple.

The main features of these dials and the progress in design of each have already been described when the clock in question was dealt with in the previous chapters. These descriptions will not be repeated here, but it is hoped that the larger illustrations of the dials here given will help to clarify any points not too clearly brought out in the smaller illustrations. Only the more complicated dials will be dealt with fully in this chapter.

Lantern clock dials were usually engraved, as we have seen in Chapter Three. Sometimes the more important pieces had the side doors engraved as well. When clocks began to be made to go eight days and to be encased, the first tendency was towards very plain dials, as we have seen in *Plates 14c* and *15a*. The next stage was the engraving of a Tudor rose around the hole pierced for the hand arbor; then followed spandrels with, as a rule, a matted centre to the dial plate (*Plate 15b*).

In *Plate 37a* we have a plain dial with the cherub spandrels, but not matted, by Ahasuerus Fromanteel. The engraved central rose just referred to has been replaced by a cast and finely tooled ornament. Today, when with high-powered rolling mills, sheets of brass are turned out many tons an hour, all with a highly polished finish, it is perhaps not fully realised just how difficult it would be to get a smooth and flawless surface as that illustrated. Matting the surface after it had been hammered and scraped reasonably flat would hide any minor surface defects, but in this case we have a piece of flawless brass casting, about one-sixteenth of an inch thick. There were no rolling mills in those days, all larger sheets being beaten out from castings by hammers worked by water-power. Batteries they were called, because there were frequently four or six hammers falling in rotation on to the anvil as the water-wheel turned and, by means of cams, lifted them in turn. The highly placed bell and the long upright hammer rod are typical of Dutch practice in the second half of the seventeenth century. This clock was made by a Dutchman working in London, who probably fled from the Spanish oppression in Holland in the sixteenth and seventeenth centuries.

The dial on *Plate 37b* is one that caused a great deal of speculation for many years. The actual minute ring is a loose friction fit and can be moved in either direction by inserting a peg in any of the little holes pierced midway between each five-minute figure. There is no XII, only a diamond; this is presumably to give an exact point to correspond to the lower point of the smaller diamond in the minute ring. Each minute is subdivided into six ten-second spaces. In the illustration the minute ring is indicating fifty seconds slow on the hour ring. The author's explanation of this peculiar dial is that it is for the purpose of measuring the equation of time before the equation kidney was invented, which invention enabled the equation to be recorded mechanically. According to the equation tables of the time, the minute ring could be set daily, or at any other desired interval, so that the diamond of the minute ring would be fast or slow by the diamond of the hour ring by the amount shown in the tables for the day selected. When opportunity arose to check the clock by the sundial, a direct reading on the minute ring would indicate the same as the sundial, if the clock were keeping good time.

The seconds dial also moves freely; since the minute ring

is only graduated to ten-seconds intervals, the exact seconds adjustment could be made on this dial. The lower subsidiary dial is also loose; the hand slips on to the winding square and has to be removed before the clock is wound; it does not bring into action any type of maintaining power. It revolves with the barrel round which the gut carrying the weight is wound; thus with an eight-day clock the hand would revolve sixteen times, once every twelve hours. It will be noted that the hours are marked anti-clockwise; unless the clock be wound exactly at iii, vi, ix, or xii it would be necessary to stop winding the last turn of the drum in such a position as would enable the hand to be replaced on the square at the correct hour. In the photograph this has not been done.

It will be noticed that there is a micrometer screw for adjusting the pendulum length; Clement is usually credited with being the first to use this and it is not thought that the application on this Fromanteel invalidates Clement's claim.

Plate 37c and *d* shows the dials of the clocks illustrated in *Plates 16a* and *20a*. From, or rather conjointly with, the latter part of the period of very plain dials we get a few wholly engraved dials, as seen in this plate. There was one particular engraver who was working at this period, mainly for Edward East, but the author has seen dials by him on a clock by Samuel Knibb, and two anonymous clocks as well as that by John Hilderson, one of the subjects of our illustration. While penning these lines, the author cannot recollect any wholly engraved dial at this period that is not by this particular artist. He is believed to be of Dutch origin and working in London, as his style is quite distinctly in the Dutch genre: a floral pattern always perfectly balanced, flower balancing flower and bird balancing bird, but his designs never symmetrical. He never uses a straight line, and in his earlier work he cannot abide an empty space, every little plain spot being filled in with dots or small circles. These are not so marked in his later work. The author has an idea that he may be John Droeshout, who on January 31st, 1671–2, engraved and signed the brass plate affixed to the cover of the engrossment of the Clockmakers' Company Charter which was presented to the Company by Richard Morgan, but has so far not been able to confirm this. The author would appreciate any further information from those possessing engravings known to be by John Droeshout which would enable him to check his theory.

Plate 38a shows a dial very similar to that shown in *Plate 37a*, but the matted centre has appeared; this is another Edward East dial, delightful in its simplicity and its clarity. The narrow chapter ring and even, proportionately, narrower seconds ring appeal at once to the eye. The ratio of width to diameter is 1 : 12 for the seconds ring and 1 : 8 for the chapter ring. There is a very high degree of elegance and finish in the hands, and the hour hand is nicely chamfered, always the sign of a good hand and a good clock. The additional decoration of the minute hand changes its production from a straight filing job to that of an artist. Also should be noted the J-shape of the 1 in the five-minute numerals; when this shape is used it is always an indication of early work. The clock to which this dial belongs is shown in *Plate 22c*.

The dial below in the same plate is a little later and by William Clement. The chapter ring is getting broader, the ratio of width to diameter being 1 : 5⅓. All the dials illustrated so far, as well as those illustrated on the next plate, are signed on the bottom of the dial plate below the VI of the chapter ring.

This style of signature is general until about the sixteen-nineties, when as will be seen in *Plate 39a* it is usually placed on the chapter ring itself, although at times it appears upon a special cartouche, or even on a specially affixed plate. The five-minute numerals of this dial are still within the minute ring and the 5 has no curl at the bottom; this is indicative of 'before 1700' as compared with the 5's of *Plates 39c, 39d, 40c, 38d, 41b* and *41c*, which show the progression of the shape of the 5. The hands, although well shaped, have not the rounded finish of the hour hand referred to in the last example.

Plate 38c shows the dial of Tompion's first equation clock illustrated in *Plate 25*. It is a superb piece of workmanship. Starting at the top, we have in the first sector opening an annual dial showing the position of the sun in the ecliptic, indicating the name of the 'Celestial House' or sign of the Zodiac in which the sun is in on that day. The dial is read by carrying the eye up from the small pointer affixed to the dial above the '45'. The next dial is an annual calendar dial indicating February 15th, the sun being 25° of Aquarius – the Water-carrier – in its journey towards Pisces – the Fishes. It will be recollected, as explained in Chapter Four, that it was to enable this dial to be read that Tompion introduced the arch into the hood door, which gave birth to the arched dial and hood with which we are so familiar today. Next comes the moving minute ring showing sun, or apparent time, which moves backwards or forwards in relation to the fixed minute ring, showing mean time, by means of the rack actuating the toothed wheel on to which this moving minute ring is mounted (*Plate 25c*). In the illustration the clock shows the sun approximately 14 minutes 40 seconds slow on mean time; it is around mid-February that mean time has its maximum rate in excess of apparent time. The minute hand revolves once in two hours; this is a year clock, and this disposition enabled Tompion to reduce the number of turns on the barrel round which the gut carrying the weight is wound, and thus reduce the distance the weight has to drop during the year. The upper XII is replaced by a small arabic 12 to allow for the hole for the winding square, covered by the maintaining power shutter which is actuated by releasing the lever at the right-hand side of the dial. The hands are about as perfect as can be conceived, and the delicate tracery of the hour hand and its openwork base are quite exceptional, as is also the hollowing out of the decoration of the minute hand. This has a counterpoise to reduce the amount of power needed to raise it during the upward part of its two-hourly circular journey. The very fine degree of matting of the dial centre should be noted; the spandrels are of the ordinary type of developed cherub's head found on the best-quality clocks made during the period 1695–1700. The signature *Thos. Tompion, London, Inventit*, signifies a first production of this type of equation clock.

Plate 39a shows a typical dial of the first half of the first decade of the eighteenth century. It is from the author's clock illustrated in *Plate 24b*. The chapter ring is broadening, the ratio of width to diameter is now $1 : 4\frac{3}{4}$, and the seconds ring is broadening too. The ringed winding holes and the decorated calendar aperture have appeared. In the spandrels, the cherubs, poor dears, are no longer regarded as bodiless heads blowing the winds from the four cardinal points. They are allowed bodies, and to earn their keep they have to support a crown and orb. The five-minute numerals have taken up position outside the minute ring and there they will remain. The 5's have not yet developed their final curve and there are marks at seven-and-a-half minute intervals where these do not coincide with a multiple of five. The hands are very finely worked and are a good fit.

Plate 39b shows another early example of the arched dial, this time definitely dated 1708. The history of this clock is related in Chapter Five, and the whole clock illustrated in Plate *25b*. The arching both top and bottom is, in the author's experience, quite unique. The hour hand is very 'Tompionesque' but has not the delicacy of that seen in Plate *38c*. The minute hand is counterpoised, as the period of going is one month. As in the case of the Tompion equation clock, the escapement is below the movement, and the lower arching of the dial is to provide a seconds dial, which Tompion omitted in the Buckingham Palace clock, but this clock was designed for astronomical observations, hence a seconds dial was essential. The dial in the upper arch is a dummy put in to balance. The inscription reads *Collego St.* TRINITATIS *Cantab* ISAACUS NEWTON *Equis Auratus Don. D.*, and the signature *R. Street London 1708*.

Plate 39c shows a Quare year dial, also with equation movement, but, as in the case of all such movements by Quare, the equation portion is quite separate, having been made by Joseph Williamson. In this case the equation dial is situated below the movement and shows through a glass plate in the door of the trunk. This dial is fixed to two bearers coming from the main plates of the movement which are clearly seen (*Plate 40a* and *b*), and the drive is through a rod and endless worm seen in the back view; this, when in position, gears with the wheel carrying the plain calendar hand revolving once a year, on the axis of which is fixed the equation kidney. The follower arm, bearing on this, turns the larger wheel, which in turn gears into a pinion fixed to the arbor of the hand bearing the effigy of the sun, moving it the necessary amount backwards or forwards each day. For the sake of symmetry the inner edge of the upper semicircle is marked fifteen minutes each side, actually the maximum variations are approximately minus fourteen minutes and plus sixteen minutes. It will be seen that the teeth in the upper part of the big wheel have not been finished, since they are never used. A wheel is really unnecessary; a rack segment as in *Plate 25c* is all that is needed; but a wheel gives better balance.

This year clock appears to have been designed for Queen Anne, as it bears the Royal Arms. The dial is not standard in size, hence the specially cast spandrels. The subsidiary dial upper right is for pendulum regulation. The clean and precise design of the hand is very pleasing. It will be noted that the curl of the 5 is developing and that the seven-and-a-half-minute signs are lozenges. The very large eccentrically placed winding square indicates a year movement. A very heavy weight is required to overcome the friction caused by the introduction of two extra trains from the ordinary eight-day movement, i.e. eight-day to month, and month to the thirteen months which is usual for a year movement. This very heavy weight necessitates a thick gut with deep grooves on a long and extra heavy barrel; hence the big winding square.

The dial on *Plate 39d* is by George Graham, the clock being shown on *Plate 26b*. It is one of the finest dials the author knows, plain, simple, dignified and clear. The half-hour marks have now gone from the chapter ring as have the seven-and-a-half-minute marks. The quarter-hour marks on the inner edge of the chapter ring have given way to half-hour marks. The proportions of the width to diameter for the chapter and seconds rings are $1:5\frac{1}{3}$ and $1:9\frac{1}{3}$ respectively. The lever for the maintaining power is seen on the right; the spandrels have the head of a bearded man wearing a kind of rabbinical turban as the central *motif*; this design was favoured by Graham.

Plate 40c shows a dial of a clock by William Tomlinson dated about 1735. The herring-bone engraving round the edge is late for this kind of decoration; it is usually found before 1700. The spandrels based on a female head and on a dolphin in the arch are correct for the period and are exceptionally well finished. Here we have a reversion to ringed winding holes and quarter-hour divisions on the inner edge of the chapter ring, clear evidence that these minor changes took place slowly and overlapped. The curl of the 5 is developing a little further, as is that of the 3. In the arch is a tidal dial; this is universal – that is to say it can be set for any port desired. The inner ring is a loose friction fit, the little lugs for moving it can be seen at xii, iiii, and viii. In the illustration it is set for London Bridge, high tide at iii, at new and full moon. By putting the appropriate hour under the 29½ for high tide at new moon for the port in question, the daily time of tide is read off the hand which clicks forward every twelve hours.

The dial of the clock shown in *Plate 40d* is astronomical. Firstly, in the arch is an aperture showing the day of the week and its appropriate deity as described in Chapter One; then come subsidiary dials for, left, the age of the moon, and right, the day of the month. The hour hand revolves once in twenty-four hours and the minute hand once an hour. These hands are thought to be early nineteenth-century replacements, for their style is not contemporary nor do they match the seconds hand; neither do they fit. The minutes between fifty-six and four have to be approximated. Each side of the minute ring are two pairs of shutters which rise and fall once a year. The outer one on the right when fully raised uncovers, as it descends, the appropriate sign of the zodiac, which is indicated by the edge of the shutter as it falls during the first six months. As the shutters rise during the next six months the signs are read off the ascending edge of the left-hand shutter. In the same way the outer pair of shutters descend, and on the right is read off the edge the date of the month from December 29th to June 25th; as they ascend, on the left are read off the days from June 26th to December 28th. This odd division of dates is to agree with the dates on which the sun passes from one sign of the zodiac to another. Against the day of the month, at intervals, are painted how many minutes fast or slow, by the sun, the clock should be. The painted spandrels represent the seasons; this is a very early appearance of this type of decoration, if original; it is thought that when the new hands were fitted the painted spandrels were added; both are of the same period, early nineteenth century.

The inner pair of shutters read off against the hour ring, indicates the time of sunrise and sunset.

Plate 41a shows the dial of the clock on *Plate 33c*. It is a year movement by one of the Finney family of Liverpool. The clock is only a timepiece, the second winding hole is a dummy, put in for symmetry. The hour dial revolves and is read off the numeral that is uppermost, then comes the minute hand and a centre seconds hand. The other hand protruding from behind the hour dial, revolves once a year and indicates the day and month of the year. On the extreme outer edge are marked, at intervals, the difference of the equation.

This dial contains a curious mixture of ecclesiastical and secular commemorations, the abbreviations for some of which proved a little puzzling. August 12th. *PWB*, is the Prince of Wales's birthday. George IV was born August 12th 1764. July 31st. *Do. Beg.* and September 5th, *Do. dae.*, Dog days begin and end. January 31st. *KCM*, King Charles, Martyr, May 29th. *KCRe*, Restoration of Charles II. On June 4th and May 19th are recorded the birthdays of George III and Queen Charlotte. *C. Day*, February 1st. Candlemas Day. April 1st is marked *AF*, which needs no explanation. Of the Feasts of the Church, only *CSP* gave any difficulty, January 15th. Conversion of St. Paul. Inside the door is written in ink the date 1769 which fits well with the date recorded for the Prince of Wales's birth.

Plate 41b shows the dial of the clock shown in *Plate 22b*, which, we have come to the conclusion, was made by a London maker, Mr. Benson of Whitehaven merely being the supplier to the final purchaser. It has the odd number of thirteen tunes, thus the hour at which any tune is played is advanced two hours daily. The spandrels have become of the nondescript type belonging to the late eighteenth century. The hour hand is much lighter in design and the serpentine minute hand has appeared. These types of hands will persist on practically all long-case clocks and on many bracket clocks. The hand with the sun's effigy is not, as might be supposed, an equation hand but an annual calendar hand, the date being read off the outer ring, which again bears a curious mixture of ecclesiastical and secular dates, e.g. *Christmas Dav, Epiphany, St. Paul, Charles I (Martyr) beheaded, Lady Day, St. George (Martyr), Longest Day, Visitation of Mary, Dog Days begin, Lammas Day, John the Baptist beheaded, London Burnt (old style), King George III born, Prince William Henry born*, appearing amongst other notifications. The author has not been able to ascertain which of the fifteen children, otherwise unrecorded in history, Prince William Henry was, but since George III married in 1761, a date of 1770–75 can be assigned to this clock. The third winding hole is for the musical train.

Plate 41c and *d* shows an ingenious and simple perpetual-calendar movement, made by Helm of Ormskirk, which records not only the short months but also leap year. The slotted wheel revolves once in four years; in four years there are twenty months of less than thirty-one days. When the pin is bearing on the edge of the slotted wheel, as seen in the photograph, the toothed wheel goes forward one tooth at the end of a month, from 31 to 1. When the rocker arm goes into a slot, according to the depth of the slot, the centre toothed wheel will actuate the moving of the calendar dial one, two, or three extra teeth as may be required. In the photograph it is evidently the early days of December; we have just passed the November notch, needing the turning of the calendar dial one extra day. During December and January the rocker arm will be bearing on the circumference, so passing from 31 to 1 at the end of these months; on February 28th it will drop into the deep slot to enable three teeth to be moved forward on the dial. Three scribing lines appear for the three different depths of slot, and it will be noted that all the three long slots in focus in the picture are of the same depth, so that that of middle depth, to allow for two days' shift in leap year, must be that on the far side of the picture.

This rear view of the dial plate is interesting inasmuch as it shows from the edges of the apertures in the plate that this was cast and not rolled, as was explained in the earlier pages of this chapter. Accidental holes sometimes appear when one examines the back of a dial plate, but this one seems to have been so planned, as there are three holes in the plate shown in the photograph. A complaint against these northern provincial makers that the author has is that they must 'mess up' their dials with useless ornamentation thus impairing their clarity; patchwork-quilting is all right on a bed, it has no place on a clock dial. It is a pity hands to fit the dial were not selected.

Plate 42a, shows a painted dial from a large musical clock by Charles Lister of Halifax. There is nothing much to describe in this dial – day of the month, month of the year calendar dial; there are evidently fourteen tunes which can be selected by turning the hand on the subsidiary dial on the left. On the right, pendulum regulation. The photograph is included mainly to show the nesting of the bells in a complicated musical clock. It is a large, spring-driven bracket clock.

The dial (*Plate 42b*) is probably unique. It is a tidal dial made for the little Lincolnshire port of Fosdyke on the Wash. Here at the time that the clock was made there was a very deep estuary and correspondingly long tides. The subsidiary dials are for the day of the month and the age of the moon on each side, and for seconds in the centre. There is no hour hand; the hour is read from the low point of the aperture in the seconds dial. Minutes are read direct off the minute hand, and finally we have the bottom dial around which is written *The Influence of the Moon on the Waters*. This shows the state of the tide at half-hourly intervals and indicates how far it was safe to ride in the estuary or the need to bring cattle in. The inscriptions read:

Full Sea at Fosdike	*Drover's Wash*
Reflux	*Drover's Wash*
Reflux	*Drover's Wash*
Reflux	*Drover's Wash*
Reflux	*Wash just spent at Cross Keys*
Reflux	*Wash ends at Cross Keys*
Wash begins at Fosdike	*Wash just spent at Fosdike*
Good Riding	*Wash ends at Fosdike*
Good Riding	*Flux*
Good Riding	*Flux*
Good Riding	*Flux*

BACK PLATES

In dealing with back plates we have, of course, only to consider bracket clocks; naturally the back plates of long-case clocks were never decorated.

Lantern clocks sometimes had their side doors decorated, but the back plate which went against the wall was, of course, plain, and so when the spring-driven bracket clock came into being it was usual to have a solid wooden door at the back concealing a quite plain plate except for the maker's name and a slight touch of decoration, as seen in *Plate 42c*, which is the back plate of the clock shown in *Plate 15a*. It will be noticed that the decoration of the cock is by the same engraver as that of the

dials on *Plate 37c/d*. The design is balanced but is not symmetrical. Another early feature of this clock is the baluster pillars. As
already explained, all spring clocks heretofore have been horizontal table clocks standing dial up, with the winding squares
protruding through the bottom plate. If we lay this clock movement so that the winding squares face downwards, we get a
logical position for the baluster pillars. These are neatly riveted
on to the front plate, which would have been the visible bottom
plate in a table clock, and they are untidily pinned on to the
now visible back plate, which in the table clock would have been
the top plate hidden by the dial. Later, as we shall see, the
pillars will be neatly riveted into the back plate and pinned on
to the front plate; the pillars themselves will take on a straight
form with turned feet and a turned central boss. The vertical
bell and the high position of the locking plate and its positioning
outside are all early features.

The other back plate this plate shows is that of the clock seen
in *Plate 16a*. It will be recollected that this clock had a unique
system of Dutch striking. This photograph shows the two bells
which swivel upon their support to come in front of the hammer
at the right time. It will be noticed that the locking plate has
twice the number of notches, enabling the clock to repeat the
hour at the half-hour. All the remarks regarding early features
applied to the East clock on the left apply equally to the Hilderson clock on the right. The early makers were not able to tap
a small thread inside the pendulum bob; this was drilled and
bushed with a piece of wood, which in turn was drilled with a
hole just fractionally smaller than the threaded base of the
pendulum rod. The bob then cuts its own thread in the wooden
bushing as it is screwed on.

After the plain back plate with the solid wooden door we
have glass coming into the back door as well as in the front
door, inducing decorated back plates. At first, floral designs
were usual; four are illustrated in *Plate 43*. In the top two we
have examples of the work of another engraver who was at
work at this period; his designs are always symmetrical. Note
how the pinned pillars have gone from the back plate.

Plate 43a shows the back plate of the clock illustrated in
Plate 18b, which, it will be remembered, was the clock in which
Knibb made his early effort at *grande sonnerie* striking. The

locking plate for quarter-striking is on the right, and when this has struck, the count wheel tips down the cross-bar, the other end of which rises and releases the locking arm of the hour strike. It will be noted that there are four repetitions of each hour up to six, enabling the hour to be repeated each quarter up to six, as explained in Chapter Two. *Plate 43b* shows a plate where the floral design is converging into the conventional and is on a clock by Henry Jones, an apprentice of Edward East. This clock has now rack-and-snail striking which was invented by Edward Barlow in 1675. The setting-up ratchet wheels for the main springs are usually on the front plate, but in some early cases, as in this instance, they are placed on the back plate.

Plate 43c shows another example of the floral type merging into the conventional and also the passing of the floral *motif* and the adoption of the purely conventional; *Plate 43d* is the back plate of the clock shown in *Plate 18d*. The cast cock of the Watson clock represents a fashion of the latter part of the seventeenth century. As is seen in the Quare clock, the size of these cocks became very overdone; in this case the cock is a restoration. The faceted bob of the Watson clock to facilitate regulation is interesting; the author had a similar bob on a clock by William Clement he formerly owned.

Plate 44a shows a clock by Claude du Chesne. The flat disk bob has been adopted, and since this can only be turned a full 180° if the bob is to swing true, some means of lesser regulation had to be found. This takes the form of an eccentric snail, seen upper right, which can be turned by a hand on the dial, so adjusting the essential flexing point in the suspension spring.

Plate 44b shows about the maximum degree of back-plate decoration before the tendency for this to lessen, and finally to disappear, sets in. It is on a clock by George Graham and is on lines very similar to Tompion, which is, of course, not surprising since he worked so many years for him. The winged and crowned semi-angels should be noted. The clock is a repeater and can be pulled from either side, though the pull cords are missing.

Plate 44c is the back plate of the Vulliamy clock illustrated in *Plate 28c*. The degree of decoration is now considerably less.

It is a pull repeater from one side only. Our final illustration shows the back plate of the clock given in *Plate 29c*. Here we have merely a decorated edge. The decoration on the pendulum bob is unusual. Note that a gong, giving a deeper tone, has replaced the bell; this is a feature of the end of the eighteenth century.

CHAPTER EIGHT

Night Clocks

THE earliest record that we have of a clock to record night hours is the biographical tablet of Amenemhe't, Prince and Holder of the Royal Seals, who lived at the beginning of the eighteenth Dynasty, and who was born about 1565 B.C. In his memorial tablet he describes his invention of a water clock to tell the time at night, and the hieroglyphic he uses to describe it is ▽, that is an inverted truncated cone, in common parlance a vessel somewhat like an ordinary flower pot, which corresponds to the shape of all known Egyptian water clocks. That found in the Temple of Karnak, of which a plaster reproduction is to be seen in the Science Museum, London, was made about 1450 B.C. The Egyptians divided the day and night each into twelve equal periods and Amenemhe't states in his tablet that he has taken this into account. His clock formed the model for all subsequent Egyptian water clocks.

To drop an equal amount vertically, in spite of decreasing pressure, during a given period would need a container with a wall of about 77°, all the known Egyptian water clocks have walls of nearer 70°, and Dr. F. Hoepper, in an article in the *Deutsche Kolloid Zeitschrift* for January 1942, related a series of experiments with a container with walls of 70°. He had calculated that with walls of 77° and water subjected to the average fall in temperature for the Egyptian night, errors up to three-quarters of an hour would creep in, an error far too big to pass unnoticed by the proficient Egyptian astronomers. He reduced the temperature of the water in his container thermostatically by the $1\frac{1}{2}°$ per hour that he had calculated as the average fall in night temperature in Egypt and found that he succeeded in getting equal falls in level for equal periods of time. The Karnak clock is marked on the inside with a series of vertical dots at unequal intervals, representing the length of the hours of the night during the different months.

This clock, of course, needed an artificial light by which to read it; later we get the appearance of touch knobs. *Plate 45a* shows a clock from the church of St. Sebaldius, in Nuremberg, and now in the Germanusches Museum there. It will be seen that it has sixteen touch knobs, that at the top being longer than the others, as a point of reference. *Plate 45b* shows the under-dial work where a pinion of 3 engages a wheel of 48, a 1 : 16 ratio, thus proving that this clock was designed for use during the night hours, which are at a maximum of sixteen at the winter solstice. Had the clock been intended for day use the touch knobs would not have been needed. In later years the dial has been painted over to mark twelve hours only and all descriptions that the author has seen of this clock assume that there is a pinion of 4 into a wheel of 48, giving a 1 : 12 ratio, but the pinion of 3 has not lost a tooth, it is undoubtedly original.

Now the Egyptian clock required an artificial light and both these clocks call for the proximity of the observer; it is not until the seventeenth century that we get night clocks that can be read at a distance. They are of two kinds, those that were made for use in large salons, which often had striking trains, and could be used as day or night clocks, and those for bedrooms where silence was a primary consideration. Of the latter one of the earliest is in the Museum at Kassel. It is by Johann Philip Treffler and is one of the only two signed pieces by this maker known. Mr. Silvio Bedini, of Salem, Massachussets, has recently published in the Journal of the National Association of Watch and Clock Collectors of the U.S.A. a most exhaustive study of this maker's Life. Treffler was at one time attached to the Court of Archduke Ferdinand II of Tuscany. This clock (*Plate 45c*) is dated about 1675–80. It will be seen that it has an ordinary chapter ring and can be used by day; above is a small hinged plate covering a small transparent glass dial which is marked with the twelve hours. The back view *Plate 45d* reveals a lamp and reflector and chimney. In *Plate 46a* is seen a closer view of the back plate and the glass dial above it. This latter is in duplicate, one sheet is fixed with the hours painted on it whilst that other, bearing the hand, revolves before it once in twelve hours. It will be noted that the pendulum hangs from the bottom of the movement necessitating an inverted crown wheel. This is also found in the other Treffler clock known and was also shown in the sketch of the clock at the Medici Palace sent to Huygens in 1658. It would seem to be an Italian conception (see *Plate 10d*).

Judging from those still to be found in Italy, thirty-hour night clocks were fairly usual at this period; a day and night clock of Italian origin is seen in *Plate 46b*. With the poor illumination available in a large room, it would not be possible to see across to a clock on the other side of the room, so an hour dial, fixed to the arbour of the hour hand and of a larger diameter than the day-hour ring, shows through a slot above the chapter ring. In the illustration the clock is recording 3.15.

In England night clocks of the seventeenth century are known by East, Fromanteel, Knibb, Bartlett, Seignior and possibly others. One by Joseph Knibb *Plate 46c* and *d*, burns each night in the author's bedroom. The main dial revolves once in two hours, on its reverse side it carried 180° apart, two subsidiary dials, one with the even numbers and one with the odd. As these pass the low point a small arm knocks them one place forward. In the illustration it is just 11 o'clock, 10 is disappearing and 11 is coming up. The objection to a verge movement in a bedroom is the noise it makes, but in this clock this disadvantage has been overcome by fixing a piece of very thin spring steel under the pallets and letting it protrude a fraction, so that the spring takes up the impact with the crown wheel. The result is almost complete silence, only in the dead of night can a faint sound be heard. There is a small screw for adjustment of the depthing.

In the quest for quietness in the bedroom Peter Thomas Campini invented a pendulum clock that actuated an eccentric balance which had a continuous, instead of an intermittent motion, the result being an entirely silent movement. This is seen in *Plate 47a* and *b*. The clock is signed on the back of the movement *Petrus Thomas Campanus Inventor, Roma 1683*. In *Plate 47b* it will be noted that the pendulum hangs from a curved arm that is connected on one end with a weighted bar, and at the other eccentrically on to a small disk on the hub of the escape wheel, if so we may call it, since that is no escapement proper. This arm is set in motion by the forked piece on the top of the pendulum rod; once in motion the weighted bar continues to give the impetus to the balance wheel. Modern attempts to make the clock function to time have not been very successful, but the idea is ingenious.

An illustration exists of a very ornate French bedroom of about 1725, where an elaboration of Treffler's transparent glass dial is seen in a 'magic lantern' clock projection of the dial on to the wall of the room. This idea of projection was revived about one hundred years later; *Plate 47c* shows two early-nineteenth-century clocks which can be used as ordinary clocks by day and which are fitted with dials for projection by night; yet electric clocks, that on the press of a switch, projected the dial on to the ceiling were hailed as a great novelty some twenty years ago. The third clock on this plate is a very simple idea, a night light is placed on a shelf behind the slotted dial. This type was used in Scandinavia.

This concludes the chapters on European clocks, merely a brief outline; to be exhaustive would need several volumes resulting in a work so expensive that no one would want to buy it. Nevertheless it is hoped that the Reader's interest has been stimulated and that what has been omitted may be the incentive to others to fill the gap.

In our final chapter we shall take a look at those clocks in which our cousins across the Atlantic take an interest and collect.

CHAPTER NINE

American Clocks

AS MENTIONED in the preface, Mr. Walter M. Roberts, President of the National Association of Watch and Clock Collectors, has been largely responsible for the gathering together of the examples illustrated, for the historical details of their makers and the general evolution of American Clockmaking, the author is duly appreciative of his help.

Little is known of American clockmaking during the early days of the Colonies. A few English-trained clockmakers came to America during the period of 1620–1700. It is known that Boston had a tower clock in 1650 cared for by Richard Taylor but nothing is known of his clocks. William Davis worked in Boston in 1683 and Edward Bogardus was active in New York in 1698. There are no known examples of seventeenth-century American clocks.

During the eighteenth century clockmaking became well established in Boston, Newport, New York and Philadelphia. Since the demand for clocks was slight the American clockmakers required other talents to insure an adequate income. They were usually silversmiths and often gunsmiths, metalmen, traders, locksmiths and tinkers.

Eli Terry produced the first clocks in large quantities early in the 1800's. Daniel Burnap and Gideon Roberts used interchangeable parts but in no great volume. American clockmaking then developed into big business for the times. Many new clockmaking shops came into existence in the Bristol, Connecticut area. Along a stream in Bristol there were eleven clock-manufacturing plants within an eighth-mile.

The introduction of low-cost brass in America made possible low-priced clocks. Wooden movements disappeared and thousands of brass-movement clocks were produced where hundreds of wooden-movement clocks had formerly been made. Cases became styled for price production and markets were enlarged.

Salesmanship as such and mass production can be credited to the American clockmaker. Terry and Jerome were good organisers but themselves poor craftsmen.

Clock work was done under great difficulties. Many makers made all of their tools. Many wheel and pinion cutters were made by hand of rough material yet with accurate results. Communication was difficult; transportation facilities poor, yet the 'Yankee Trader' was born and prospered. He was resourceful and ingenious. He extended his markets on horseback and stagecoach; later on sailing ships.

In this chapter a few types and styles are shown to give an idea of the clocks that were produced and are today respected by the collector of American pieces. There were thousands of styles, many of which can be found in the works to which reference is made later.

The clockmakers in America during the late 1600's and 1700's were, for the most part, English-trained. Their work reflected this training and it was not until the late 1700's that modifications of the traditional type appeared. A few tower clocks were built during this period, but the tall clock accounted for the greater portion of clocks built, each being individually made until possibly Daniel Burnap and certainly Gideon Roberts followed by Eli Terry arranged their shops to make clocks in quantity. This founding of mass production led the way for a strong manufacturing economy in America.

American production can conveniently be divided into three categories: tall clocks, wall clocks and shelf clocks, each variety of which will be examined in turn.

Until the turn of the nineteenth century the bulk of the clocks produced in America were tall clocks made in the Atlantic seaboard states, but many of the surviving pieces from this period bearing American names were, in fact, either imported complete from England or imported as movements and cased in the States.

In the main movements with straightforward going and striking trains, anchor escapement and rack and snail strike were produced, although occasionally a movement with calendar or other simple astronomical indications was made. The most famous maker of these more complicated movements was David Rittenhouse (1732–96) whose name is a household word among American collectors, although the number of pieces from his hand is very limited.

Plate 48 illustrates a clock by Rittenhouse. On its case is a ticket describing it as an astronomical clock, but as there are in fact no astronomical indications, it should be more correctly described as a clock made by Rittenhouse for use in astronomical observations.

It is reputed to have been used by Rittenhouse when observing the transit of Venus on June 3rd, 1769.

This is said to be the most accurate timekeeper made by Rittenhouse, but full details as to the improvements introduced to give it that superiority in timekeeping over his other productions are lacking. Mr. Robert A. Franks who examined the clock some time ago reported that the movement had a Graham dead-beat escapement, but of a most unusual type, the escape wheel being planted behind the back-plate of the movement engaging directly with the upper portion of the pendulum rod which is 'expanded' to encompass the escape wheel and which holds the two pallets, thus eliminating the customary anchor and fork, consequently reducing friction. The perfection of the workmanship is striking, one notes the high number of leaves on the pinions, a refinement that reduces friction and uneven power delivered to the escape wheel. No mention is made of the type of pendulum and the nature of its compensation, which must be assumed if such accurate results are to be achieved.[1]

Plate 49 shows four tall clocks: *a* is by Simon Willard of Roxbury, Massachusetts and is of date about 1785. It is a good example of a mahogany case with Sheraton style inlay, fret top and ball and spire finials. The painted dial indicates seconds and has a calendar opening. In the arch is a lunar dial that will revolve once in two lunar months and carries landscape and seascape scenes. The movement is brass, eight-day and weightdriven.

Plate 49b is a scroll pediment clock by R. Shearman of Philadelphia about 1800. This scroll top followed on after the fret trimmed top and reflects Chippendale styling. The pediment is finished with urn and flame finials in wood with a fluted block below the centre finial. It has free standing columns on the hood, fluted quarter columns on the trunk and base and

[1] The author recently saw a clock by Ellicott with the escape wheel embraced within the expanded pendulum in Lord Harris' collection.

bracket feet. The dial is painted and shows seconds and calendar. It will be noted that the hands have passed from the mid- to late-eighteenth-century style of *a* to the Regency style. The brass movement is eight-day, weight-driven.

Plate 49c is a corner tall clock by John Osgood of Andover, Massachusetts, of about 1797. This is a case of a movement being given to a country carpenter to have the case made; a man who evidently had no idea of introducing style or proportion into the pine case with butternut hood that he made. The hands too would seem to have been adapted from a larger dial. The dial is early nineteenth century but the minute hand is mid-eighteenth century and the hour hand smacks more of the later seventeenth. The hour hand should just touch the inner edge of the hour ring and the minute hand the outer edge, as is seen in examples *a* and *b*. This rule is broken in *d*, but in this case there is no doubt that the hands are original. The movement of *c* is a brass weight-driven timepiece. *Plate 49d* is a miniature tall clock or grandmother clock by Joshua Wilder of Hingham, Massachusetts, dated about 1800. In this case the case is mahogany veneer on pine with the fret pediment and urn finials of a quarter century earlier; it has free standing columns with brass mountings on both the hood and trunk. The movement is eight-day, brass, weight-driven with alarm. The illfitting hands are probably due more to the lack of appreciation of the finer points of a dial, rather than to anything else.

Space does not allow a further expansion of our study of tall clocks, we must now pass on to that of wall clocks. These, having short pendulum movements, first appeared around 1760–5. Simon Willard developed a type with a forty-hour hand-made movement of brass with the pendulum rod fixed directly to the anchor, thus saving scarce brass and lessening the time of making. Wall clocks gradually replaced tall clocks and after 1800 were made in increasing numbers following the introduction of the banjo clock. *Plates 50* and *51* illustrate a few of the many types.

Plate 50a shows a Simon Willard wall clock made at Grafton, Massachusetts about 1770. The delicate case is of mahogany with a kidney door opening, fret top and brass finials. There is a lunar dial and a dial and a day of the month calendar. These

two indications are on the same dial as the phase of the moon,
which makes one turn in two lunar months or fifty-nine days.
It is read off the top of the stationary hand fixed above the
hour dial. Since the calendar dial will have to be corrected by
hand after each short month, the lunar indications will become
very approximate after a short while. The painting of the lunar
disk and the starry sky is very crude compared with the good
finish and engraving of the rest of the dial. The brass movement
is seen in *Plate 50b*. There is no striking train, one blow on the
bell being given at every hour. This clock is one of fifteen known
examples.

Plate 50c is another clock by Simon Willard, made after he
had moved to Roxbury in Massachusetts and dates from about
1810. It takes the well-known banjo shape, a style developed
in the 1790's and patented in 1802. A glance at the movement
Plate 50d shows at once that there has been a great improvement in the workmanship employed and this resulted in much
better timekeeping, making this type of clock immediately
popular. The T-bridge in the movement, the clean lines of the
design of the case, as well as the clear dial and graceful hands
should be noted.

These banjo clocks were first made of mahogany with inlay
at the throat and door. The flat base made this type equally
suitable for wall or shelf. Later examples used a bracket base
with the entire front gold-leafed, including rope trim on the
frames. Glass panels are reverse painted, some being very
elaborate. When gold-leafed, the clocks were called 'presenta-
tion clocks'. A book on Simon Willard, dealing with his life
and work is mentioned in the bibliography given at the end of
this book.

Plate 51a shows a Banjo-lyre clock, anonymous, but typical of
the work of Sawin, *c.* 1825. This clock has a brass banjo type
movement with going, striking trains and alarm. The glass in
the carved lyre throat and base is reverse painted and there is
the typical bracket base. The feather finial is also characteristic.
Here we are losing the light and graceful lines of the true banjo
and a heavier type is developing, which is again reflected in
Plate 51b which illustrates a true Lyre clock, again anonymous,
but having a dial and hands as usually employed by Curtis. Its
date is about 1830. It is a weight-driven timepiece with alarm.

The use of a shorter pendulum had permitted a redesigning of the base. Aaron Willard Jr. is generally credited with the original design of the lyre clock.

Our last example of a wall clock is seen in *Plate 51c*, a New Hampshire Mirror clock of about 1820 by Benjamin Morrill of Boscawen, New Hampshire. This design is unique to this state and proved very popular at the time. The brass movement seen in *Plate 51d* differs from others in that the pendulum is placed at the side, earning for this type the name of 'side wheeler'. As will be seen there are going and striking trains. Vermont and Massachusetts makers copied the case style but used banjo-type movement.

We now pass to the last of our three categories, shelf clocks. Mass production was responsible for the wide popularity of American shelf clocks. Shortly after 1800 Eli Terry designed and produced a 30-hour wooden movement using oak plates, laurel wood pillars and black cherrywood gears. Since brass held a premium price and these woods were locally available, it was possible to sell wooden-movement clocks at a much cheaper price. It was not until 1839 that brass became available at a low price. After that date the low-priced brass-movement clock became a reality. The variety of styles produced between 1810 and 1910 is almost without limit, seven of these are reproduced here.

Plate 52a illustrates a Massachusetts shelf clock by David Wood of Newburyport, Mass. *c*. 1800, an eight-day timepiece in a nicely inlaid mahogany case, possibly by Pillsbury, who made many cases for Wood. The design here, in the upper portion, follows the English broken-arch type, very popular in England in the latter half of the eighteenth century. Clocks of this type invariably had fine cases, well proportioned, some with kidney dials, others with glass panels or tablets for the door and lower case. Glass-panelled cases often used deeply dished dials. The Willards made many fine case-on-case and shelf clocks.

In *Plate 52b* we see a very rare Willard clock, known as a lighthouse clock. It was made about 1822 by Simon Willard at Roxbury, Massachusetts, but the style did not prove popular and very few were made. Aesthetically one does not wonder at this; nevertheless today, since it is a Willard production and so few are available, they are much sought after. The movement is eight-day, brass, some having strike and alarm.

In *Plates 52c* and *52d* we have two Terry Shelf clocks, that in *Plate 52c* being the pillar and scroll type while *Plate 52d* is the experimental box cased model. Terry was working at Plymouth, Connecticut at this time, about 1816. This pillar and scroll clock was the first of its kind that Terry produced, and was the third model in his series of production. This model has the escapement in front of the dial with the solid plate wooden movement fastened to the dial. The movement is wood throughout with weights compounded and often with drop holes cut in the case bottom to permit operation for a full day. The hands which are very similar in design to those in England at this period were usually of cast pewter with a counterbalance as part of the minute hand.

Plate 52d shows the experimental model having the strap type wooden movement but with brass rack and snail strike control, as a carry over from Terry's tall clock work. The first clocks produced used a nicely engraved label which was changed to a printed label when the outside escapement model was dropped and the design modified to the same style case, but slightly higher, to permit a full thirty hour operation with non-compounded weights of cast iron.

The pendulum bob has been taken off in order not to hide the name paper inside the case. The hour ring of this clock is reverse painted on the glass of the door, which then shuts in front of the hands and movement.

These pillar and scroll shelf clocks are a classic American design and are considered one of the most graceful. Later designs somewhat increased the height of the case and the escapement was moved on to the front plate. Terry's original patents can be seen at The Bristol Clock Museum, Bristol, Conn.

Plate 52a gives a mirror shelf clock by Atkins & Downs for George Mitchell, Bristol, Conn. about 1831. It has an eight-day wooden movement with compounded weights. The case is mahogany veneer on pine with stencilled half columns and top. *Plate 53b* shows a typical clock of this type with the front plate removed revealing the wooden movement with going train, strike and alarm; the double-headed hammer for the latter appearing at the bottom of the illustration where it would fit inside the bell striking it on the inside on both sides, as opposed to the single strike on the outside of the bell for the hour strike. These thirty-hour cheap clocks were sold throughout the world, many being sold in England.

So far we have been dealing exclusively with weight-driven clocks; the production of spring-driven clocks was hampered by the difficulty of getting good homogenous spring steel. To overcome this the ordinary waggon spring was very ingeniously adapted to horology and such a clock is illustrated in *Plate 53c*. It is a waggon-spring clock by Joseph Ives, of Brooklyn, New York about, 1825. As will be seen from *Plate 53d* the movement is brass strapped with an unusual train lay-out, the waggon spring is seen in the base. It has a mahogany Phyfe-type case with a reverse painted glass panel in the door.

The waggon spring was a patent of Joseph Ives; other patents of his were for roller pinions for both wood and metal movements to reduce friction, on the lines of John Harrison's work a century earlier, although it is probable that this was not known to Ives; the printed descriptions of Harrison's work was probably circulated to a scientifically interested few. Ives also made a wall mirror clock with a seconds pendulum with steel and brass movement, roller pinions, square toothed gears. He produced a tin plate movement with squirrel cage escapement for low price production and was responsible for improved methods of brass rolling. Case types were double steeple for thirty-hour and eight-day movements, square and moulded cases for thirty-day shelf clocks and wall clocks housed in octagonal cases. Joseph Ives was a good inventor but a poor man of business; he was associated with many partners through his career.

Plate 54a shows the forerunner of the steeple and beehive designs that became so popular in the mid-nineteenth century. It is a Gothic Ripple shelf clock by Brewster & Ingraham and was designed by Elias Ingraham during a sea voyage in 1845. It has a spring-driven movement with stamped brass plates and wheels, a striking clock with alarm, the setting dial for which can be seen in the centre around the hand arbor. The ripple trim found a certain amount of acceptance about this period. The E. Ingraham Co. is the only American clock company still under family management, being one of the largest producers.

Plate 54b illustrated a sidearm acorn shelf clock by Forestville

Mfg. Co. Bristol, Conn. about 1845, J. C. Brown, owner. Mr. Brown's name always appears on the labels of his clocks together with the firm's name. He designed several unique cases, one of which is shown; the style was never copied. The clock illustrated has an eight-day movement, brass, with spring drive and fusees in the lower part of the case with gut connexions with the winding arbors. The glass panel shows the J. C. Brown residence.

Whilst in the early years of American Clockmaking ideas and designs were copied largely from England, the finishing note of this chapter will be an example where the American Horologist led the world. *Plates 54c* and *d* show a year torsion pendulum clock made and patented by Aaron D. Crane about 1830. Crane's first patent for torsion pendulum clocks was taken out in 1829, just about a century before their appearance in the European market. Crane made 8-day, 30-hour weight driven torsion pendulum clocks and also 400-day spring-fusee clocks. The one illustrated is marked to go for 376 days. The pendulum comprises six weights and revolves about three and a half complete turns in each direction about a stationary figure. Crane clocks are usually in Empire style cases, as in the example illustrated.

The astronomical dial is seen in *Plate 54d*. The calendar dial will revolve once a year and the day and month will be read off the stationary hand. The sun will make one revolution in a mean day and the moon one revolution in the period between two successive southings, i.e. its passing of the meridian, its globe making one complete turn in a lunation. The position of the sun at midday will show its place in the ecliptic and its 'aspect' or angular position in relation to the moon. The hand before the globe will revolve once with the moon hand and will show the state of the tide in 1/6ths at any time. Since there are no age of the moon indications, the clock will have to be set to the time of high or low tide at new or full moon for the port selected and the moon's globe adjusted accordingly. The clock will then register for the selected port. The sliding shutters, which are wrongly adjusted (their tops should be horizontal), show the proportion of the twenty-four hours in daylight and darkness, as judged by the eye. Had the hours been marked on the outer bezel, the times of sunrise and sunset would be indicated. The bottom part of the dial, the plate on which the word 'Astronomical' is engraved, marks those hours of the twenty-four which are dark at all times of the year in the latitude of the locality selected.

There is romance in the history of clock and watch-making in America – the struggle for existence – the success of an idea – the lasting effect on the economy of a country. Craftsmen from abroad became part of a new country, sharing their knowledge and training younger men, thus founding an industry that prospered.

Industry moves ahead constantly. Research on time measurement has made possible the atomic clock such as the ammonia, cesium and maser types with an accuracy of one part in ten billions. Co-operation among scientists, governments and industries makes such accuracy available. The future holds as great a romance as does our past.

Special thanks to those through whom these photographs were made available and whose names appear in the List of Acknowledgments. Also to be thanked are Cartwright F. Lane, Charles Parsons, Edwin Burt, Willard Porter and many other members of The National Association of Watch and Clock Collectors Inc. whose co-operation was given.

For the convenience of those interested in obtaining more and specific information on American clocks and their makers, a Bibliography on the subject is appended.

Bibliography

ALBRECHT, Rudolf   *Die Raeder-Uhr*, Rothenburg, 1906

BAILLIE, G. H.   *Watchmakers and Clockmakers of the World.* London, 1947
Clocks and Watches, An Historical Bibliography. London, 1951

BASSERMANN-JORDAN, Ernst von   *Die Geschichte der Raederuhr.* Frankfurt, 1906

BRITTEN, F. J.   *Old Clocks and Watches and their Makers.* 7th Ed. London, 1956

BEESON, Dr. C. F. C.   *Clockmaking in Oxfordshire.* Antiquarian Horological Society, 1962

CESCINSKY, Herbert   *Old English Master Clockmakers.* London, 1938

CESCINSKY, H. and WEBSTER, M.   *English Domestic Clocks.* London, 1913

CHAPUIS, Alfred   *L'Horlogerie, Une Tradition Helvétique.* Neuchâtel, 1948

CHAPUIS, A. and DROZ, Ed.   *Les Automates.* Neuchâtel, 1949

DEFOSSEZ, Leo   *Les Savants du 17ème siècle et la Mesure du Temps.* Lausanne, 1946

EDWARDES, Ernest L.   *The Grandfather Clock*, 2nd Ed. Altrincham, 1952

GORDON, G. F. C.   *Clockmaking Past and Present.* (Revised A. V. May). London, 1949

GREEN, F. H.   *Old English Clocks.* London, 1931

LLOYD, H. Alan   *Chats on Old Clocks.* London, 1951
Some Outstanding Clocks over 700 Years: 1250–1950. London, 1958

ROBERTSON, J. Drummond   *The Evolution of Clockwork.* London, 1931

SYMONDS, R. W.   *A Book of English Clocks.* (Penguin.) London, 1951
Thomas Tompion: His Life and Work. London, 1951

TARDY   *La Pendule française.* Paris, 1948–50

ULLYETT, Kenneth   *In Quest of Clocks.* London, 1950

169

WARD, Dr. F. A. B.   *Time Measurement*, Pt. I Science Museum,
                         London, 1961; Pt. II, 1966
WENHAM, E.   *Old Clocks for Modern Use*. London, 1951

American Bibliography

ARTHUR, James   *Time and Its Measurement*, 1909
BARNUM, P. T.   *Struggles and Triumphs*, 1872
BARR, Lockwood   *Eli Terry Pillar and Scroll Shelf Clocks*, 1952
BENSON, James W.   *Time and Time Tellers*, 1902
BOOTH, M. L.   *New and Complete Clock and Watchmakers
                         Manual*, 1860

BREARLEY, Harry C.   *Time Telling Through the Ages*, 1919
CHAMBERLAIN, Paul M.   *It's About Time*, 1941
CHANDLEE, Edward E.   *Six Quaker Clockmakers*, 1943
DREPPERD, Carl W.   *American Clocks and Clock Makers*, 1947
ECKHARDT, George H.   *Clocks of Pennsylvania and Their Makers*,
                         1954
HERING, D. W.   *The Lure Of The Clock*, 1932
HOOPES, Penrose R.   *Connecticut Clockmakers of the 18th Century*,
                         1930
JAMES, Arthur E.   *Chester County Clocks and Their Makers*, 1947
JEROME, Chauncey   *History of the American Clock Business for the
                         Past Sixty Years*, 1860
JONES, Leslie Allen   *Eli Terry, Clockmaker of Connecticut*, 1942
LYONS, Harold   *Atomic Clocks, Scientific American*, Feb. 1957
MILHAM, Willis I.   *Time and Timekeepers*, 1923
MILLER, Edgar G., Jr.   *American Antique Furniture*, Vol. 2, 1937
MOORE, N. Hudson   *The Old Clock Book*, 1911
MUSSEY, Barrows   *Young Father Time*, 1950
NEW YORK UNIVERSITY   *Time and Its Mysteries*
NUTTING, Wallace   *The Clock Book*, 1924
NUTTING, Wallace   *Furniture Treasury*, Vol. 3, 1933
PALMER, Brooks   *The Book of American Clocks*, 1950
                         The Romance of Time, 1954
WILLARD, John Ware   *A History of Simon Willard, Inventor and
                         Clockmaker*, 1911

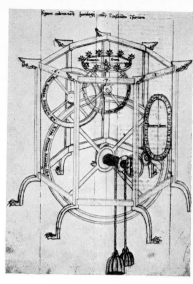

B. DONDI'S CLOCK OF 1364 PROVIDING THE MOTIVE FORCE FOR HIS ASTRONOMICAL DIALS. The earliest depiction of a mechanical clock known

A. RENAISSANCE SAND-GLASS
Recording $\frac{1}{4}$, $\frac{1}{2}$, $\frac{3}{4}$ and 1 hour

Plate 1

D. SOUTH GERMAN OR ITALIAN GOTHIC CLOCK
With foliot balance, *c.* 1550. *Ht.* 1′ 4″

C. DOMESTIC CLOCK
Fifteenth century,
probably Italian

A. ANONYMOUS. Drum clock with fusee, bearing date 1504

B. MOVEMENT OF 2A showing very early type of fusee

Plate 2

D. MOVEMENT OF 2C
Note very large and light balance

C. DRUM CLOCK WITH TRAVELLING CASE, *c.* 1550

A. FRENCH ASTRO-
LOGICAL CLOCK
DATED 1560,
MADE FOR THE
LATITUDE OF
LONDON

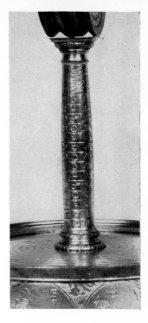

B. PILLAR WITH ENGRAVING
COLLATING A PLANET
WITH EACH OF THE
TWELVE HOURS OF DAY
AND NIGHT

Plate 3

C. FRONT DIAL
The black central tidal dial was added
by the astronomer, James Ferguson, to
whom the clock once belonged, in the
eighteenth century

D. BACK DIAL WITH ALIDADE FOR
SIGHTING THE SUN

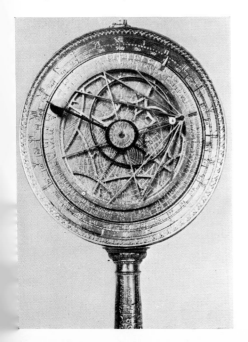

A. INCLINED PLANE CLOCK BY ISAAC HABRECHT OF STRASBURG, *c.* 1600. 3½″ dia.

B. FLAGELLATION CLOCK, *c.* 16

Plate 4

C. FRANSISCO SCHWARTZ, BRUSSELS. Small clock with cross-beat escapement, *c.* 1630. An early example of a minute hand. *Ht.* 6¼″

D. BACK VIEW OF 4C. Showing aperture for calibration marks for the setting up of the mainspring to effect regulation

A. ROLLING BALL CLOCK BY CHRISTOLPH ROHN, *c.* 1601. Period of ball, 1 minute including return

B. MECHANISM OF THE BALL CLOCK. Note the second cup (in the top shadow) ready to descend. The long chain drives the carousel

Plate 5

(See also *Plate 6* for details)

A. DETAILS OF THE TRIGGER RELEASE OF THE BALL FOR ITS UPWARD PASSAGE IN THE TUBE

B. THE CAROUSEL WHICH FUNCTIONS ONCE EVERY THREE HOURS

Plate 6

C. THE GOING AND STRIKING TRAINS

A. BOOK CLOCK BY HANS KIENING OF FUESSEN. With regulation by pallet impact angle, *c.* 1595

B. BOTTOM PLATE OF KIENING'S CLOCK (See also Fig. 9, page 53)

Plate 7

C. MOVEMENT OF KIENING'S CLOCK

D. ANOTHER VIEW OF THE MOVEMENT

A. CLOCK WITH GLOBE ATTACHED BY
NICHOLAS VALLIN, *c.* 1600
Was this an early attempt to 'find
the longitude'?

B. MOVEMENT OF VALLIN'S CLOCK
Note the pinion on top for driving the
globe

Plate 8

C. BOTTOM PLATE WITH VALLIN'S SIGNA-
TURE CLEARLY VISIBLE

D. INSIDE OF THE BOTTOM COVER OF VAL-
LIN'S CLOCK. Showing the record of
its various owners

A. TRANSITIONAL BALANCE-
WHEEL LANTERN CLOCK
Anonymous, 30-hour move-
ment, c. 1600–1610. Note decorated wrought-iron pillars

B. SILVER SHIP'S LANTERN
Late sixteenth century

C. LANTERN CLOCK
By Wm. Selwood, London,
12-hour movement, c. 1620.
Ht. 1′ 4″. Dial 6¼″

Plate 9

D. GEORGE GRAHAM. Travelling lantern alarm
clock with strong oak case, c. 1714

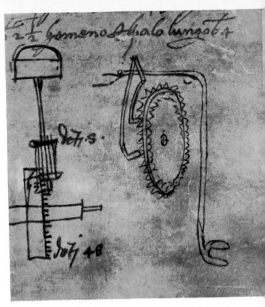

A. PENDULUM CLOCK BY CAMERINI
DATED 1656
(*Crown copyright*)

B. A SKETCH SHOWING THE PRINCIPLE OF THE
ANCHOR ESCAPEMENT FROM AN ITALIAN MANU-
SCRIPT OF ABOUT 1524

Plate 10

C. PENDULUM DESIGN FROM
Questo Benedetto Pendulo
Early seventeenth century

D. SKETCH OF PENDULUM WITH IN-
VERTED CROWN WHEEL
Early seventeenth century. Com-
pare with B

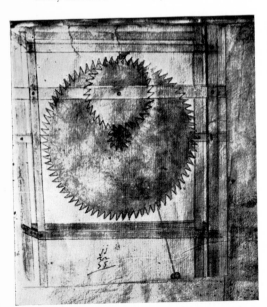

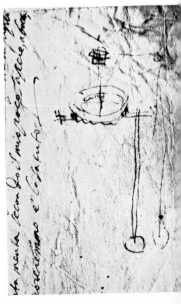

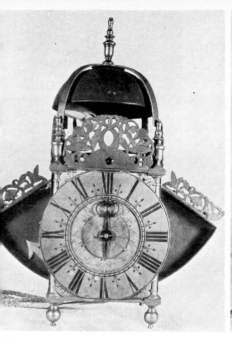

A and B. WING LANTERN CLOCK
By Thos. Wheeler, Neare ye French
Church, 30-hour movement, c. 1675–
80. *Ht.* 1′ 4″. *Dial* 6¼″. *Width over
wings* 12″

Plate 11

C and D. GERMAN TABLE CLOCK
By Christian Caroli, Koenigsberg, 30-hour movement, *c.*
1675. *Dial* 4½″ square. *Ht.* 3¼″

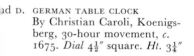

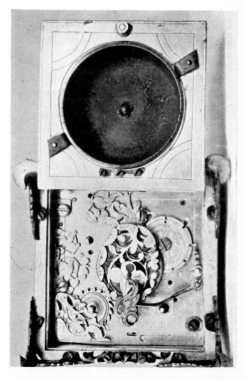

A. HANS BUSCHMANN
Year spring driven clock, *c.*
1651–52. *Ht.* 1′ 11″

Plate 12

B. BACK VIEW OF BUSCHMANN'S
CLOCK WITH DAY OF WEEK
AND YEAR DIALS

C. MAINSPRING DRIVE IN THE BASE
WITH RACK FOR THE REMON-
TOIRE WINDING OF THE SUB-
SIDIARY SPRING

D. MOVEMENT OF BUSCHMANN'S YEAR
CLOCK

J. G. MAYER, MUNICH
Complicated clock, *c.* 1660.
Shows two of the dials

B.   THE OTHER TWO DIALS OF
MAYER'S CLOCK

Plate 13

BACK PLATE OF MAYER'S CLOCK

D.   PART OF THE MOVEMENT OF MAYER'S
CLOCK

A. IRON CASED CLOCK OF LANTERN
STYLE, *c.* 1560. German

Plate 14

B. J-B. ALBERTI
Italian lantern style clock. 1685

C. EARLY DUTCH PENDULUM CLOCK
By J. Bernard van Stryp, Antwerp, *c.* 1660.
Dial 6½″ by 8¼″

D. MOVEMENT OF VAN STRYP CLOCK
Showing cycloidal cheeks

A. EARLY WOODEN-CASED PEDIMENT CLOCK
By Edward East, London, 7-day movement, c. 1660. *Ht.* 1′ 5″. (See also *Plate
42C*)

B. PEDIMENT CLOCK
By Edward East, London, 8-day movement, c. 1670

Plate 15

C. EDWARD EAST
Early cased clock, 7-day movement,
c. 1665

D. JOBST BURGI
Continental anticipation of the
'Architectural' type of case, c. 1610

A. PEDIMENT CLOCK
By John Hilderson, London, 8-day
movement, *c.* 1665. *Ht.* 1′ 6″

B. MOVEMENT OF HILDERSON CLOCK
Showing unique striking arrangement. (See also *Plates 37c* and *42*

Plate 16

C. CLOCK. By Wm. Knottesford, London. 8-day
movement, *c.* 1685

D. BACK VIEW OF KNOTTESFORD CLOC
Note the drawer for the key

WOODEN BASKET CLOCK
By Joseph Knibb, London, 8-day, quarter-
striking and repeating movement, c. 1685.
Ht. 1' 2"

B. WOODEN BASKET CLOCK
By Thomas Tompion (No. 15),
8-day, repeating and alarm
movement, c. 1685

Plate 17

BASKET CLOCK. By Joseph Windmills,
London, silver mounts, hall marked for
1698, 8-day movement

D. DOUBLE BASKET CLOCK
By John Shaw, Holborne, 8-day movement, c. 1695

A. WOODEN BASKET CLOCK
  By Samuel Watson, London, 8-day
  repeating movement, *c.* 1690. (See
  also *Plate 43C*)

B. WOODEN BASKET CLOCK
  By Joseph Knibb, with early attempt at
  Grande Sonnerie striking, 8-day movement,
  c. 1685. *Ht.* 1′ 2″. (See also *Plate 43A*)

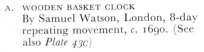

Plate 18

C. WOODEN BASKET CLOCK
  By Joseph Knibb, London, with Roman
  strike, 8-day movement, *c.* 1695. *Ht.* 1′ 2″

D. WOODEN BASKET CLOCK
  By Daniel Quare, London, made for
  use at sea, 8-day movement, *c.* 1695.
  Ht. incl. hook 1′ 2″. (See also *Plate 43*

A. PETER GARRON
Three train grande sonnerie clock in tortoiseshell veneered case, *c.* 1705

B. WOODEN BASKET CLOCK
By Thos. Tompion, London, No. 312, 8-day quarter repeater, *c.* 1705. *Ht.* 1′ 2″

Plate 19

C. INVERTED BELL CLOCK
By George Graham, London. With original bracket 8-day movement, *c.* 1715. The bracket has a drawer for the key

D. JOSEPH ANTRAM
Three train clock. Antram was clock maker to George I. This clock belonged to his disowned wife, the Countess of Ahlden, *c.* 1715

A. LANTERN CLOCK
MOVEMENT. By
Edward East,
London, dated
1664, 30-hour
movement. En-
cased about
1685. (See also
Plate 37D)

B. HANGING CLOCK
By Edward East, London, 8-day
movement, *c.* 1670. *Ht.* 1′ 9″

C. EXAMPLE OF A FINE
CLOCK SPOILT BY 'MOD
ERNISATION' IN PAST
CENTURIES

Plate 20

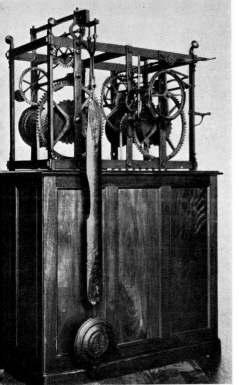

A. WILLIAM CLEMENT'S TURRET CLOCK WITH THE EARLIEST KNOWN ANCHOR ESCAPEMENT. Made for King's College, Cambridge, dated 1671. From an exhibit in the Science Museum, South Kensington. (*Crown Copyright*)

B. BACK VIEW OF WILLIAM CLEMENT'S TURRET CLOCK. (*Crown Copyright*)

Plate 21

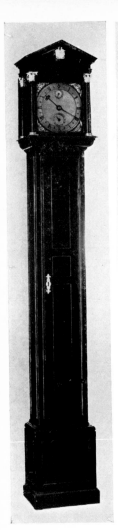

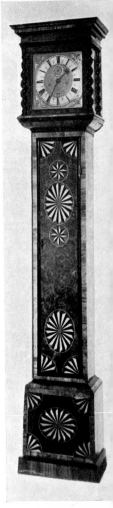

A. AHASUERUS
FROMANTEEL,
LONDON
8-day move-
ment, *c.* 1680.
Ht. 6′. *Dial*
8½″. (See also
Plate 37B)

B. JOHANNES
FROMANTEEL,
LONDON
8-day move-
ment, *c.* 1675.
Ht. 6′. *Dial*
8½″

C. EDWARD EAST,
LONDON
8-day move-
ment, *c.* 1685.
Ht. 6′. *Dial*
10″. (See also
Plate 38A)

D. JOSEPH WINDMILLS,
LONDON
8-day movement,
1690. *Ht.* 6′ 6″.
Dial 10½″

Plate 22

A. WM. CLEMENT, LONDON
c. 1685. *Ht.* 7′ 3″. *Dial*
10″. (See also *Plate*
38D)

C. JOHN CLOWES, LONDON
8-day movement, 1¼-
seconds pendulum, *c.*
1685. *Ht.* 7′ 4″. *Dial* 10″

B. MOVEMENT OF THE CLEMENT
CLOCK. Showing micrometer
adjustment for the 1¼-seconds
pendulum

Plate 23

A. CHRISTOPHER
   GOULD, LONDON.
   8-day movement,
   c. 1690. *Ht.* 8′ 4″.
   Dial 12″

B. WM. OSBORNE,
   LONDON. 8-day
   movement, *c.* 1705.
   Ht. 7′ 3″. *Dial* 12″.
   (See also *Plate 39A*)

C. JAS. DRURY,
   LONDON. 30-
   hour move-
   ment, *c.* 1710.
   Ht. 6′. *Dial* 5″

D. GEORGE GRAHAM.
   8-day long case
   clock,
   No. 681, *c.* 1728.
   Ht. 8′. *Dial* 12″

Plate 24

A. THOMAS TOMPION, LONDON. Year equation movement, *c.* 1695. *Ht. 8'. Dial* 12″. (See also *Plate 38C*)

B. RICHARD STREET, LONDON. 1-month movement, 1708. *Ht.* 10′. *Dial* 1′ 6″ by 2′ 6″. (See also *Plate 39B*)

C. MOVEMENT OF TOMPION'S YEAR CLOCK Fixed dial plate removed to show the engaging of the rocker arm rack with the wheel actuating the moving minute ring. (See also *Plate 38C*)

D. SHOWING EQUATION KIDNEY AND ROCKER ARM, *c.* 1695 (A, C & D are *by gracious permission of Her Majesty The Queen*)

Plate 25

A. DANIEL QUARE, LONDON. 3-month movement, *c.* 1695. *Ht.* 7′ 6″. *Dial* 11″

B. GEORGE GRAHAM, LONDON. Month movement, *c.* 1720. *Ht.* 8′ 3″. *Dial* 12″. (See
   also *Plate 39D*)

C. GEORGE GRAHAM, LONDON. Month equ
   movement with early mercury pendul
   c. 1730. *Ht.* 7′ 6″. *Dial* 12″

D. ANTHONY HERBERT, LONDON. Vauxhall
   plate-glass door, 8-day movement, *c.* 1
   Ht. 7′. *Dial* 12″

Plate 26

A. TRUE BELL CLOCK. George Hodgson, London, 8-day movement, *c.* 1760. *Ht.* 1′ 6″

B. TRUE BELL CLOCK. Benjamin Stennet, London. Half seconds, dead-beat escapement, 8-day movement, *c.* 1810. *Ht.* 1′ 9″

Plate 27

C. TRUE BELL CLOCK. G. M. Metcalfe, Londres, 8-day movement, *c.* 1785. *Ht.* 1′ 8″

D. ELIAS KREITMEYER, FRIEDBERG Continental anticipation of the true bell case, *c.* 1710

A. BALLOON CLOCK. Anonymous. Recoil escapement, 8-day movement. Dated 1796

B. BALLOON CLOCK. Thomas Brass, Guildford, 8-day movement, pull repeater, c. 1780. *Ht.* 1′ 7½″

Plate 28

C. INVERTED BELL CLOCK. Justin Vulliamy, London. Enamelled dial, 8-day movement, pull repeater, c. 1775. (See also *Plate 44*C)

D. DEEP BROKEN ARCH CLOCK. In Vernis Martin, Henry Fish, London, 8-day movement, pull repeater, c. 1765. *Ht.* 1′ 3″

A. SHALLOW BROKEN ARCH CLOCK
James Thwaites, London, recoil
escapement, 8-day movement,
enamelled dial, *c.* 1795. *Ht.*
1′ 4″

B. PLAIN ARCH CLOCK
Edward Baker, London, recoil
escapement, 8-day movement,
painted dial, *c.* 1815. *Ht.* 1′ 5″

Plate 29

C. CHAMFER TOP CLOCK
Anonymous, painted dial, recoil escapement, *c.* 1820. *Ht.*
1′ 8″. (See also *Plate 44D*)

D. LANCET CLOCK
Hawkins, Southampton, recoil
escapement, 8-day movement,
painted dial, *c.* 1810. *Ht.* 1′ 7″

A. ANONYMOUS. 8-day musical clock with unfolding lotus buds and waterfall, 3rd quarter eighteenth century. *Ht.* 2′ 8″

Plate 30

B. ANONYMOUS. 8-day clock with sunflower dial and cascading waterfalls. Musical train in case on which clock is standing, 3rd quarter eighteenth century

C. ANONYMOUS. 8-day musical clock with automata, waterfalls and procession, 3rd quarter eighteenth century

D. ANONYMOUS. 8-day enamelled musical clock with automata, 3rd quarter eighteenth century

ASTRONOMICAL CLOCK. Thomas Budgen, Croydon, 8-day movement, c. 1740. (See also *Plate 40D*)

CHARLES COULON, LONDON. 8-day movement, c.
1745. *Ht. 7'. Dial 12"*

C.   THE AUTHOR'S LARGEST AND SMAL-
LEST LONG CASE CLOCKS. Graham's
Successors Colley & Preist, London. Month movement, c. 1755.
Ht. 8' 6". Dial 12". (See also *Plate
38B*.) Sanders, Brinkworth, dated
15.6.1817, 30-hour movement. *Ht.
2' 11". Dial 5"*

Plate 31

A. ASTRONOMICAL CLOCK. George Margetts, London, month movement, *c.* 1780. *Ht.* 9′. *Dial* 14″

B. MUSICAL CLOCK. Benson, Whitehaven, 8-day movement, *c.* 1775. *Ht.* 8′ 6″. *Dial* 12″. (See also *Plate 41B*)

C. THOMAS BROWN, BIRMINGHAM. 8-day movement, *c.* 1785. *Ht.* 7′. *Dial* 12″

D. PHILIP LLOYD, BRISTOL. Tidal dial, 8-day movement, *c.* 1780. *Ht.* 8′ 2″. *Dial* 12″

Plate 32

RIGBY, LIVERPOOL. Tidal dial, 8-day movement, *c.* 1785

C. FINNEY, LIVERPOOL. Year clock, 1769. *Ht. abt. 6′ 6″.* (See also *Plate 41A*)

THOMAS BRUTON, BRISTOL. Tidal dial, 8-day movement, *c.* 1795. *Ht. 8′. Dial* 12″

D. ANONYMOUS. 8-day movement, *c.* 1800. *Ht. 6′ 6″. Dial* 11″

Plate 33

o

A. JOSIAH EMERY, LONDON. 8-day movement, *c.* 1795. *Ht.* 6′ 10″. *Dial* 12″

B. ROSS AND PECKHAM, LONDON. 8-day movement, *c.* 1800. *Ht.* 6′ 6″. *Dial* 12″

C. ANONYMOUS, PROVINCIAL. 8-day movement, *c.* 1800. *Ht.* 8′ 6″. *Dial* 1′ 2″

D. ANONYMOUS, OTLEY, YORKS. 8-day movement, *c.* 1810. *Ht.* 8′ 3″. *Dial* 1′ 2

Plate 34

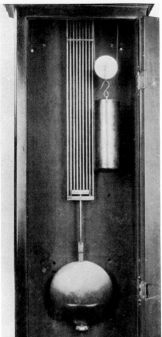

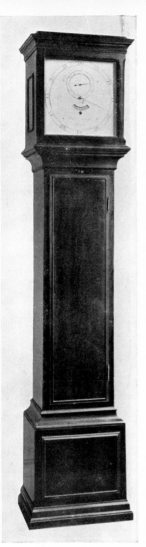

JOHN SHELTON, LONDON
Month movement, 1760.
Ht. 5′ 7″. Dial 12″

GRIDIRON PENDULUM OF
SHELTON'S CLOCK. Show-
ing the holes in the back-
board round the bob used
when clamping the bob
for travelling

D. GRIDIRON PENDULUM OR ARN-
OLD'S CLOCK. In this case the
holes in the back-board are
merely for fastening to the
wall, when the clock is in
position

C. JOHN ARNOLD
Regulator No. 1, month
movement, 1774

Plate 35

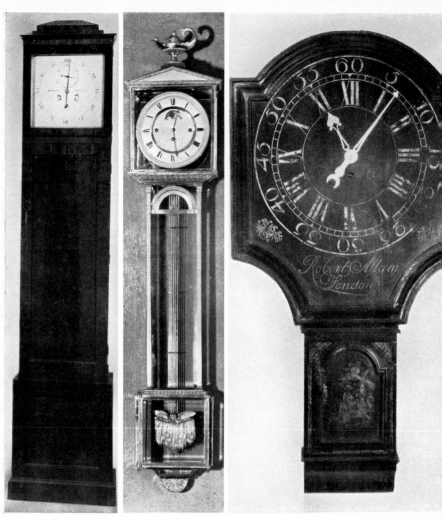

A. BARWISE, LONDON. Regulator, 8-day
movement, *c.* 1820. *Ht. 6′ 3″. Dial 12″*

B. GLUECKSSTEIN. Vienna Regulator,
8-day, 3 train with lunar dial in fire-
gilt bronze case, *c.* 1830

C. ROBERT ALLAM, LONDON. 'Act of Parliament' Clock, 8-day movement, *c.* 1760
Ht. 5′. Dial 2′ 6″

Plate 36

A. AHASUERUS FROMANTEEL, LONDON
c. 1660. *Dial* 8¼″

B. EARLY EQUATION DIAL FOR ADJUSTMENT BY
HAND. *c.* 1680. *Dial* 8½″. (See also *Plate 22A*)

Plate 37

D. EDWARD EAST, LONDON, 1664. The minute hand, added later, has to be set independently of the hour hand and is not
correctly set here. (See also *Plate 20A*)

C. JOHN HILDERSON, LONDON
c. 1665. (See also *Plates 16A* and *42D*)

A. EDWARD EAST, LONDON
   c. 1680. *Dial* 10″. (See also *Plate 22C*)

B. GRAHAM'S SUCCESSORS,
   Colley & Preist, London, c. 1755.
   Dial 12″ (See also *Plate 31C*)

Plate 38

C. THOMAS TOMPION, LONDON
   c. 1695. *Dial* 12″. (See also *Plates*
   25A, C, and *D.,* (*By gracious permission*
   of Her Majesty The Queen)

D. WILLIAM CLEMENT, LONDON
   c. 1685. *Dial* 10″. (See also *Plate 23A*)

WM. OSBORNE, LONDON
c. 1705. *Dial* 12″. (See also *Plate 24B*)

RICHARD STREET, LONDON, 1708
Dial 1′ 6″ by 2′ 6″. (See also *Plate 25B*)

DANIEL QUARE, LONDON
Year movement, *c.* 1710. *Dial* 14″ by 17″

Plate 39

GEORGE GRAHAM, LONDON
c. 1720. *Dial* 12″. (See also *Plate 26B*)

A. (Front view) QUARE EQUATION MOVEMENT
SEPARATE FROM THE CLOCK MOVEMENT
c. 1710. (See also *Plate 39C*)

B. Back View of A

C. WILLIAM TOMLINSON, LONDON
Universal Tidal Dial, *c.* 1735. *Dial* 12″

D. THOMAS BUDGEN, CROYDON
c. 1740. (See also *Plate 31A*)

Plate 40

DIAL OF FINNEY YEAR CLOCK
(See also *Plate 33C*)

B. JOHN BENSON, WHITEHAVEN
   Dial 12″, *c.* 1775. (See also *Plate 32B*)

Plate 41

C. HELM, ORMSKIRK
   Perpetual calendar movement,
   c. 1785

D. DETAILS OF PERPETUAL CALENDAR
   Note holes in the brass casting
   forming the dial plate

A. THOMAS LISTER, HALIFAX
Musical bracket clock, *c.* 1805

B. WILLIAM BOTHAMLEY, KIRTON
Unique tidal dial, *c.* 1785

Plate 42

C. EDWARD EAST, LONDON
c. 1660. (See also *Plate 15A*)

D. JOHN HILDERSON, LONDON
c. 1665. (See also *Plates 16A* and *37C*)

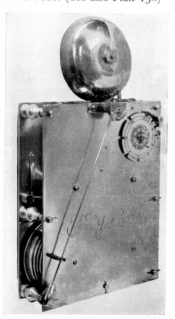

JOSEPH KNIBB, LONDON
Grande Sonnerie movement, *c.* 1685. (See also *Plate 18B*)

B. HENRY JONES, LONDON
    c. 1680

Plate 43

SAMUEL WATSON, LONDON
c. 1690. Note facetted bob. (See also *Plate 18A*)

D. DANIEL QUARE, LONDON
    c. 1695. (See also *Plate 18D*)

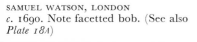

A. CLAUDE DU CHESNE, LONDON
   c. 1715

B. GEORGE GRAHAM, LONDON
   c. 1725

Plate 44

C. JUSTIN VULLIAMY, LONDON
   c. 1775. (See also *Plate 28C*)

D. ANONYMOUS
   c. 1820. (See also *Plate 29D*)

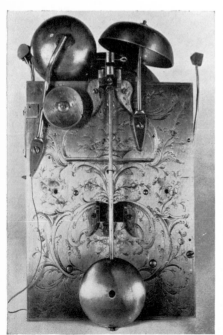

EARLY MONASTIC NIGHT ALARM CLOCK
FROM ST. SEBALDIUS CHURCH, NUREM-
BERG. 16-hour movement, *c.* 1400

B. BEHIND THE DIAL OF 45A
Showing pinion of 3 meshing with wheel
of 48

J. P. TREFFLER, NIGHT CLOCK
c. 1675

Plate 45

D. BACK VIEW OF TREFFLER'S CLOCK

A. DETAIL OF NIGHT DIAL AND BELOW
   MOVEMENT PENDULUM IN TREFFLER'S
   CLOCK. (See also *Plate 45D*)
   Plate 46

B. ANONYMOUS
   Italian Day and Night Clock, *c.*

C. & D. JOSEPH KNIBB, LONDON
       Night Clock, *c.* 1685.
       Ht. 1′ 8″

B. DETAILS OF CAMPANI'S SILENT MOVEMENT

P. T. CAMPANI'S SILENT NIGHT
CLOCK, 1683

Plate 47

THREE EARLY NINETEENTH-CENTURY NIGHT CLOCKS

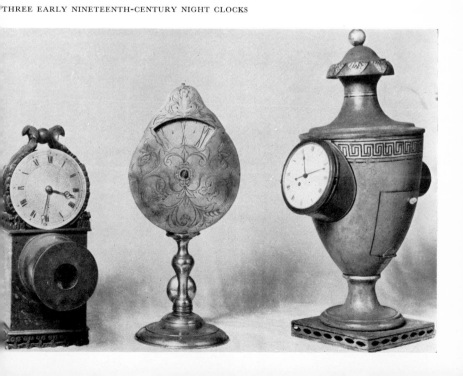

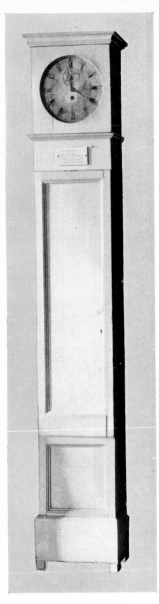

B.   DIAL OF A

A.   DAVID RITTENHOUSE USED
     FOR HIS OBSERVATIONS OF
     THE TRANSIT OF VENUS IN
     1769

Plate 48

TALL CLOCK BY
SIMON WILLARD,
ROXBURY, MASS.
c. 1785

B. TALL CLOCK BY R.
SHEARMAN,
PHILADELPHIA
c. 1800

C. CORNER TALL CLOCK
BY JOHN OSGOOD,
ANDOVER, MASS.
c. 1797

D. GRANDMOTHER
CLOCK BY JOSHUA
WILDER, HINGHAM,
MASS., *c.* 1800

Plate 49

P

A. WALL CLOCK BY SIMON
WILLARD GRAFTON, MASS.
c. 1770

B. MOVEMENT OF 50A

Plate 50

C. BANJO CLOCK BY SIMON
WILLARD ROXBURY,
MASS., *c.* 1810

D. MOVEMENT OF 50C

A. ANONYMOUS BANJO
    LYRE CLOCK, *c.* 1825

B. ANONYMOUS LYRE
    CLOCK, *c.* 1830

C. MIRROR WALL CLOCK BY BENJ.
    MORRILL, BOSCAWEN, NEW
    HAMPSHIRE, *c.* 1820

D. MOVEMENT OF 51C
    'A side Wheeler'

Plate 51

A. SHELF CLOCK BY DAVID WOOD, NEWBURYPORT, MASS., *c.* 1800

B. SIMON WILLARD, ROXBURY, LIGHTHOUSE CLOCK, *c.* 1822

Plate 52

C. SHELF CLOCK BY ELI TERRY, PLY-MOUTH, CONN., *c.* 1816

D. TERRY SHELF CLOCK. WOODEN STRAP TYPE

A. MIRROR SHELF CLOCK BY
   ATKINS AND DOWNS FOR GEO.
   MITCHELL, BRISTOL, CONN.
   c. 1831

B. TYPICAL WOODEN MOVEMENT FOR
   53A

Plate 53

C. WAGON SPRING CLOCK BY
   JOSEPH IVES, BROOKLYN, N.Y.
   c. 1825

D. MOVEMENT OF 53C

A. SHELF CLOCK BY BREWSTER AND
   INGRAHAM, *c.* 1845

B. SHELF CLOCK BY FORESTVILLE M
   COY., BRISTOL, CONN., 1845

Plate 54

C. YEAR ASTRONOMICAL TORSION PEN-
   DULUM CLOCK BY AARON D. CRANE
   c. 1830

D. DETAIL OF ASTRONOMICAL DIAL OF
   CRANE CLOCK

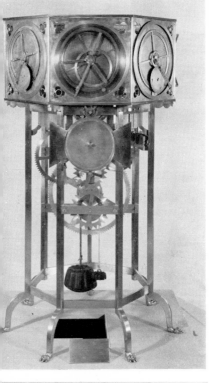

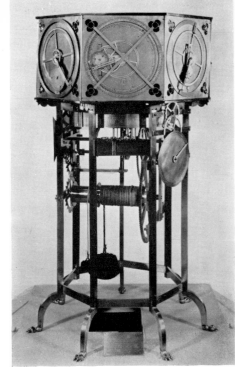

Plate 55

A. THE RECONSTRUCTED CLOCK
Meantime dial with sunrise and sunset wings, dial of Mars *left*, Venus *right*

B. The dial of Mercury with the Perpetual Calendar for Easter below, dial of Venus *left*, Moon *right*

C. The dial of Jupiter with dials of Saturn *left* and Mars *right*

Plate 56

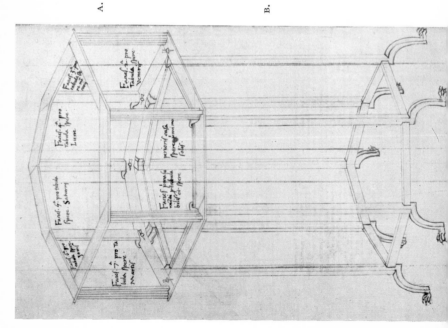

A. DONDI'S SKETCH OF THE FRAMEWORK

B. THE RECONSTRUCTION

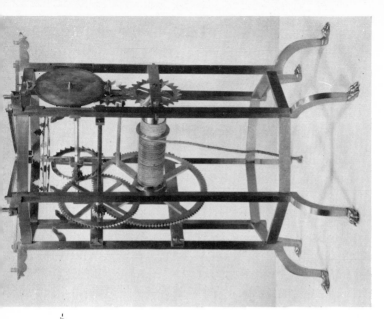

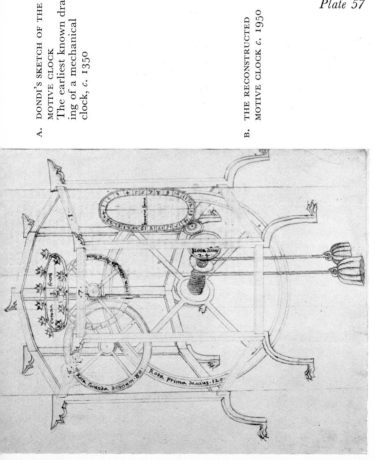

Plate 57

A. DONDI'S SKETCH OF THE
MOTIVE CLOCK
The earliest known draw-
ing of a mechanical
clock, *c.* 1350

B. THE RECONSTRUCTED
MOTIVE CLOCK *c.* 1950

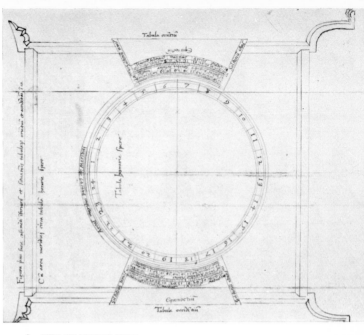

A. THE MEANTIME DIAL
    with the wings for the rising and setting of the sun

Plate 58

B. THE RECONSTRUCTED DIAL
    showing part of the train for the conversion of mean to sideral time

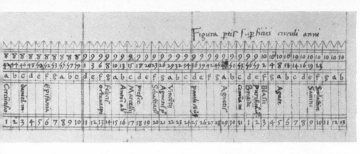

Plate 59

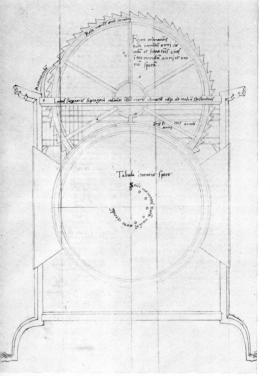

A. DONDI'S DETAIL OF THE ANNUAL CALENDAR WHEEL

B. The reconstructed wheel with one of the the racks for actuating the Calendar on the inside

C. The method of communicating the daily motion to the Annual Calendar wheel

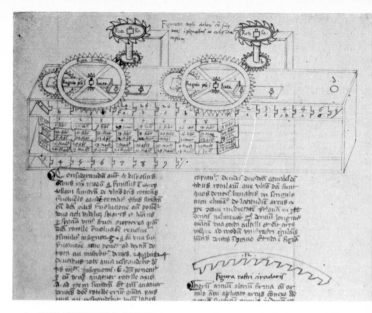

A. THE PERPETUAL CALENDAR FOR THE MOVABLE FEASTS OF THE CHURCH

showing the rack to be fitted inside the annual Calendar wheel

Plate 60

B. THE RECONSTRUCTED PERPETUAL CALENDAR

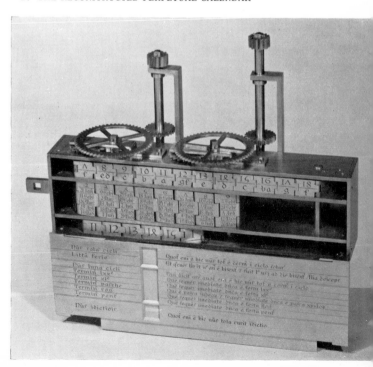

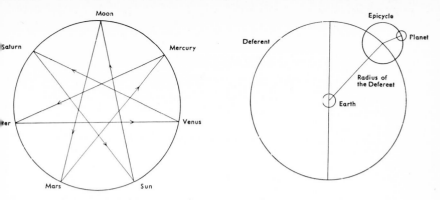

Diagram showing the derivation of the names of the days of the week

The first concept of planetary motion

Plate 61

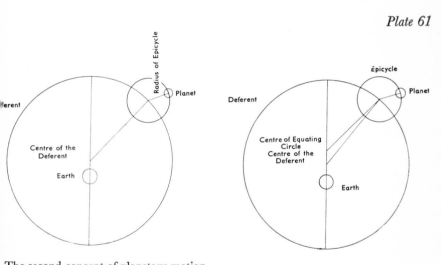

The second concept of planetary motion

The third concept of planetary motion

B. THE RECONSTRUCTED DIAL of the *Primum Mobile*

Plate 62

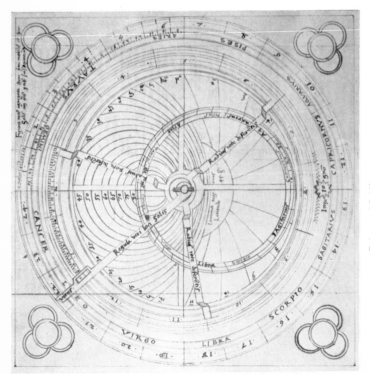

A. THE DIAL OF THE *Primum Mobile*
sideral time

C. THE RECONSTRUCTION

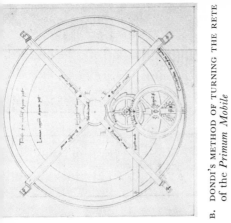

B. DONDI'S METHOD OF TURNING THE RETE
of the *Primum Mobile*

Plate 63

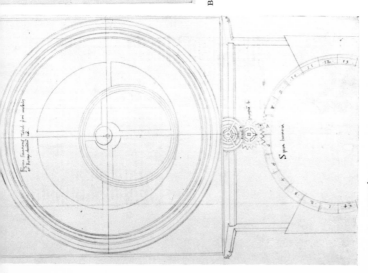

A. DONDI'S METHOD OF CONVERSION
from mean to sideral time (for
reconstruction see *Plate 58B*)

Plate 64

B. THE RECONSTRUCTION

Note the small window in which appears the Saints' day of the year

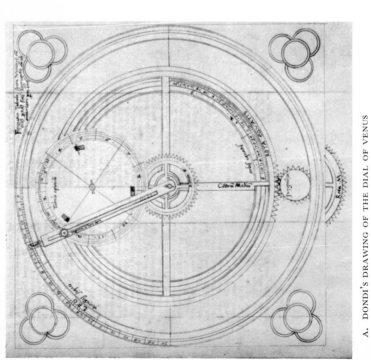

A. DONDÌ'S DRAWING OF THE DIAL OF VENUS

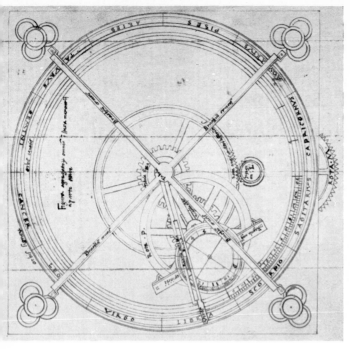

B. DONDI'S DRAWING OF THE DIAL OF MERCURY

Plate 65

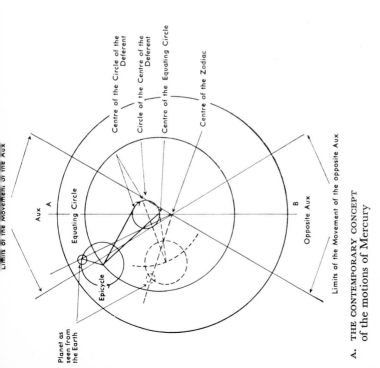

A. THE CONTEMPORARY CONCEPT
of the motions of Mercury

A. RECONSTRUCTION OF
THE DIAL OF
MERCURY
below, the Perpetual
Calendar for Easter
in position

[The next clock with a
perpetual calendar for
Easter was the third
Strasburg clock by
Schwilqué in 1842]

Plate 66

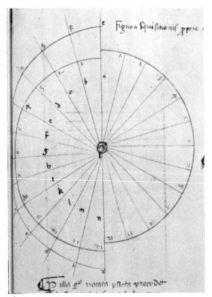

B. DONDI'S DIAGRAM FOR MAKING
THE OVAL WHEELS
to achieve the believed motion
of Mercury

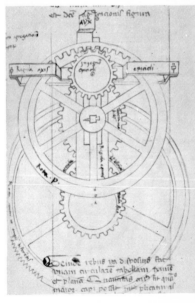

C. UNDER DIAL WORK FOR MERCURY
Note the wheel with internally
cut teeth, this may well be a
first application

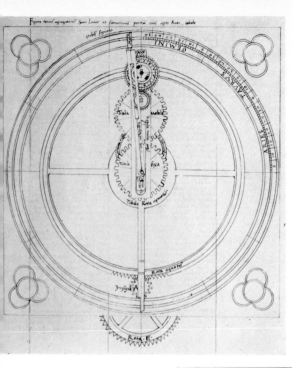

A. DONDI'S DRAWING OF
   THE LUNAR DIAL
   Note the upper oval
   wheel with an unequal
   number of teeth in
   equally sized sectors

Plate 67

B. THE RECONSTRUCTED
   LUNAR DIAL

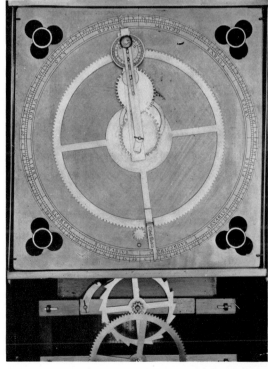

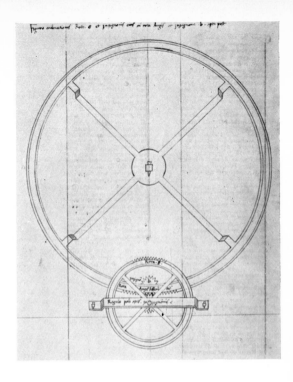

A. BEHIND THE DIAL WORK FOR THE MOON

Plate 68

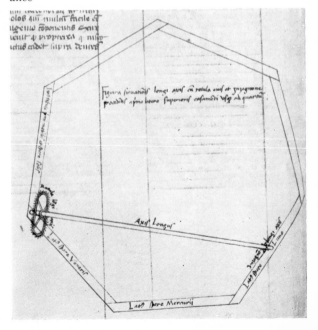

B. DONDI'S SKETCH OF THE DRIVE FOR THE MOON
off the *Primum Mobile*. On a seven-sided frame this involves a skew gear, again possibly a first appearance

Plate 69

THE RECONSTRUCTION OF THE SKEW GEAR DRIVE
and interior view of the clock, with dials of Jupiter and
Saturn removed

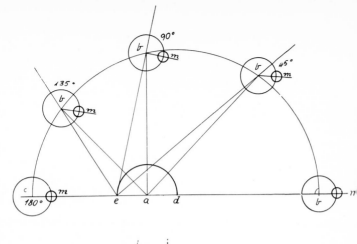

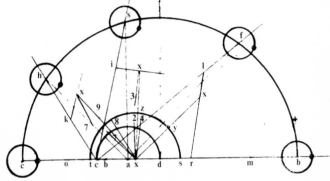

Plate 70

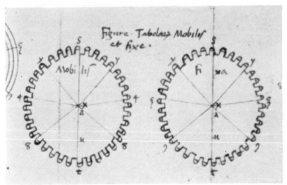

A. DIAGRAM TO SHOW THE MOON'S PROGRESSION
   through equal angles in equal periods of time over unequal arcs

[The next clock to provide for the Moon's eliptical orbit was made by Thomas Mudge nearly 400 years later *c.* 1755–60]

B. DIAGRAM FOR THE OVAL WHEELS
   needed for the lunar dial (*modern lettering added*)

C. THE WHEELS
   resulting from the reconstruction of 70B

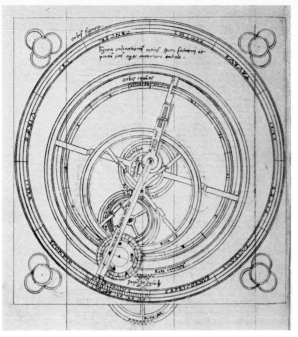

Plate 71

A. DONDI'S DRAWING OF THE DIAL OF SATURN

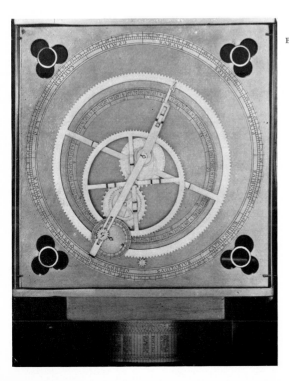

B. THE RECONSTRUCTED
DIAL OF SATURN

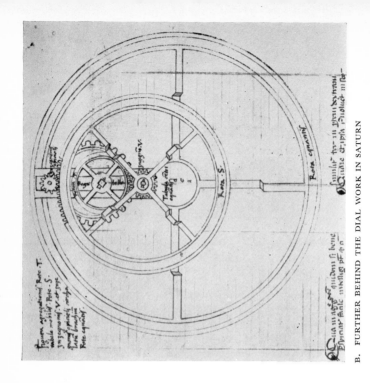

B. FURTHER BEHIND THE DIAL WORK IN SATURN

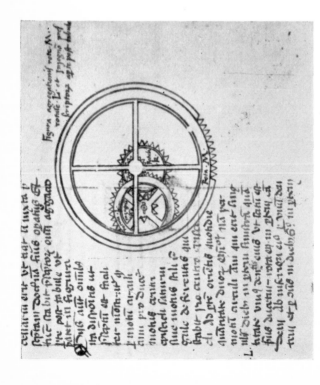

Plate 72

A. BEHIND THE DIAL WORK IN SATURN
to attain the long period of revolution

B. THE RECONSTRUCTED DIAL OF JUPITER

Plate 73

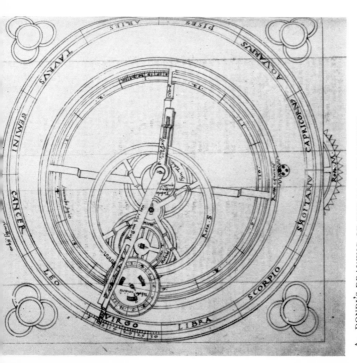

A. DONDI'S DRAWING OF THE DIAL OF JUPITER
This is driven by the only stub pinion in the clock

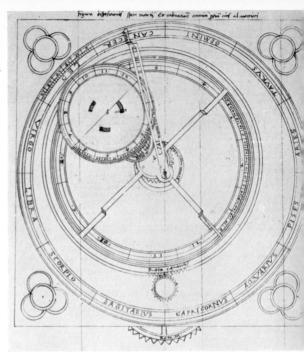

A. DONDI'S DRAWING OF THE DIAL OF MARS

Plate 74

B. THE RECONSTRUCTED DIAL OF MARS

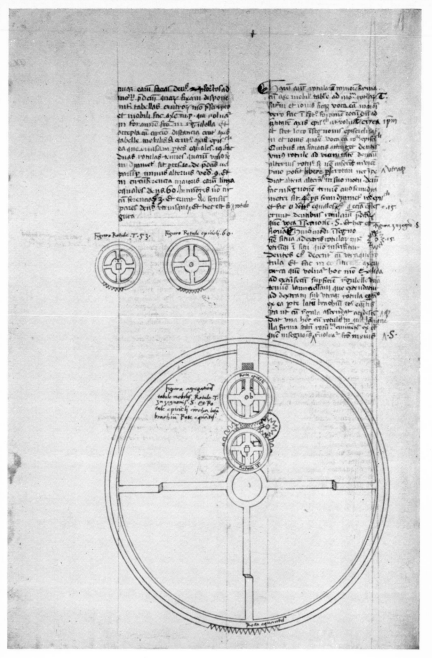

Plate 75

UNDER DIAL WORK FOR MARS

This also serves to show how appearance of the actual MS. taken from the
Bodleian copy (reduced by half)

B. THE RECONSTRUCTED NODAL DIAL, which is driven off the Lunar dial

Plate 76

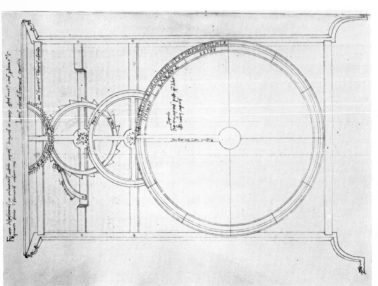

A. DONDI'S DRAWING FOR THE NODES
Period of revolution of the hand approximately 28 years

Plate 77

PROSPECTUS INTRA CAMERAM STELLATAM

The Octagon Room at Greenwich *c.* 1680 in Flamsteed's time,
showing the two 'Great Clocks' and a long telescope in use

APPENDIX II

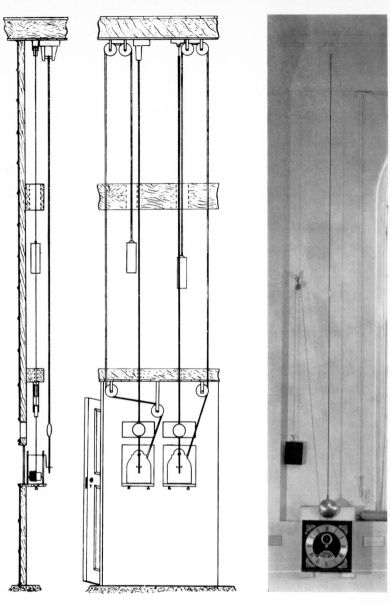

A. Possible lay-out of the two clocks presented by Sir Jonas Moore with their 14ft pendulums suspended above the movements and the pendulum bobs showing through the small windows

B. The reproduction clock with pendulum suspended above, in a temporary position at Greenwich

Plate 78

A. The reproduction of Tompion's original clock now in the British Museum

B. Connection between escapement and pendulum in the reproduction clock

C. One of Tompion's original clocks now in the British Museum

Plate 79

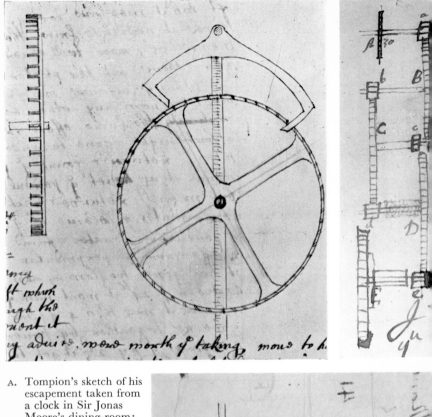

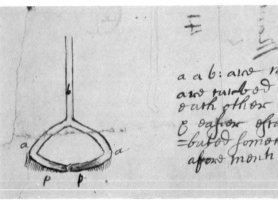

A. Tompion's sketch of his escapement taken from a clock in Sir Jonas Moore's dining-room; a semi dead-beat. From Flamsteed's letter of Dec. 11, 1675 to Richard Towneley

B. Flamsteed's description of the trains of Flamsteed's Greenwich Clocks given to Towneley in a letter Feb. 15, 1678

C. Tompion's pin pallet escapement described in his letter to Towneley, Feb. 9, 1678

Plate 80

Giovanni de Dondi's Horological Masterpiece 1364

This Appendix is based on a description of the Dondi Clock written by the Author which appeared in the *Suisse Horlogère* in July 1955. The line drawings are from the copy of the MS in the Bodleian Library, Oxford, Laud MS 620.

THE DOCUMENT that we are about to consider is probably the most important that is ever likely to be found in connexion with the early history and development of mechanical clocks. It is just about six hundred years old and details, to the minutest degree, the construction of an astronomical clock, the like of which had probably never before been attempted, and which was many centuries before its time. It adds very appreciably to our knowledge of the state of horological understanding at that time. In the first place it portrays the earliest construction of a mechanical clock that has come down to us; for this reason alone it is worthy of record; and indeed has been so recorded by Drummond Robertson and Baillie.[1]

That this was regarded as an exceptional document is shown by the fact that the original MS, or the earliest surviving copy, if it be not the original, that which is preserved in the library of St. Mark's, Venice, and is ascribed to the fourteenth century, has been copied at least five times within the next two centuries. There are two copies in the Ambrosia library, Milan, one in the library in Padua, one in Eton College library and one in the Bodleian. Thorndike[2] states that the two copies in Milan belonged to V. Pinelli (1531–1601). One is in a gothic fourteenth-century hand the other, not so good or nearly complete, is a fifteenth-century MS. The Eton College copy states that it was copied from one dated 1397. The Bodleian copy was done by two people, the text by John of Leyd (?Leyden) and the titling of the chapters, the diagrams and their explanatory notes by Jacomo

---

[1] *The Evolution of Clockwork*, Robertson, 1931. *Clocks and Watches*, Baillie, 1951.
[2] Lynn Thorndike in *Archeion*, 1936, pp. 308–19. *Isis*, Vol. 10, 1928. *History of Magic*, Vol. III, p. 740.

Politus, who describes the termination of his labours very exactly as on the 8th day of November 1461 at the 4th hour, which we must remember would be, in Italy, the fourth hour after sunset. Another MS, probably also a copy, is in Cracow University, 577 (DO. III. 28); it is of sixteenth-century date and is entitled 'Johannes de Dondi, Fabrica horarii magistralis'.

The clock itself was the subject of a description by Philip de Mézières in his 'Le Songe du vieux Pèlerin', c. 1389, and also by Giovanni Manzini, Podestà of Pisa, in 1405. These two records show that the clock actually existed, and was not merely a design.

Coming to later years, the Bibliographie Universelle, published in Paris in 1814 (Vol. II), contains a short article on the work of Giovanni de Dondi and his father, Jacopo. In 1896, the Royal Institute of Venice for Science, Letters and Art, published an article by Andreas Gloria, running into 61 pages, on the 'Two marvellous clocks invented by Jacopo and Giovanni Dondi.'[1] The Biographie Universelle says that the son wrote a description of the father's clock, which led to his being identified with the work; but the MS is, in the writer's opinion, certainly the work of the actual maker of the clock.

According to Thorndike, Jacopo, the father, was born in Padua in 1293, and was appointed municipal physician of Chioggia in 1313. He was recalled to Padua in 1342, and made a clock which was placed in the Carrace Tower in 1344. This earned for him the title of 'Dell'Orologio', which his son and later descendants inherited. The son, Giovanni, has usually been credited as being the first recipient of the title. This clock was probably just a simple mechanical clock, which at that time was in itself considered an achievement, especially if it embodied a simple lunar dial. Gloria illustrates the memorial tablet to Jacopo in the Baptistry of the cathedral at Chioggia, in which his achievements are catalogued. This uses the words 'horas inventum', which, he assumes, indicate something more than a simple clock. In any event, we see that the son had some introduction to horology through the efforts of the father, who is also reputed to have computed some astronomical trains.

The inscription, which is in medieval ecclesiastical Latin, has been translated as follows: 'I Jacobus was born in Padua and having crept back to earth whence I came, this confined urn conceals my cold ashes. My work was useful enough to my country and known to many a city. My art was medicine, and to know the sky and the stars, whither I now proceed, released from the prison of my body. And

[1] *Atti del Real Istituto Venito di Scienze, Lettere, Arti*, Series 7, Vol. 7, 1896, pp. 675–736.

truly each art remains, adorned with my books. Yet indeed, dear Reader, know it is my invention that, from afar, shows at the top of the lofty tower the time and the changing hours that you count. And pray in silence for my peace and pardon.'[1]

Since a clock striking the hours is mentioned as being in the church of Beata Virgina in Milan in 1335[2] it is more probable that this reference is to a clock dial, the date of the invention of which has never been established.

Sarton[3] states that Giovanni was born in 1318; in 1349 he was appointed personal physician to the Emperor Charles IV (1347–78). In 1350 he was lecturing in astronomy at Padua; in 1367–70 he was lecturing in medicine at Florence, and from 1379–88 he was again connected with the University at Padua. He died at Genoa in 1389.

All these references deal either with the lives of the father and son biographically, or with the MS as a MS; none of them attempts to treat it from the horological point of view. This was first done by the late G. H. Baillie. From the Venice MS he had made a translation, which has generously been put at my disposal by its present owner, Mr. Charles Drover; but although, as is clear from the very able way in which the translation is edited, Baillie evidently studied the whole matter very carefully, he never published any full description, a brief report in the *Horological Journal* for 1934 being his only record. This description has been left, after all these centuries, for the present author to do, working from the translation above referred to for the text and for the illustrations from the Bodleian copy, which are much clearer, and better for reproduction. The two correspond very well, both contain the same number of chapters, but their headings do not always occur in the same places.

The drawings and diagrams are faithfully reproduced, even to errors noted by Baillie.

In the present description an attempt will be made to record all the various dials in order that a due appreciation may be shown of the immensity of the genius of this fourteenth-century savant, and the extremely complicated trains he devised in order to portray accurately, not only the exact motions of the then-known planets, but also for the layman and cleric, all the feasts of the Church, both fixed and movable. Nothing comparable in complexity is known to the writer until we come to the mid-sixteenth century, when a somewhat similar clock was made by Baldewin, in Kassel, from thence to Samuel Watson's clock of 1690. In 1769, David A. Cajetano of

[1] *Mechanical Universe*, Bedini and Maddison. Am. Philosophical Soc. Phila., Oct. 1966, p. 18.
[2] Britten, 7th ed. p. 6.
[3] *Introduction to the History of Science*, Baltimore, 1948.

Vienna made a clock incorporating differential gearing. There is also at this period the work of Aureliano, whose masterpiece is in the National Museum, Munich, and that of Father Philip Matthaeus Hahn, *c.* 1780, in Vienna. All these are some 200 to 400 years later than Dondi, during which time the sciences of horology and astronomy had made vast strides.

While giving details of the train of the timepiece portion of his clock, Dondi gives no details as to how this should be fixed within the framework of the clock. The clock has the usual revolving 24-hour dial of the period, registering before a fixed pointer; this he states is an ordinary common clock, of which several varieties are known. Its function is confined to the demarcation of the 24 hours of the day through the regular revolution of its wheels. He adds that if the student is not capable of devising for himself the general layout of this part, he had better not attempt to make the parts that follow.

This raises the point, how long must mechanical clocks have been in general use, in this part of Italy at any rate, for them to need no description as to how they should be made? For the planetary dials Dondi gives the most detailed instructions how to make the most simple parts, such as cocks and bridges, just where to drill holes for bearings, the thickness of the sheets to be employed, the length of studs, etc. The standards of measurement taken by Dondi are interesting: a thumb's breadth, two fingers' thickness, the size of a goose quill, as big as a cock's quill, a knife's or half a knife's thickness, etc. Another interesting point is that iron is never mentioned. Terms translated as bronze, brass and copper are occasionally used for the materials for the framework and dials, but no mention is ever made of the material employed in the trains. Philip de Mézières, who was Chancellor to the King of Cyprus, says that the clock was made entirely of brass and copper, and that its construction took Dondi sixteen years.

But to revert to the query concerning the earliest mechanical clocks. We must remember that about this time, 1350, the first of the famous series of clocks in Strasbourg cathedral was being constructed. Little is known as to the details of this; according to Ungerer[1] it probably contained an annual calendar dial, an astrolabe, and possibly a lunar dial. The upper portions would be occupied with figures moving at the hours or their subdivisions, doing obeisance to the Virgin and the infant Christ, etc. The whole was surmounted by a cock which, at the hours of mid-day and midnight crowed and flapped its wings, in commemoration of St. Peter's denial of Our Lord. This was a monumental clock, many feet high

[1] *Les horloges astronomiques et monumentales etc.* Strasbourg, 1931.

and was the much cruder blacksmith's work when compared with Dondi's, which was more of the nature of work by a locksmith, goldsmith, or precision instrument maker. The Strasbourg clock would, no doubt, make a greater impression on the devout and credulous, with its moving and bowing figures, than would Dondi's, with the movements of its dials imperceptible to the eye.

Here then we have in Italy and in South Germany, in the middle of the fourteenth century two clocks of great complexity, in which a 24-hour timepiece is incorporated as a prime mover.

THE FRAMEWORK OF DONDI'S CLOCK

This consists of a heptagonal frame in two parts, *Plate 56,* the lower, which should not be less than about two feet high, contained the clock dial proper, the annual calendar dial showing the fixed feasts, the dial giving the dates of Easter and the movable feasts dependent upon it, and the dial of the Nodes. The other three frames in this part were presumably blank. In the upper frames, which were about one foot square, were the dials of the *Primum Mobile*, Venus, Mercury, the Moon, Saturn, Jupiter and Mars.

MEAN TIME MOVEMENT AND 24-HOUR DIAL (PLATE 57)

Dondi details his train, 144 teeth on the revolving hour circle, meshing with a pinion of 12, which carries a wheel of 20 meshing with a wheel of 24 fitted to the winding drum. Thus for every revolution of the dial in 24 hours, the winding drum revolves 10 times. This drum carries the great wheel of 120 teeth, meshing with a pinion of 12, which in turn carries the second wheel of 80 teeth. This second wheel therefore revolves 100 times a day. It meshes with a pinion of 10 carrying the escape wheel of 27 teeth. This latter, therefore, makes 800 revolutions a day. Each revolution of the escape wheel calls for 54 oscillations of the balance wheel, giving a total of 43,200 oscillations a day, or 1,800 per hour. That is a 2-second beat. This Dondi describes as the usual rate of beat in his day. The pinion of 12 meshing with the hour circle was made to slide out, so that adjustments could be made easily as and when required. It should be remembered that the Italian hours were calculated 1–24, starting at sunset, which would mean daily adjustment. Dondi remarks later in the manuscript that it is more convenient to use the clock in the astronomical method, starting the day at midday.

It will be noticed that there is a balance wheel and not a foliot with adjustable weights. Regulation was by means of adjusting the driving weight if the clock were slow, but, as will be seen later, if the clock were fast, small weights were to be fixed to the balance.

We have then, here, a common clock, 'of which there exist many varieties', with a 2-second beat which is the 'usual rate'. How many years would it have taken with the comparatively slow spread of knowledge of those days, combined with the small number of horological craftsmen and their known secrecy, for such knowledge to be considered 'general' and not worthy of detailed description? The writer suggests that Alfonso X, the Learned, who died in 1284, would certainly have known of a weight-driven clock had it existed; so that a date around 1290–1300 is not an unreasonable guess as that of the first mechanical clock.

As we have seen, of the material used in the construction little is said, but iron is not mentioned at all. Words translated: brass, bronze and copper are used very occasionally. We can assume that, in the main, the clock was made of brass for the trains and dials and bronze for the frame, although in one case a dial is referred to as being made of bronze sheet and in another as of copper. There is nothing to guide us as to whether the standard practice of brass wheels and iron pinions had been adopted at this date. The process of annealing is also mentioned. These details may, therefore, possibly modify the view, very generally held, that all the earliest mechanical domestic clocks were made of iron. The writer is tending to the view that brass was, possibly, more usual in Italy and that iron was more generally applied in that other cradle of horology, South Germany.

It is also to be noted that although Dondi sketches all his pinions showing the number of their leaves, not once is a lantern pinion shown, and only once a 4-studded pinion in the drive of the dial of Jupiter, *Plate 73*.

We can now pass to the indications given in the other panels of the lower framework.

The first of these is, naturally, the 24-hour dial with which we have already dealt. On each side of this were set the scales by which the rising and setting of the sun could be determined for every day of the year, *Plate 58*. Dondi gives very lengthy details for the construction of these scales. The figures indicate the hours starting in each case at the dividing line on the left, as the dial rotates anti-clockwise.

If the clock is set at sunset, so that the line between 24 and 1 is just registering with the date, then (*a*) treating the date as the fixed pointer, the clock will continue to indicate hours since sunset; and (*b*) treating the meridian mark as the fixed pointer, it will indicate hours since noon. In either case, when the division between 24 and

1 reaches the same date over on the right, it will be sunrise, and similarly for sunset on the scale on the left.

In considering this clock throughout it must also be remembered that it is constructed for the latitude of Padua, 45° N, where the length of the day at summer solstice is 15 hrs. 33 mins., while here in England we are used to considering clocks made for London, 51½° N., with the length of the day at summer solstice 16 hrs. 45 mins. At the time this clock was made the dates of the solstices were June 13th and December 13th; by 1582 when the Gregorian calendar was introduced, a further two days had been lost, making the solstices June 11th and December 11th.

THE ANNUAL CALENDAR DIAL WITH THE FIXED FESTIVALS

Dondi's next care is the annual wheel, which is to show the fixed feasts of the year and to drive the various planetary dials. He makes a large and broad band wheel of as large a diameter as will be accommodated within the framework. Midway in depth inside the band is a stiffening circle with six radial arms terminating in a central plate carrying a vertical upward-pointing arbor. The wheel is supported by brackets fixed to the uprights of the frame and the upper pivot for the arbor revolves in a central plate carried by radial arms fixed to the seven corners of the base of the upper framework. The supporting brackets are so fixed that the teeth of the wheel are level with the top of the lower part of the framework.

Its broad and now vertical flange is divided into the 365 days of the year, *Plate 59*. To get his 365 divisions, Dondi divides the circumference first into six parts one of which he subdivides into three, and this 1/18th part he subdivides again by four, giving a 1/72nd part. He then takes the remaining 71/72nds and divides this similarly into 72 parts. He thus gets 73 virtually equal parts, which he again subdivides by five, giving him his necessary 365 divisions.

On the upper edge of this wheel are then cut 365 teeth to correspond with the days of the year. On the vertical surface of the wheel are inscribed, first the length of each day of the year in hours and minutes, next the dominical letter, then the name of the Saint commemorated on that day, and finally the date of the month, the actual name of the month not appearing. In the diagram the band starts at January 1st, the Feast of the Circumcision, dominical letter *a*, length of daylight 8 hrs. 42 mins. in Padua.

The frame of this dial is covered with a plate in which is cut a slot just wide enough for a single day to appear, *Plate 64b*. The alternate months were to have been gilded and silvered, with the engraved letters and numbers alternately in red and blue enamel.

He communicates motion to the annual calendar wheel from the time train in the following way: A pinion of 10 has its bearing in the inner side of the upper bearer of the lower No. 1 frame, i.e., that carrying the 24-hour dial, and at such a distance that it can mesh with the 365 teeth of the annual calendar wheel. This pinion has to be capable of easy removal so as to allow for any adjustment of the annual calendar dial. This pinion is then affixed behind the large wheel having 60 saw-like teeth and which is let into the thickness of the cross bearer of the frame. This wheel in turn is engaged by 6 studs set in the rear of the 24-hour dial wheel. These 6 studs will therefore turn the large wheel 1/10th of a turn a day, which is one tooth of the pinion of 10, which will turn the annual wheel 1 tooth or 1 day. When not actually in engagement with the studs, the large wheel is steadied by a detent, *Plate 59c*.

Dondi points out that if the whole of the seven dials for the planetary motions he is considering, as well as the annual dials for the fixed and movable feasts, are to be driven from the annual calendar wheel via the 6 studs mentioned, there will be a heavy strain on the train during the night, when the studs are in engagement, consequently the clock will go slower at night than by day. To overcome this he adopts the following measures. An auxiliary weight, seen end-on in *Plate 69* has a click bearing into the teeth of the annual calendar wheel and is just insufficient to turn the wheel when it is loaded with all the dials. When the pins behind the meantime dial, *Plate, 59c* come into action and begin to take up the drive of the annual calendar wheel, they have practically no work to do as the necessary power has been provided by the auxiliary weight.

CALENDAR OF THE MOVABLE FEASTS

In the third section of the lower frame was shown the table of the movable feasts, and this is a most ingenious conception. From the dominical letter can be ascertained on which day of the week any particular calendar date will fall. January 1st is *a*, and the next succeeding six letters, *b–g*, are used for the dates, January 2nd to January 7th, the dominical letter being that in the sequence on which the first Sunday in January falls. The days of the month fall on the same sequence of days of the week once every solar cycle of 28 years. The same dominical letter is kept throughout the year, except in leap years, when the first preceding letter is taken up to leap year day and the next preceding letter for the rest of the year. Incidentally Dondi gives February 24th, the feast of St. Matthew, as leap year day. As will be seen later, Dondi intended to stop the clock for a day on February 24th in leap year.

February 24th was the sext of March in the Roman Calendar and its repetition gave rise to the term bis-sextile year.

The cycle starts with the dominical letter f (i.e., a year in which January 6th is the first Sunday of the year) and the letters are taken in the reverse order, thus the letter for the second year of the cycle is e, that of the third year d, and that of the fourth up to leap year day c, and b for the rest of the year. The 28th year of the cycle, also a leap year, will then end with the two letters a and g, leaving the cycle to recommence with the letter f.

Of the five movable feasts, two, Septuagesima and Quinquagesima, are seven and five Sundays before Easter, and Rogation and Whitsun five and seven Sundays after. Once therefore Easter Day is fixed, these other feasts all hold fixed positions in relation to it. In order to find Easter it is necessary to know the dominical letter.

Dondi takes Easter as the first Sunday after the 14th day of the 1st lunation, i.e., the 1st full moon, after March 7th. The beginning of the critical lunation varies each year, but the Greek astronomer, Meton, discovered that the days of full moon fall on the same days of the month every 19 years. This is called the lunar cycle. The Greeks considered this discovery so wonderful, that they caused it to be carved in stone in letters of gold, hence the numbers of this cycle, 1–19, are known as the Golden Number. In the first year of this cycle the new Paschal moon was, in Dondi's day, on March 23rd, resulting in Easter Sunday being in April 5th, and in the 19th, or last year of the cycle, on April 17th. *Plate 60* shows how Dondi met this problem.

He makes a series of hinged linked chains; the top one has 28 links, marked on top with the 28 years of the solar cycle, and below the corresponding dominical letter, with two letters every fourth, or leap year. The central and broad chain has 19 links, corresponding to the lunar cycle, each link being engraved with the dates of the five movable feasts, that of Easter being in the middle. The bottom chain has 15 links, and deals with the period of the Indiction which will be discussed later.

Each chain runs in a separate compartment of the box enclosing the whole on three sides, and there are two separate drives. That on the left drives the chains of the solar and lunar cycles and that on the right, the chain for the Indiction.

The two wheels with 20 teeth placed on the outer surface of the box carry on their arbors pentagon pinions, each side of which corresponds to the length of one link of the chains. These wheels of 20 mesh with pinions of 10, which carry the larger wheels of 60 teeth. These, in turn, mesh with pinions of 24, which carry vertical arbors supporting wheels having 12 saw-like teeth.

Thus for every turn of the saw-tooth wheels the large wheel is turned 24 teeth, i.e. 2/5ths of a turn. This causes the pinion of 10 to turn through 4 teeth, turning the wheel of 20 through 4 teeth correspondingly, or 1/5th of a turn. Thus the pentagon pinion will make a 1/5th turn, advancing the chains one link.

The Indiction is a period used in Roman law and was frequently applied to leases and other contracts, but it started on September 1st not on January 1st. Dondi had, therefore, to provide for the annual changes of his chains at different times. In order to do this he does not gear his chain drives direct into the teeth of the annual calendar wheel, but he affixes to the inner surfaces of this two rake-like shoulders, each having 12 teeth, and so places them that they finish their engagement with the saw-tooth wheel on January 1st and September 1st, respectively. One of these racks can be seen on the inside of the annual calendar wheel (*Plate 59b*).

Before considering the remainder of the dials, it will be as well to recall the state of astronomical knowledge at that time. Also to be considered is astrology, since it had played an important part in the lives of all men from time immemorial. How often do we not find it recorded in the Bible that the King sent for his astrologers, magicians and soothsayers? This belief in the influence of the planets on the daily, or even hourly, progress of one's life was still commonplace until about the end of the seventeenth century; after which the science of astronomy began to replace that of astrology in the daily life of the people. We owe, however, the names of our days of the week to the astrological superstitions of our ancestors. They believed that every hour of the day was influenced in turn by the planets, in succession, in their order of distance from the earth. Thus, if we take 1 a.m. Monday as our start, we have 24 hours to be divided by the seven planets, which gives each planet its influence three times during the day, with three hours over. *Plate 61a* will show that this leads to Mars being the planet to influence the first hour of the next day, Tuesday, in French mardi, then Mercury, Wednesday (mercredi), and so on throughout the week.

The serious attention paid in those days to astrology is illustrated by a remark Dondi makes. He says that there are very few people who are capable of understanding astronomy or the reading of his clock. He ascribes the capacity of the few to the fact that they were born when the stars were propitious.

Dondi summarises the knowledge of those he calls the ancients substantially as follows:

In their observations they had noted that besides the fixed stars there were seven stars that wandered, i.e., the planets, which in those days included the sun and the moon. The fixed stars were only fixed in their relative positions, while they continued in an unceasing motion in one direction in what they termed the firmament. They noticed that the sun and moon followed this same motion; they therefore attributed the same motion to the other five planets.

However certain differences were observed between the apparent motions of the fixed stars and those of the planets; the ancients therefore thought that beyond the firmament and all the stars there was another sphere, which they called the *Primum Mobile* because it was a law unto itself. This sphere, having the swiftest motion of all, carried round all orbs and spheres and stars and influenced them. Another name for this was simple or rational motion, since it was uniform in time; it was also sometimes called the diurnal motion, because its movements were repeated every 24 hours.

Two immovable points were accepted, about which the sphere of the *Primum Mobile* turned, and which they called the poles of the world, one in the north, which they called arctic after Arctus, or Ursa, which is near it, and the other in the south, antarctic, because it was diametrically opposed to the arctic.

The measure of motion of the planets was taken along an imaginary circle midway between these points the equator, it being the more pronounced in this plane. They noted that the seven planets made the whole passage of the firmament in unequal periods of time and with motions proper to themselves. Therefore, other spheres than those of the *Primum Mobile* and the firmament of the fixed stars had to be taken into account.

It was considered that these planets had their motions about other poles, since their distances from the poles and the equator varied. It was also observed that the planets never proceeded outside a band of a certain depth in the heavens. They therefore imagined a band of this breadth, the 'Zodiac' on the surface of the *Primum Mobile*, and crossing the circle of the equator at two opposing points, one passing from the north and the other from the south at an angle of about 24° in relation to the equator. They also discovered a proper motion to the firmament and the fixed stars (this was the precession of the equinoxes; Dondi states that as this motion is so slow, he ignores it in his clock. It amounts to about 1° in 100 years). They noticed that this motion rotated in the inverse direction to that of the *Primum Mobile*; they consequently called it the eighth sphere. It was the orderly and harmonious movements of these spheres that later gave rise to the expression 'the music of the spheres'.

It was noted that none of the planets preserved a fixed rule in its course, but each traversed unequal distances of the zodiac in equal spaces of time, and that their distances in the firmament and from the earth varied. The five planets, other than the sun and moon, were observed to have not only irregular forward motions, but also at times to be stationary and even to have retrograde motions.

Having made these postulates, the astronomers of the day had to devise a means of the representation by circular motions, as such only were considered suitable for celestial bodies in those days. The variety of the motions of the stars led to the postulation of the plurality of the spheres and the irregularity of the planetary courses, the theory of epicycles[1] and of other eccentric circles. (*Plate 61b.*)

However, it was found that the motions of the planets did not conform exactly to the theory of perfectly circular motion, consequently the centre of the circle of the deferent was considered as a point outside the earth, *Plate 61c*. The irregularities of the eccentric motions were further corrected by equating circles. The centre of the epicycle was taken to revolve with a variable speed around the deferent circle, but with a constant speed, its *mean motus*, from the centre of the equating circle, that is to say it moved with constant angular velocity. *Plate 61d*.

This was the state of knowledge in Dondi's time, and it so remained until the coming of Copernicus, in the sixteenth century, who recognised the Sun as the centre of the universe, and so founded the heliocentric theories of today.

Dondi's lengthy exposition of the state of astronomical knowledge of his time, of which the foregoing is a very brief summary, concludes with the expression of his wish to make a work that should show the motions of the stars, as they have been taught by the authorities on the subject; so that at any time of the day, the correct position of any of the planets could be seen at a glance, just as if their positions at that moment had been worked out laboriously from tables. He also hoped to induce 'the vulgar' to have more respect for astronomy.

With this brief description of the state of the astronomical thought

---

[1] An epicycle is the circular motion of a planet, the centre of which circle travels round the earth in a circle the radius of which springs from the centre of the earth, and which circle is called the deferent.

of the time before us, we can better appreciate the construction of
the dials of the *Primum Mobile* and the several planets.

In the upper frame, above the 24-hour dial, was placed the dial of
the *Primum Mobile, Plate 62*. On the extreme outside we have the
sidereal 24-hour circle, superimposed upon the square basis plate
and divided into 10-minute intervals. Within this lies the circle of the
zodiac, marked off into the twelve signs, each subdivided into 30°.
Dondi divides the radius of this circle into 26 parts, and strikes a
centre 1/26th up from the centre of the zodiacal circle. This point
will be the centre of the deferent of the sun, which will be a circle of
radius from this point to the inner edge of the zodiacal circle. The
dial of the sun's deferent is the next circle, divided into twelve and
subdivided into 30 for each of the twelve divisions. This is carried
round by the three arms marked 'Radius rotae deferentis', its centre
being, as explained above, eccentric to the extent of 1/26th part of
the radius of the circle of the zodiac.

Fixed behind the dials is a four-armed bracket carrying the central
plate, which carries the arcs of circles called almucantars or parallels
of altitude in the upper half, and in the lower half the semi-circle is
divided into 15° of arc to represent, between 6 a.m. and 6 p.m.,
temporal or unequal hours used in monastic life; these are calculated for the latitude of Padua, i.e. 45° N.

The ring of the sun's deferent carrying with it the circle of the
ecliptic, is now free to revolve across the plate of the temporal hours,
as in the case of an astrolabe.

Dondi communicates the correct movement of the dial of the
Primum Mobile from the 24-hour dial in the following way. He takes
a wheel of the same diameter as the outer circle of the zodiac and in
it he cuts 365 teeth. Into this he gears a wheel of 61, *A* in *Plate 63c*,
meshing with a pinion of 24 *b*, *Plate 63a*, which communicates the
drive from the 24-hour ring of 144 teeth. Both *A* and *b* carry on their
arbors wheels of equal diameter, each of 60 teeth. Thus during the
24 hours the pinion *b* is turned 6 times and, through the two wheels
of 60, turns *A* 6 times or through 366 teeth of the hour wheel of the
sidereal hour dial. Thus this makes one revolution plus one tooth
each day, so that it will complete the 366 sidereal days during the
period of 365 mean days.

He recognised that the true ratio was $366\frac{1}{4}$ to $365\frac{1}{4}$, corresponding to a daily difference of $59'\,8''$ of arc, or 3 m. 56 secs. each
day. To correct this he stops the clock on leap year day.

Dondi's next care is to record the eccentric motion of the sun's deferent (what we should today call the eccentricity of the sun's apparent orbit). The outer edge of the ring of the sun's deferent is divided into 183 parts, first by dividing into 60, then dividing 59/60ths again into 60, thus obtaining 61 very nearly equal divisions These are again subdivided into 3, giving the 183 required. Into this wheel of 183 he meshes a pinion of 10, not seen in *Plate 63b*, which is on the same arbor as the wheel *E* of 20 teeth, *Plate 63b*. This meshes with a pinion of 15 *f*, *Plate 63b*, which carries the wheel *g*, of 60 teeth. This in turn meshes with a pinion of 8 which carries a wheel having 8 'humps'. As the wheel of the *Primum Mobile* revolves once a sidereal day, it carries this train with it so that the humps come into contact with the 4 studs on the bracket (in the sketch the diameter of the hump wheel is too small). Thus this wheel of 8 humps makes half a revolution a day, which equals 4 teeth of the pinion of 8, that is 4 teeth or 1/15th of the wheel *g*, equals 1 tooth of the pinion *f*, turning the wheel *E* 1 tooth, i.e., 1/20th turn, communicating 1/20th turn or $\frac{1}{2}$ tooth to the invisible pinion of 10, which is driving the dial of the sun's deferent. Thus the deferent dial advances 1 tooth every 2 days; 2×183 teeth equals the 366 days of the sidereal year. The hump wheel is provided with a detent to steady it when not in engagement, and the pinion of 10 can be slipped out, to allow for adjusting the dial.

The circle of the deferent carries a pin, not shown in *Plate 62a*, that engages in the slot in the arm marked 'Verus' which is twice the length of the eccentricity of the sun's deferent. This arm is keyed to the arbor of the centre dial, so that as the deferent dial makes its eccentric turn, the pin in the slot, which should carry the effigy of the sun, *Plate 62b*, will show the true position of the sun, hence the inscription 'Verus'. It was intended that the constellations of the zodiac should be gilded and silvered alternately, and the engraving thereon be filled with red and blue enamel, as before.

Next we have to consider the six planetary dials, that of the sun being incorporated in the dial of the *Primum Mobile*, as we have seen.

THE DIAL OF VENUS

For the Venus, *Plate 64a*, Dondi takes the *Aux*[1] as in the same position as that of the sun, in the beginning of Cancer, and the *motus* of the centre of her epicycle as exactly equal to that of the sun in its eccentric deferent, i.e., 59′ 8″ of arc a day; the argument of Venus i.e. its movement around the circumference of the epicycle, measured from the line of the *Aux*, he takes at 36′ 59″ of arc a

[1] The *Aux* is the point on the Zodiac struck by a line from the earth through the centre of the epicycle, when this latter is farthest from the earth.

day. He therefore arranges to show these motions. For this dial
the material used is translated as bronze.

The vertical radius of the zodiacal band is divided into 54 parts,
and the centre of the equating circle is 1/54th part above the centre
of the zodiac. Basing his calculations on Ptolemy, the centre of the
deferent is halfway between these two points, its radius being
30/54ths of the radius of the zodiac. From the point of intersection
of the vertical radius of the zodiac by the deferent circle, the
epicyclic circle is described with a radius of $21\frac{7}{12}$/54ths of the zodiacal
radius (we must remember that at this time the decimal notation for
fractions did not exist). The equating circle is divided into 12,
beginning at the *opposite Aux* and running anti-clockwise. These 12
are again divided into 30 to give the 360° of the equating circle.

The wheel at the bottom, *M*, has 60 teeth meshing into the 365
teeth of the annual calendar wheel and carries a pinion of 24 meshing with the 146 teeth of the equating wheel of Venus. Thus with a
daily motion of 1 tooth of the annual wheel, in 5 days it turns *M*
through 1/12th of a turn, i.e. 2 leaves of the pinion of 24, which
corresponds to 2 teeth of the equating wheel every 5 days or 1/73rd
of a mean year. Thus in 365 mean days the equating wheel turns
through 2 × 73, i.e 146 teeth, one complete revolution.

On the arbor of the equating circle is fixed the wheel *E* of 45 teeth.
Behind the dial of the epicycle is the wheel of the epicycle of 72
teeth. The teeth of wheel *E* should be unevenly cut to the maximum
extent that will allow them to mesh. The teeth should be wider (or
larger) on the side opposite to the *Aux* than on the side of the *Aux*.
This method can be used for Venus because the distance between
the centres of the equating circle and the deferent is small. Other
steps will be taken for the other planets.

During the 365 days forming one rotation of the equating wheel,
the wheel *E* of 45 teeth turns the wheel of the epicycle, not visible in
Plate 64, through 45 of its 72 teeth, i.e. 5/8ths of a turn of 360°, or 225°,
which is equivalent to $7\frac{1}{2}$ signs of the zodiac. By calculation Dondi
gives the actual motion of Venus as 36′ 59″ 32‴ daily for the 365
days of a non-leap year, to this he adds 9′ 15″ for the odd 6 hours,
calculating that his dial is out by about 11 minutes of arc a year.

THE DIAL OF MERCURY
For this dial, which, with that of the moon, is the most complicated, Dondi gives three motions; the first eastwards, equal to
that of the sun in its eccentric, viz. 59′ 8″ almost daily. This
motion is not uniform over the circle of the deferent or across the

zodiac, but is uniform around the equating circle, and a straight line running through the centre of the epicycle will describe equal angles at the centre of the equating circle in equal periods of time. The second is the motion of the centre of the deferent. With Venus the motion of the planet was depicted by its travel around its epicycle, of which the centre travelled around the deferent, as modified by the equating circle. The centre of the deferent was fixed at a point eccentric to the centre of the zodiac; but with Mercury the centre of the deferent is taken to be in motion, moving in a circle in the contrary sense to the epicycle, and having its centre at a point on the line to the *Aux* of the equating circle, at such a distance that the centre of the equating circle lies midway between it and the centre of the zodiac. The motion of the centre of the deferent is the same as that given above for the centre of the epicycle, 59′ 8″ almost, daily, but in the opposite, westerly, direction, as seen in *Plate 65a*. It will be clear then, that when the centre of the epicycle cuts the vertical line leading to the *Aux* of the zodiac, *AB*, the centre of the deferent cuts the same line at the same time, since they have equal but contrary motions.

The third motion is that of the planet's centre around the circle of the epicycle, 3° 6′ 24″ a day.

When the centre of the deferent cuts the line *AB* at its high point, the four centres will be in line; when at its low point, the centres of the deferent and equating circles will coincide and the two circles will be of equal area.

While the centre of the deferent makes a complete revolution of the small circle, neither its *Aux* nor its *opposite Aux* traverse the whole of the equating circle, but are confined within two diameters of the zodiac tangential to the small circle. Further, no one point remains the *Aux* or the *opposite Aux*, but each point successively occupies those positions, for every part of the deferent goes round the zodiac, but the *Aux* and *opposite Aux* are confined within the limits just given.

Further, while the centre of the epicycle goes round the equating circle and the band of the zodiac once a year, in the same period it goes twice round the deferent.

Having thus summarised Dondi's explanation of Mercury's movements, let us see how he proposes to put them into effect. At the time that the clock was made, the *Aux* of the equating circle on the zodiac was 29° 2′ 14″ of Libra, according to the Alfonsine tables; a line is therefore drawn from the centre of the zodiac circle to this point, *Plate 65b*. On this line lie the four centres, *Plate 65a*.

The radius of the zodiac is divided into 33 parts, the centre of the equating circle and the centre of the circle of the centre of the deferent being 1/33rd and 2/33rds distant from the centre of the zodiac, respectively. The radius of the deferent is 20/33rds measured from the centre of the circle of the centre of the deferent, *Plate 65a*. The radius of the epicycle is 7½/33rds, measured from the circumference of the deferent.

The first two motions of Mercury are produced in the following way. The wheel *M* of 60 teeth, *Plate 65b*. carries behind it a broad pinion of 24 which engages the equating wheel of 146 teeth placed behind the dial. Thus each 365 days *M* turns $6\frac{1}{12}$ times, the pinion of 24 equally so, thus advancing the equating wheel of 146 teeth, which carries the arm marked 'Verus', i.e. the true position of the planet in the zodiac, one whole revolution.

In a slot in the arm of the deferent, that seen in the centre of the V (*Plate 65b* and again in *Plate 66c*) slides a pin fixed behind at the centre of the dial of the epicycle.

The pinion of 24 on *M* which meshes with the equating wheel, is sufficiently wide to engage simultaneously a pinion of 24 on the far end of the arbor of the pinion *L*, also of 24, *Plate 65b*. This latter meshes with the deferent wheel, having equally 146 teeth. This wheel is, therefore, turned equally through one revolution in 365 days but in the opposite direction. These two motions are slightly fast, as the revolution is completed in 365 instead of $365\frac{1}{4}$ days, but Dondi states that it is his intention that the clock should be stopped on leap year days, so that this error will be corrected when the clock is restarted.

The third motion, that of the epicycle of Mercury, is more complicated and cannot be reproduced by pure circles. Its *motus* is eastwards, i.e. 3° 6′ 24″ daily, but as we have seen, the centre of the deferent of Mercury is not fixed, but moving in a circle in the contrary sense. What has to be depicted is two uniform contrary motions one to the left due to the equating wheel, and one to the right due to the rotation of the circle of the deferent. These two motions begin together from the diameter of the *Aux* of the equating wheel and at the same moment on that diameter.

To do this Dondi constructs elliptical wheels in a most original manner. He takes a line, the length of the diameter of the equating circle and marks its centre *b*, *Plate 66b*. Above this he strikes off, in its correct position, the centre of the circle of the centre of the deferent *c*, and describes a circle of radius *cb* which will represent the circle of the centre of the deferent. From *c* he describes a semicircle to the right, and divides this into 12 equal parts. He then describes an

s

equal semicircle on the left from *b*, equally divided into 12 parts, producing the dividing lines beyond the circumference. The divisions on the left are those that the arm of the equating circle should traverse in equal periods of time, and with it the centre of the epicycle, represented by the pin sliding in the groove in the arm of the deferent, because these divisions contain equal angles at the centre of the equating circle. The 12 divisions on the right are the 12 arcs of the circle of the centre of the deferent that will be described in equal periods of time. The centre of the deferent and that of the equating circle meet on the *Aux* diameter of the equating circle, move away in opposite directions at equal speeds, meeting again at the *opposite Aux* diameter of the equating circle.

From the top of the small circle is struck off a point *e* at a distance equal to the radius of the deferent. Taking each of the divisions on the circumference of the small circle on the right-hand side in turn as centre, equidistant points *f*, *g*, *h*, etc., are struck off on the left. This gives the path the centre of the epicycle will travel from its *Aux* to its *opposite Aux* and back again. The twelve lines on the left are then reduced by 2/5ths of the radius of the deferent, to the points *a–n*, bisected and joined up to give the contour of the wheel on that side; the other side being made symmetrical. Two wheels are cut, one to be fixed and the other revolving around it. Each wheel has 24 fixed blunt nosed teeth cut in it, *Plate 66c*. These teeth will be of unequal size, but since the two wheels are symmetrical, the two wheels will mesh harmoniously. In *Plate 66c* these two wheels do not appear to be symmetrical, but they are so in the working sketches.

The wheel of the epicycle has 63 teeth cut internally and is driven by a pinion of 20, *Plate 66c*. The motion of the epicycle to the left should amount to 3° 6′ 24″ daily or three times round the zodiac, or 36 constellations, plus 54° 43′ 23″ each solar year.

The movable of the two wheels will be carried round by the arm of the equating circle once a year, so that the internal-toothed wheel of 63 teeth fixed to it, will equally turn once a year. This will turn the pinion of 20 carrying the epicycle wheel three times and 3 teeth over. Three times equals 36 constellations; each tooth equals 1/20th of 360, i.e. 18°, giving a total of 36 constellations 54°, being 43′ 23″ of arc too slow in the year. In *Plate 66c* will be seen a wheel with internally cut teeth. We have no other contemporary clocks with which to make comparison, but in view of the imaginative nature and complexity of Dondi's clock the writer feels justified in claiming a first appearance of an internally cut wheel or at any rate the earliest known example.

DIAL OF THE MOON

The astronomers of Dondi's day attributed to the moon four motions. First a daily *motus* westwards of 13° 11' 39" by the centre of the epicycle along the circumference of its eccentric deferent. This movement was not uniform along this circumference or about its centre, but was uniform about the centre of the earth and the zodiacal belt. Second, the centre of the deferent was taken as moving about the centre of the zodiac in a circle of radius of the distance between these two centres. Third, was the argument of the moon around the circumference of the epicycle of 13° 3' 54" daily in a contrary direction to that of the other planets. Fourth, the motion of the intersection of the two deferents of the sun and moon, known as the dragon's head and tail (the Nodes), of 3' 11" westwards daily.

The eccentricity of the centre of the moon's deferent, which is itself describing a circle, is $12\frac{1}{2}$/90ths of the radius of the zodiac. The radius of the deferent is 2/3rds of that radius and the radius of the epicycle of the moon $6\frac{1}{3}$/90ths.

The wheel of the equating circle, which is centred on the centre of the zodiac, has 164 teeth. To get this number of teeth Dondi divides by 11, then 3 and 5, getting 165ths. Then he divides the circumference plus 1/165th into 165, which gives him 164 virtually equal teeth, since one has been taken in twice over.

At the lowest point of the dial and on its face is fixed a pinion *A* of 12, meshing with the equating wheel of 164, *Plate 67a*. The arbor of the pinion *A* projects behind the dial and has squared on to it a pinion *b* of 16 affixed to the back of the dial and between it and the wheel of the *Aux* of the deferent of 257 teeth. A bridge, *Plate 68a* carries a wheel of 72 slightly oblique teeth, which is designed to revolve once in two days, having on its arbor a broad pinion *c* of 16 meshing simultaneously with *b* and the wheel of 257. The reason for the oblique teeth will be seen presently.

Thus when *E*, *Plate 67a*, makes half a turn, 36 teeth, to the East, or in the direction of the signs of the zodiac, the wheel of 257 moves westwards carrying with it the hub of the centre of the deferent. At the same time the wheel of the equating circle is moved eastwards 6 teeth, i.e., half a turn of pinion *A*, which is on the same arbor as pinion *b*.

In one day the wheel of 257 advances 8 teeth, therefore it makes a complete revolution in $32\frac{1}{8}$ days, or 32 days 3 hrs., in which time the hub of the centre of the zodiac will have moved through the 12 signs. The *motus* of the *Aux* of the moon is actually 11° 12' 18" daily, or in 32⅛ days 11 signs 29° 57' 15", or only 2' 45" short of 12 signs.

As we have just seen, each day the equating wheel moves 6 teeth in the direction of the signs. This wheel of 164 teeth will, therefore, make a complete turn less two teeth in 27 days. The two teeth of *A* equal 1/3rd of half a rotation of *E*, or 8 hrs. Thus the centre of the epicycle of the moon will perform the circuit of the band of the zodiac in that time. In 27 days 8 hrs. the moon actually passes through 12 signs 0° 9' 18".

The main drive for this lunar wheel is not off the annual calendar wheel, as in the case of Venus and Mercury, but off the wheel of the *Primum Mobile* which, it will be recollected, has 365 teeth and turns through 366 teeth in a day. A wheel of 61, *Plate 68b*, meshes with the 366 teeth of the *Primum Mobile* and is thus turned 6 times a day. A long arbor stretching across the framework carries a pinion of 6, its teeth being cut somewhat obliquely, and meshing with the wheel *E*, which it will be remembered, also had slightly oblique teeth, and turns the wheel *E* of 72 teeth, one revolution every two days. Since Dondi had to deal with a seven-sided frame he could not get a straight drive and had to cut a skew gear. On the same basis as that given for the internally cut wheel, a first appearance is claimed for the skew gear.

In connexion with the argument of the moon in its epicycle, Dondi makes the following remarks. Firstly the moon moves westwards in the upper part of its epicycle, while the other planets move eastwards. Their motion is equal about the centre of the equating circle, but that of the mean *Aux* of the moon is not measured in a line drawn from the centre of the epicycle to the centre of the equating circle, but from a line drawn from the centre of the epicycle, passing through the centre of the circle of the deferent and terminating on the far side of its circumference, *Plate 70a*.

With the other planets, the motion of the centre of the epicycle at times is less than that of the planet, so that the planet's motion becomes retrograde, but with the moon, the centre of the epicycle dominates, so that the moon always moves to the east, albeit with irregular speeds.

As we have seen, the centre of the deferent of the moon takes a circular course, as was the case with Mercury, *Plate 65a*, but the motion of the centre of the moon's deferent and that of its *Aux* are slower than the centre of the epicycle, consequently they never coincide in the same place or position in the band of the zodiac. To portray this requires a different treatment from that of Mercury.

The means taken by Dondi to reproduce this motion are very elaborate, in fact he says 'it is suited to the intellect of the few only'. *Plate 70a* shows briefly the motion Dondi wishes to reproduce; *d* is the centre of the zodiac and *a* the centre about which the arm of the deferent turns clockwise, *b* is the centre of the epicycle, *m* is the moon at its *Aux*, *be* therefore is the line about which the angle formed by the radius of the moon in its epicycle will increase uniformly by 13° 3′ 54″ daily. The motions about the centres *a* and *b* have already been provided for.

In *Plate 70a de* is the diameter of the hub of the centre of the deferent, *ab* is the arm of the deferent, when the centre of the epicycle is at its *Aux* and *ac* when it is at its *opposite Aux*; the semi-circle represents half the hub of the centre of the deferent. This is divided into four parts and since the arbor of the epicycle is driven round uniformly about the centre *d*, the four points shown will be reached in equal periods of time. The lines drawn from *e*, through the centre of the epicycle and cutting its circumference on its outer edge, are those against which the angle formed with the radius of the moon will uniformly increase.

The working-out of the profiles of the fixed and mobile wheels, with blunt-nosed teeth, is long and complex. The centre of the mobile wheel is taken at *m*, *Plate 70b*; 1/3rd of *bd* is struck off at an equal distance from the zodiac on each of the other lines at *l*, *i*, *k* and *o*. From these points lines are drawn at 45°, 90° and 135° respectively, and down these lines are struck off *lx*, *ix* and *kx* respectively, equal to *dx* on the base, *x* being the centre of the fixed wheel, which for the moment is assumed to be circular. The corresponding points from *m* and *o* will lie on the base line and are not separately indicated. The point *x* on the base line is joined to the *x*'s of *lx*, *ix* and *kx* and the distances between these points and *x* on the base is bisected, giving five points of contact for the two wheels. These are joined up. They do not form a true semicircle, but the junction of two arcs passing through *syz* and *zgt*, the centres of which are very near to the centre of the true circle. To find the half-periphery of the mobile wheel one proceeds in a similar way, working from the points *l*, *i* and *k*.

The movable wheel has to turn 45° through each of the irregular intervals on the deferent, and this is not consistent with a rolling action. To effect this an equal number (five) of unequally sized teeth are cut in each section of the wheels, as shown in *Plate 70c*. Thus when turning round the fixed wheel the moving wheel will turn through equal angles in relation to the line running from the centre of the epicycle to the point *e, Plate 70a,* in equal periods of time.

During the period of lunation, that is from conjunction to conjunction occupying 29d 12 h 44′ 3″ the moon travels through 12 signs 25° 48′ 59″, during which time the centre of the epicycle travels the whole of the deferent twice, once from the mean conjunction of the moon with the sun to its mean opposition and once from the mean opposition to the mean conjunction.

Thus, while the movable wheel is making two turns round the fixed, *Plate 67a,* it carries the wheel *c* of 45 teeth round with it twice. This gears into the wheel of the epicycle of 84 and therefore turns it twice plus 6 teeth or $2\frac{1}{14}$th turns, which is equivalent to 12 signs 25° 42′ 51″ 26‴, being slower than the theoretical given above by 6′ 8″, which may be corrected when it has accumulated.

DIAL OF SATURN

The planet Saturn has only two motions in longitude, one being the *motus* of the epicycle along the deferent and the other the argument of the planet along the circumference of the epicycle. The former, in the direction of the zodiac, is uniform about the equating circle which is eccentric to both the deferent and the zodiac; its eccentricity being double that of the deferent measured in a straight ine fro m the centre of the zodiac. The eccentricity of the equating circle is given as $6\frac{5}{6}$/80ths of the radius of the zodiac, and that of the deferent, half of that amount.

The second motion is eastward in the upper part of the epicycle and is uniform from its mean *Aux.*

In Saturn the first motion is 2′ 0″ 36‴ which, when subtracted from that of the sun, viz. 59′ 8″ 20‴, leaves 57′ 7″ 44‴. The line of the *Aux* of Saturn passes through the 12° of Sagittarius, and on this line lie also the centres of the deferent and equating circle.

The motion of the centre of the epicycle is governed by the annual calendar wheel through the wheel *M* with which it gears, as is the case with the other planets, except the moon. The wheel *M* of 60 teeth, *Plate 71a,* engages with the annual calendar wheel of 365 teeth, which is turned by it one tooth daily. Behind the dial on the arbor of *M* is a pinion of 6 *n, Plate 72a,* meshing with a wheel of 30, *L,* which will therefore make 1/5th of a turn i.e. 6 teeth in 60 days. *L* carries a pinion *g* of 10, which will therefore move the wheel *K* of 20, with which it meshes, 2 teeth or 1/10th of a turn. *K* carries on the front of the dial, *Plate 71a*, a pinion, *h*, of 10 which engages with the equating wheel of 180, which will, therefore, move 1 tooth or 2° in 60 days, or 2/60ths of 2°, i.e., 2′ daily, which is very close to the daily movement of the epicycle of Saturn.

The pin of the centre of the epicycle will travel upwards from *Aux* to *opposite Aux* and downwards from *opposite Aux* to *Aux*, because the centre of the equating circle is farther from the centre of the zodiac than the centre of the deferent.

The second motion, that of the planet in its epicycle, is faster than the first, being in a non-leap year 11 signs 17° 32′ 4″, this being the result of the subtraction of the planet's *motus* from that of the sun. Saturn, therefore, in a year goes round rather less than the whole epicycle by 12° 27′ 36″.

The first motion of Saturn, that is its mean *motus* for the passage of the whole ecliptic, is 29 years 5 months 4 days 8 hours nearly. During this period, while the centre of the epicycle is traversing the whole circumference of the deferent, the argument of Saturn, that is its motion in its epicycle, is 28 complete revolutions 5 signs 3° 3′ 24″.

In order to show this much accelerated motion, when compared with the first, Dondi proceeds as follows: he takes two equal-sized wheels of 30 teeth cut with blunt-nosed and spaced teeth as on the fixed and elliptical wheels of Mercury and the moon. One of these is fixed to the hub of the equating wheel and the movable one on to the cursor in one of the arms of the equating wheel; the diameter of the fixed wheel at right-angles to its two points of fixture being in line with the diameter of the moving wheel, both diameters being on the line to the *Aux*. All this train is placed on the front of the dial.

When the equating wheel is turned to the left, it will carry with it the movable wheel with blunt teeth around its fixed complement in a uniform motion about its arbor in relation to the centre of the equating circle. Since the equating circle has a uniform motion about its centre, the line just referred to will move through equal angles at that centre in equal periods of time. Similarly around the arbor in the centre of the movable wheel.

Then follows a somewhat complicated reasoning to demonstrate that the movement of the epicycle can be correctly derived from the movable wheel. The motion of the epicycle is as follows. As the movable blunt-toothed wheel turns, it carries wheel *T* of 60 teeth, *Plate 72b*, which is squared on to it. This turns the pinion *v* of 20 fixed to the arbor of the wheel *S* of 114 teeth, three times; which wheel now turns the pinion of 12 carrying the dial of the epicycle 28½ turns, or 28 revolutions 6 signs, which corresponds closely to the figure 28 revolutions 5 signs 3° 3′ 24″ quoted above.

In connexion with the dial of Saturn, Dondi says that he copied his calculations from elsewhere. Later in the MS he gives his own, somewhat simpler method. Was the calculation referred to one of his father's?

THE DIAL OF JUPITER

For Jupiter the *Aux* is given as 22° Virgo and on a line from this point to the centre of the zodiac will lie the centres of the deferent and equating circles. In this case, the wheel *M*, *Plate 73a*, meshing with the annual calendar wheel has 72 teeth and carries on its arbor in front of the dial a pinion of 4 which engages with the equating wheel of 240 teeth, so that one stud of this pinion drives the equating wheel through $1\frac{1}{2}$° or 90′. Therefore with a forward motion of *M* of 1 tooth daily, it will take 18 days to move the pinion one stud, corresponding to 1 tooth in the equating wheel, in 18 days for 90″ or 5″ a day, which corresponds very nearly to the daily motion of the epicycle calculated as 4′ 59″ 16‴. Wheel *T* of 24 is fixed to the arbor of the movable wheel with blunt teeth. It meshes with a pinion of 12 on the arbor of wheel *S* of 65 teeth, which in turn meshes with the pinion of 12 of the epicycle. Thus for each turn of the equating wheel, *S* is turned twice or through 130 teeth, turning the epicycle through 10 complete revolutions plus 10 signs, which compare with a theoretical of 10 signs 8° 33′ 36″. This gives a daily motion of the epicycle very nearly equal to the theoretical of 74′ 9″ 4‴, the time for the centre of the epicycle to traverse the whole deferent being given as 11 years 10 months 9 days 17 hours 20 minutes.

The train depicted is an alternative train; another, which involved an internally toothed wheel as was used for Mercury, to drive the pinion of the epicycle, is described but not illustrated in the Bodleian copy.

THE DIAL OF MARS

This has to be constructed along the lines of those for Venus and Jupiter, with especial regard to that of Jupiter. The *Aux* is given as 14° of Leo. The wheel *M*, *Plate 74a*, taking up the drive from the annual calendar wheel, has 72 teeth with a pinion of 18 engaging with the equating wheel of 172 teeth. For the *motus* of Mars in its epicycle fixed and movable wheels with blunt teeth, the latter travelling on a cursor, as made for Jupiter and Saturn, are provided for. These can be seen in *Plates 73a* and *71a*.

The wheel, *T Plate 75*, has 53 teeth and the wheel of the epicycle 60 teeth. The teeth of these two wheels approach very closely, but do not engage. They are driven by a common pinion, *s*, of 15, which can follow them in their course up and down the cursor. The index arm is placed at the centre of the zodiac on a protuberance on the hub of the equating circle, owing to the greater eccentricity of Mars, *Plate 74a*. This arm will be carried round by the pin bearing the image of the planet, which is set at the commencement of the first sign of the epicycle, and which will slide up and down the groove in the arm.

Wheel *M* moves forward 4 teeth in 4 days, so that the pinion of 18 turns, in the same direction, eastwards, 1 tooth and consequently makes a complete revolution in 4 × 172, i.e. 688 days or 1 year 10 months 19 days, and the mean *motus* of Mars as given in the tables amounts to 12 signs in amost exactly this period of time.

In the same time the wheel *T* makes one complete revolution, whilst the movable wheel turns about that fixed, and since it has 53 teeth, by means of their common pinion, it will turn the wheel of the epicycle also through 53 teeth. As each tooth correspond to 6°, this equals 10 signs 18°. In the time taken for the centre of the epicycle to traverse the whole band of the zodiac, which is 1 year 10 months 17 days 22 hours 22 minutes, the mean *motus* of Mars is 12 signs as given in the tables, and its argument is 10 signs 14° 4′ 26″, the actual motion of 10 signs 18° being a little fast.

DIAL OF THE DRAGON'S HEAD AND TAIL (THE NODES)

This dial, *Plate 76a*, is situated in the fourth panel of the lower frame and, as may be supposed, is driven off the lunar dial, which is directly above it. The circle of the zodiac is inscribed on the dial and a hand affixed so that the left edge of the pointer is in line with the centre of the zodiac. The pointer is squared on to a wheel behind the dial having 204 teeth. This meshes with a pinion of 12 on its upper periphery, which pinion carries wheel *C* of 100 teeth. This in turn meshes with a pinion of 10 carrying on its arbor a wheel *F*, with 20 saw-like teeth. This wheel is driven, a tooth at a time, by a pin fixed at the back of the wheel *E* of 27 teeth in the lunar dial, *Plate 67a*.

Thus, since *E* turns once in two days, *F* takes 40 days to make one revolution, pinion *d* of 10 therefore takes 400 days to turn wheel *C* of 100. Hence the pinion of 12 will take 17 turns to turn once the wheel of 204 teeth carrying the indicating arm. Therefore the period of revolution for this arm is 400 × 17 days, 6,800 days or 18 years 7 months 14 days, including leap years, during which time the

Dragon's Head, or ascending Node, travels through 12 signs 0° 5′ 21″, as against the 12 signs exactly of the clock.

This concludes the description of the clock proper. It will be recollected that the slight irregularity in the *motus* of Venus was met by cutting unequal teeth in a circular wheel. Dondi now gives a train for providing the *motus* of Venus with a pair of fixed and moving blunt-toothed wheels and a common pinion for the latter and the wheel of the epicycle, as provided for in the dial, of Mars, *Plate 75*. Taking the lettering of this *Plate 75*, the wheel of the epicycle has 48 teeth, wheel *T* has 30 teeth; these two nearly touch but do not mesh. Their common pinion, *s*, has 12 teeth. Then, while the moving blunt-toothed wheel is turning round the fixed by the equating circle, *T* is turning the wheel of the epicycle through 30 of its 48 teeth, which equals 7½ signs; this is the same result as is given in the description of the dial of Venus.

The remaining 28 pages of the MS contain three chapters devoted to the detailed descriptions as to how to set the various dials, how to read them and how to correct the various errors that creep in by reason of the inability of the various trains to portray exactly the motions of the various planets.

Dondi first deals with the general maintenance of the 'common clock', its regular winding and with the daily setting of the hour dial which in accordance with the then Italian custom, was to be set daily at sunset, although Dondi states it is far more correct to set the clock right daily when the sun crosses the meridian, as that point never varies and can be ascertained accurately by instruments or from a sundial.

Then there follow very detailed instructions as how to free various keyed wheels in the different trains, to liberate them for the setting of the dials, and details of how this should be done.

The second chapter deals with the reading of the various dials, the ordinary 24-hour dial, the number of hours left in the 24-hour day as shown by the scales for the rising and setting of the sun, *Plate 58a*, the calendar dials, etc.

In the dial of the *Primum Mobile*, in addition to the motion of the sun, can be read through the rete of the astrolabe at every hour of the day or night, the four cardinal points of the heavens, the degrees of the ascendant, descendant, zenith, nadir; from which four corners can be ascertained, at any hour, the beginnings of the 12 celestial houses, be it by day or by night, 'which cannot be learnt from any other instrument so far as known'. In view of the importance of astrology in the lives of the people at this time, such an easy

and continuous method of indication must have been considered a
great asset. Dondi then gives detailed instructions for the reading of
the astrolabe, rising and setting of the moon and the planets, the
altitude of the sun, the temporal hours, etc.

For the three 'higher planets', i.e., Mars, Saturn and Jupiter, as
well as for Venus, the mean centre is obtained by noting the position
of the arm of the equating circle (that which carries the centre of the
epicyclic dial) in the scale of signs of that circle; the extent to which
that arm has traversed the signs from the opposition of the *Aux* of the
equating circle, indicates the mean centre of the planet. To get the
mean *motus* you read the distance of the *Aux* of the equating circle
from the 1st point of Aries on the zodiacal circle and add this to the
mean centre; if the result exceeds 12, you subtract that number,
leaving the mean *motus*.

The argument of the planet is the extent to which the planet has
moved in its epicyclic dial to the left of the line through the mean
Aux. The true position of the planet in the zodiac is seen from the
image of the planet as it slides in the slotted arm. (The calculations
for Mercury are slightly different.)

The direction, retrogression and stations of the four planets, and
for Mercury as well, is found as follows. If a line drawn from the 1st
and 7th signs of the epicyclic dial is at right-angles to the arm marked
'Verus', the planet is stationary. If when this happens the planet is on
the left of the epicyclic dial, i.e. on the east, the planet is in the
1st station, and if on the right, i.e. the west, the planet is in the 2nd
station. But if this diameter cuts the pointer at an acute angle, or if
the angle be obtuse, or if the line and the pointer coincide, with the
planet being opposite the *Aux* of the epicycle, then the planet's
motion is retrograde.

As regards the Moon, since this has no stations, direction or
retrogression, the motion of the moon is medium in its course when
the indication would be stationary for a planet, slow when the
indication for a planet would be 1st or 2nd station, and fast when the
indication for a planet would be retrograde.

The third chapter deals with the various corrections to be made.
In dealing with the clock proper, if it be slow additional weight is to
be added, and although the illustration shows a balance, if the clock
be fast, small weights are to be added to the balance, which 'when
they hang are tossed by its beat and which are inserted, as it were in
its motion'. Dondi recommends that a supply of these small weights
be kept handy.

As already stated, the annual calendar wheel is to be corrected by stopping the clock for 24 hours on February 24th in leap year.

The different lengths of the day due to the eccentric course of the sun are referred to, the sun taking nearly 186 days to traverse from the 1st point of Aries to the beginning of Libra and 179 days from that point back to Aries. Dondi naturally does not know of the influence of gravity in this connexion; he states that the part of the circle of the zodiac corresponding to the orbit of the sun in the deferent is smaller at the zenith, which is at the beginning of Cancer, and is greater at the part opposite to the zenith, but that these inequalities equalise in 182½ days as between the semi-orbit of the sun from *Aux* to *opposition Aux* to the *Aux* and back again.

He then deals with the equation of time and with the varying daily differences between sun and mean time, giving the days of equality as the beginning of Capricorn, December 23rd, the beginning of Cancer, June 14th, early September and at an unspecified date in October. As far as can be ascertained from the somewhat verbose text, these dates are those where approximate equality will be reached as a result of the somewhat rough and ready corrections he advises, viz: set the dial of the *Primum Mobile* one tooth forward on the 1st of January, February, November and December and one tooth back on the 1st of May, June, July and August.

Provision is also made for the dial of the *Primum Mobile* for the correction of the annual deficit of 5 h 50 m according to the Alfonsine tables. Dondi proposes a correction of 6 hours, leaving an overplus of 10 m. 25 secs. p.a. This he reckons to be equal to 15″ arc or 6 hours in 35 years; the correction is therefore to be omitted in the 36th years.

For the dial of Venus the annual error of 5 h 50 m will be met by stopping the clock in leap year. The residual error is to be met by setting the wheel M one tooth forward in the 46th year.

There is deficit in the period of the argument of Venus; this should be 7 signs 15° 10′ 41″, but the clock is 10′ 41″ slow p.a. In 6 years this will amount to 1° 4′ 6″. The plate of the epicycle should be freed by loosening the keys in the slots and the dial advanced 1° every 6 years, the residual error being corrected after 90 years by advancing the dial additional 1°.

For Mercury there is, beyond the correction at leap year, provision for a secondary correction after 144 years by setting the wheel M forward 1 tooth. In the argument of Mercury there is an annual deficit of 42' 5", so that the dial should be set forward 2/3° annually with a residual correction of 1° in 29 years.

For the moon Dondi calculates about 2 hours in the moon's mean *motus* in 7 revolutions of the moon's epicycle, i.e. 19 d. 8 hrs. The wheel E of 72 teeth which turns once in 2 days, should be set forward 3 teeth. There is a residual error of 27" of arc, which after 28 years equals 21' 56" of arc or 40 m. of the moon's mean *motus*. Therefore after 27 adjustments, on the 28th, i.e. after 5,357 days: 14 years, 8 months after the first setting, the wheel E should be advanced by only 2 teeth instead of 3. This adjustment will upset the wheel of the *Aux*, which should be set back on the pinion c every third adjustment of the wheel E.

There is a deficit in the moon's argument of about 6' 8" each lunar month; the dial of the epicycle is to be set forward 1° every 9 months 22 days 7 hours. This will leave a residual error of 1° every 44 years, therefore after 45 corrections, the plate of the epicycle should be set forward 2: instead of 1:, and so the argument of the moon will be entirely corrected.

Similarly corrections are given for the dials of Saturn, Jupiter, Mars and the Nodes.

Having seen the 'long-term' view taken by Dondi for the care of his clock, it is not surprising to find in the summing-up of the various corrections to be made, a strong emphasis laid on the necessity for a reliable clock-keeper who will note accurately the time at which the clock was started and those of subsequent corrections.

The thought may arise; why take all this trouble to get such accuracy in the astronomical trains when the errors inherent in the motive clock are so great? But we must remember that the astronomical trains, with the exception of that of the moon, were only moved on 1 tooth a day through the annual calendar wheel so that the errors of the clock, which were to be corrected daily, could accumulate for a long time before it became a day out.

Again one wonders what would be the effect of friction on such a vast assemblage of dials and complicated trains. True, Dondi provided a subsidiary drive sufficient to take from the annual calendar wheel the strain of moving the dials, also that the motions are very slow: one tooth of the calendar wheel a day at the most. It is this slow motion that makes workable his dynamically bad elliptical wheels.

Perhaps Dondi's long-term policy was justified, for we hear that about 70 years after it was made, in 1440, Michele Savonarola wrote of the difficulty of getting the clock repaired. Eventually a French astronomer was found capable of doing this. According to Baillie it was still working in 1470 just 100 years after it was made but in another half-century, in 1529, it was again out of order. Von Basserman-Jordan in his *Alte Uhren und ihre Meister*, Leipzig, 1926, said that Charles V had Dondi's clock repaired, which it very badly needed, by one Juanelo Torriani, subsequently taking the clock and Torriani with him to Spain when he abdicated, where it remained at the monastery of San Juste until the building was burned by the orders of Marshall Soult on August 9th, 1809.

This version has been contradicted by Bedini[1] who states that no reference has been found to Dondi's clock after 1529–30, Torriani is believed to have made another astronomical clock with eight dials and a globe, which went to Spain with Torriani and Charles V.[2]

Of the ultimate fate of Dondi's clock nothing certain is known.

How fortunate we are Dondi left us this rich legacy, so revealing of the state of the knowledge of the sciences of horology and astronomy at this early period. The writer has had completed the translation of that part of the MS omitted by Baillie, this now runs to some 130,000 words with about 180 drawings and working sketches. Together with Mr. Drover he hopes some day to be able to publish the whole translation. Mr. Drover also has a translation of the Astrarium which it is hoped also to publish.

One can only regret that the MSS Richard of Wallingford is believed to have written, dealing with his great astronomical clock, made about 1320, some 35 years before Dondi, has not survived.[3] A comparison between the two would be most enlightening.

Those of my readers who have had the interest and the patience to collate the printed descriptions with Dondi's drawings cannot fail to have been impressed with the accurate state of knowledge of astronomy at the middle of the fourteenth century and the magnitude of the genius of this great savant. The more he reflects, the greater his gratitude that it was possible for him to rescue in the 50's the result of Baillie's researches of the 30's after twenty years of neglect and relegation to oblivion by an unappreciative horological world in general. In this expression of gratitude he must include the names of Mr. Geoffrey Buggins, Managing Director of Messrs Thwaites and Reed, London, who had the courage to take the risk

---

[1] *Mechanical Universe*, op. cit., p. 39.

[2] *Morpurgo Tractus Astrarii*, p. 41.

[3] Since this was written, a Richard of Wallingford MS has in fact been discovered by Dr. J. G. North of Oxford.

of quoting for building the clock where others were not willing and to Mr. Peter Haward, his co-Director and senior Clockmaker who actually carried out the work. Mr. F. N. Fryer, an instructor at the Sir John Cass Technical College, London, for engraving a faithful reproduction of contemporary script.

This first hurdle over, remained the problem of disposing of the clock when made. A disappointing lack of appreciation of the importance of Dondi's work in the evolution of the horological and engineering fields, was encountered in the museums of England, Italy and Germany; only in the U.S.A. was this appreciation found, resulting in the clock now being in the Smithsonian Institution in Washington D.C.

Whilst the work of Messrs Haward and Fryer whose names are engraved at the bottom of the Dial of Venus rightly acclaims them as Masters of their Crafts, we have to admit that they had detailed instructions before them, whereas Dondi had to work *ab initio* Planning, Calculating and Designing.

Dondi, whose manuscripts have ceased to be copied and referred to horologically since about the middle of the sixteenth century now lives in the minds of horologists in all the principal countries of the world and this the writer feels is his most important contribution to Horology; but according to reports the visitor to Washington will look in vain for any reference to this.

The Original Greenwich Clocks

UP TO THE PRESENT very little has been known regarding these two clocks except from Baily's *Life of Flamsteed*, London 1835, from which we learn that these clocks had 14-ft. pendulums beating two seconds and that one had a spring suspension and the other a pivot suspension. These two clocks are seen to the left of the door in the well-known engraving of the Octagon Room at Greenwich which is believed to date about 1676. *Plate 77.*

In the absence of further details it was assumed that these long pendulums hung down the stair well to the left of the door until, when restoring the Octagon Room to its original state in 1959, the Ministry of Works established that the floor below the clocks had never been disturbed, but that the beams above the clocks had been hollowed out to allow the passage of a weight suspended by a single cord. *Plate 78a.* The object of the small windows above the clocks in *Plate 77* had always been a mystery since the windows were behind the clock dials and so could not be used for illumination, until a replica of the British Museum original Greenwich clock was made (*Plate 79a*) and fitted with a 14-ft. pendulum above it when it was found that the pendulum bob appeared exactly behind the window. A temporary position of this clock and pendulum seen in *Plates 78b & 79b* shows the method of connecting pendulum and escapement. The excursion of this pendulum is so small that it is often necessary to watch the seconds hand to be sure that the clock is going.

In the absence of any further information the assumption was made that Tompion recalled Hooke's experiment recorded in the Minutes of the Royal Society dated 28.10.1669 where he showed that a freely-suspended pendulum 14 ft. long with a heavy bob could be kept in motion by a pin set in the rim of the balance wheel of a pocket watch threaded to a wire loop fixed below the pendulum. This gave the desired combination of a long period of swing and a small arc, but it must be noted that the pendulum was freely suspended and that the escapement actuating it was below the bob and was a verge, the only type of escapement in a pocket watch at that time.[1]

[1] *Horological Journal,* April 1962.

Some horological writers have wrongly taken this combination of long period and small arc to connect Hooke's name with the invention of the anchor escapement.

Recent researches by Lieut.-Commander Howse of the National Maritime Museum, Greenwich have revealed quite a different state of affairs and he has kindly given the author permission to use this information.

He unearthed an extensive correspondence between a Mr. Richard Towneley, a landowner of Towneley Hall, Towneley, a village near Preston in Lancashire, and a friend of Sir Jonas Moore, who in 1676 ordered these two clocks to be made by Tompion, as is seen from the inscriptions on them (*Plate 79c*). Towneley was well known at the Royal Society, but was not a Fellow, possibly as he was a Catholic.

Towneley's end of the correspondence, i.e. Flamsteed's letters to him, is in the files of the Royal Society who have kindly given permission for it to be drawn upon. The whereabouts of Towneley's letters to Flamsteed, if they still exist, is not known.

In a letter dated January 22nd, 1676, mention is made of the Octagon Room being 20 ft. high which would allow a long pendulum to be hung above the clock. Tompion's two clocks presented by Sir Jonas Moore were not delivered until July 7th, 1676 (letter July 6th, 1676). Flamsteed notes in this letter that the clocks had 'pallets partly after, your (Towneley's) manner'.

Whether the height of the room was decided upon to accommodate the long pendulums or the long telescopes is an open question, probably the latter as the long pendulums above the clock were an innovation and long telescopes were in current use.

Heretofore the writer has given Tompion the credit for adapting Hooke's experiment of 27.10.1669 and applying it to these two clocks, but it would seem this may not be the case. In a letter dated February 11th, 1676, to Towneley Flamsteed writes: 'I cannot hope to have it go perfectly well till I have got a bigger weight on the swing and a room to get it in that may permit it to be hung, as in yours, above the clock, which is doubtless the only way to make them move regularly [this cannot be one of the two clocks delivered 7 July 1676] and after which contrivance, that that Mr. Tompion fits for us, will be made up' – i.e. the two Jonas Moore clocks. Thus it will be seen that Towneley's use of a long pendulum with a heavy bob hanging above the clock probably had an influence on Tompion in designing the two clocks made for Sir Jonas Moore.

Another interesting point that has emerged is that the two original clocks do not appear to have been delivered with standard anchor escapements, those now existing being presumably substituted when

T

the clcoks left Greenwich and had the existing 39″ one seconds pendulums fitted.

In a letter dated March 2nd, 1675, Flamsteed writes: 'I have a pendulum (clock) making by Mr Tompion' and on December 11th, 1675: 'the Pallets of my watch (clock) are in the old form', presumably standard anchor escapement.

Something quite new in horological history is a drawing of a semi-dead-beat escapement by Tompion which is now revealed for the first time. Flamsteed relates in a letter dated December 11th, 1675, how he removed it from a clock in Sir Jonas Moore's dining-room, took a paper impression of it, measured it and sketched it (*Plate 80a*).

He writes: 'the pallets are applied and play upon it with the true chamfer given to the teeth and by this way Sir Jonas thinks there is little check given to the second finger.' The date of this escapement is about 40 years before 1715, the date always taken about that of Graham's introduction of his dead-beat escapement, but as Graham did not join Tompion until 1695, it is possible that this escapement was dropped. Towneley had evidently here designed an escapement of this type since Flamsteed continues: 'but he thinks your pallets may do better and therefore intends to write to you to get us a movement made . . . with pallets after your way'. This clock did not need a high room, a pendulum 6 ft. $7\frac{7}{10}$ inches is suggested, 44 beats to the minute, period a week or more. Flamsteed adds: 'Sir Jonas desires only the bare movement, for the face and fingers made to be added here (Greenwich) without further troubling you.'

Another unknown Tompion invention is described in a letter dated February 9th, 1678. Tompion changes the two part-Towneley pallets in the two 'great' clocks for an escapement of his own (*Plate 80c*) It will be seen that this escapement is a forerunner by about three-quarters of a century of Amant's pin-wheel escapement of *c.* 1749, modified by Lepaute a few years later. Flamsteed writes: 'The pendulums vibrate now not much more than half as much as formerly. The form of the pallets I have sent you coarsely deliniated.'

'*a a b* are in the same plane, but the pallets *p p* are curved backwards and stand slipping from each other as in yours (Towneley's). Perhaps the less vibrations and easier escaping in this way may have contributed something to the extraordinary acceleration before mentioned.'

On February 15th, 1678, Flamsteed fulfils a belated promise to give details of the trains of the two 'great clocks' (*Plate 80b*).

·　　·　　·　　·　　·

The diameter of the barrel on the axis of the last wheel on which the cord is wrapped is $1\frac{7}{8}''$ bore. I forgot to count how many times it was wound round it but you will find it an easy calculation.[1]

[1] Pendulum wheel A teeth 30 diameter $\frac{3}{8}''$ cogga 8

	B	48	$1\frac{1}{2}''$	8
	C	80	$2\frac{7}{8}''$	8
	D	96	$3\frac{7}{8}''$	8
	E	112	$6\frac{3}{4}''$	8

Thus we see much new light is thrown on to this question of the design, making and supply of these two original Greenwich Clocks. Perhaps Towneley's letters to Flamsteed may some day be uncovered at Herstmonceaux to fill in the present gaps in our knowledge.

Note on Symbols of Measure in Horology

Of time
OhO′ O″ = hours, minutes, seconds

Of arcs and angles
O° O′ O″ = degrees, minutes, seconds

Of watch movement diameter
″ ′ = ligne = one-twelfth of an inch

Of large clock movement
‴   = one-sixtieth
′ ″ ‴   = minutes, seconds, sixtieth parts of seconds

Glossary

ALMACANTARS Parallels of altitude.

APOGEE The point where an orbiting body is farthest from the earth.

ARGUMENT The angular distance travelled by a planet in its epicycle.

AUX That point on the zodiac struck by a line drawn from the earth through a planet when the latter is farthest from the earth.

AUX, OPPOSITE A point at 180° from the Aux.

AZIMUTH Vertical arc of sky from the zenith to the horizon; the angular distance of this from a meridian.

BALANCE An oscillating wheel, which is controlled by the balance spring and regulates the going of a watch, or of a clock.

CELESTIAL HOUSES The astrological term for the twelve signs of the Zodiac.

CHRYSTALINEUM A sphere in the Ptolemaic system that represented the year of $365\frac{1}{4}$ days.

COLLET A dome-shaped washer used to render firm the hands of a clock.

COLURES The two principal meridians of the celestial sphere which pass through the solstices and equinoxes respectively. They are therefore at 90° to each other.

COPERNICAN THEORY The heliocentric (i.e. with a central sun) theory as developed by Copernicus.

COUNT WHEEL *See* Locking plate.

CROWN WHEEL The escape wheel in a verge escapement.

CYCLOIDAL CURVE The curve traced by a point on the circumference of a circle that is rolling along a straight line. It is the isochronous curve developed by Christiaan Huygens.

DAY
Mean: The day of 24 equal hours.
Sidereal: The period between two successive passages of a star across the meridian.
Solar: The period between two successive passages of the sun across the meridian.

DECLINATION The angular distance of a star, or the sun, north or south of the equator.

DEFERENT   The radius of a circle whose centre is placed outside the earth, to account for the departure of the planetary orbit from the true circle.

DOMINICAL LETTER   January 1–7 are allotted the letters A–G. The letter for the first Sunday for January is the Dominical Letter for the year. In leap years two letters are required, one up to February 29th and the next preceding letter for the rest of the year. The Dominical Letter is used in connexion with the ascertaining of the date of Easter Sunday.

DUTCH STRIKING   The repetition of either the past or coming hour at the half hour, on a different toned bell.

ECLIPTIC   The sun's apparent orbit.

EPACT   The age of the moon on January 1st.

EPICYCLE   The supposed circular course of a planet, the centre of which travelled round the circle of the deferent.

EQUANT   An adjusting circle to provide equal angular motion at its centre for a planet, to be combined with its eccentric motion.

EQUATION OF TIME   The difference between mean time and solar time, as shown on a sundial.

EQUATORIUM   An instrument for computing geometrically the position of the planets.

ESCAPEMENT   The means of control over the driving force of a clock or watch. It is an alternating motion allowing one tooth of the wheel to escape at a time.

FOLIOT   An early form of controller for a clock, an alternative to the balance.

GOLDEN NUMBER   *See* Metonic Cycle.

GRANDE SONNERIE   Where, in a quarter striking clock, the hour is also repeated at each quarter.

GREGORIAN CALENDAR   The amended calendar introduced by Pope Gregory XIII in 1582 whereby leap years are omitted in three out of every four centennial years. This was not adopted in England until 1752 when the correction amounted to eleven days, the omission of which caused the financial year to end on April 5th instead of March 25th.

INDICTION   A Roman period of 15 years for taxation purpose. It is used in ecclesiastical contracts.

LEAVES   Pinions have leaves, not teeth.

LONG-CASE   Another term for 'Grandfather Clock'.

LOCKING PLATE   A wheel with notches at increasing intervals which allows a clock to strike the necessary number of blows at each hour before an arm falls into a notch and stops the striking.

LUNAR CYCLE   *See* Metonic Cycle.

MAINTAINING POWER   A subsidiary force that comes into action for a few minutes when the driving force of the clock is nullified during winding.

MERIDIAN   A circle passing through a place and the north and south poles.

METONIC CYCLE   The Greek astronomer, Meton, discovered that the days of full moon are repeated in a cycle of nineteen years. The Greeks considered this so wonderful that they had it carved on stone in letters of gold, hence the term Golden Number.

MOTUS (MEAN)   The angular distance, measured from the 1st Point of Aries, travelled by a planet round the ecliptic.

NODES   Two points of intersection 180° apart where the apparent orbit of the sun intersects that of the moon, to which it is inclined by about 5°. When the sun, moon, earth and a node are in line an eclipse of the sun or moon will occur.

PERIGEE   The position of an orbiting body when it is nearest to the earth.

PTOLEMAIC THEORY   The ancient theory of the Universe evolved by the Greek astronomer Ptolemy on the geocentric principle, i.e. with the earth in the centre.

RATING NUT   A nut below the pendulum bob for regulation.

REGULATOR   An extra accurate clock, usually a timepiece fitted with a compensated pendulum, jewels, &c.

RIGHT ASCENSION   The co-ordinate of a heavenly body as measured by the angle the meridian passing through it makes with the prime meridian through the vernal equinox.

RISE AND FALL   A device for regulating the length of a pendulum.

ROMAN STRIKING   A method using two different toned bells, one for the I and one for the V as used in roman notation.

SHEEPSHEAD   A late form of lantern clock in which the dial protrudes materially beyond the clock body.

SOLAR CYCLE   A period of twenty-eight years, after which the days of the month fall on the same days of the week.

SOLSTICES   Those two points where the sun reaches its greatest declination North and South of the celestial equator, June 21st and December 21st. The solstices are mid-way between the equinoxes, and so at 90° to them.

SOUTHING   The passage of a body, say the moon, across the meridian.

SPANDRELS   Decorative cornerpieces found on clocks.

SPOON LOCKING   A hook with a flattened tail fixed inside a long case so that when the door was closed, it pressed in the flattened tail causing the hooked end to go forward and catch the hood frame, so preventing it being raised.

TEETH   Wheels have teeth, but pinions have leaves.

TIME

> *Equation of:* The difference between mean time and solar time, as shown on a sun-dial.
>
> *Mean:* The artificial division of the day into exactly twenty-four hours.
>
> *Sidereal:* The measurement of time by the successive passage of stars across the meridian. The sidereal day is 3 minutes 56 seconds shorter than the mean day.
>
> *Solar:* The time as calculated by successive passages of the sun across the meridian, as shown on a sundial. (*See* Time, *Equation of*)

TRAIN   A series of wheels and pinions geared together in a clock, e.g. going train, striking train.

ZODIAC   A belt in the heavens, about 18° wide, outside which the sun, moon and planets do not pass. It is divided into twelve signs, each of 30°. Aries (The Ram), Taurus (The Bull), Gemini (The Twins), Cancer (The Crab), Leo (The Lion), Virgo (The Virgin), Libra (The Balance), Scorpio (The Scorpion), Sagittarius (The Archer), Capricornus (The Goat), Aquarius (The Water Carrier) and Pisces (The Fishes).

Index

Printed in Great Britain by
Cox & Wyman Limited
London, Fakenham and Reading